The Old Man's Guide to a Brand New Ride: Learning and Loving to Ride a Motorcycle

Rodney A. Ellis

Rodney A Ellis

Copyright © 2013 Rodney A. Ellis

All rights reserved.

ISBN-10-1490954790
ISBN-13-978-1490954791

Dedication

There are lots of people that I should thank, but here are the folks who have made this book possible.

My son, Cody Ellis, who got me started riding and who is my favorite riding companion.

Gary Ellis, my brother, who insisted that I write it and made me buy an iPad to use. Hopefully, I'll sell enough copies to pay for it.

Judy Rice Covington, who has encouraged and helped me every step of the way. She edited, and prepared the book for publication. Judy is my publisher of choice and a dear friend.

Terry Fisher and Bill Burke, who served as pilot readers and offered lots of encouragement. Bill and I are planning a fist fight about which of us will be played by Harrison Ford in the movie.

Kathy Sprinkle, Debbie Blackwell Buckley, Tim Babb, and Jamie Tucker. (Terry Fisher is also a part of this group.) These folks support me in many, many of my endeavors. They love me, tell me when they think I'm right, tell me when they think I'm wrong, and are family in every way that matters.

The Old Man's Guide is dedicated to every one of you...

the "wind beneath my wings"

Rodney A Ellis

**The Old Man's Guide to a Brand New Ride:
Learning and Loving to Ride a Motorcycle**

Table of Contents

**The Old Man's Guide to a Brand New Ride:
Learning and Loving to Ride a Motorcycle**

Introduction

The kids are gone or going (at least as much as kids ever go). You're stable and can spare a few bucks. You've mastered the challenges of earlier life (at least as much as they ever get mastered) and are looking forward to new and different things. You'd like to see new places, meet new people, and experience your newly found freedom. You're looking for something, but you aren't sure what. Then, one day, standing at the corner of Something and Elm, you hear it: a distant rumble, growing in decibels with every passing second. Almost involuntarily you turn toward the sound. At first you can see only a single, glowing light, quickly expanding into a fetching mass of steel and chrome. A helmeted rider speeds past you on his steed of metal and you know that you have found what you were looking for: you want to be a biker.

Of course, you've known about motorcycles for years. Maybe you rode one as a kid, surrendering it grudgingly to the demands of college or the responsibilities of a family. Maybe you never operated a bike, but have ridden behind a friend from time to time. Maybe your hips have never graced the seat of a bike, but you've wondered how it might feel. Regardless of your past experience, you have heard the call. You want to ride.

Therein lies the rub. You're not a kid any more. You're way too old to start riding now... aren't you? After all, kids ride bikes and wear leather. Old people ride rocking chairs and wear flannel. Right? If you're 40 something or older it's too late, right?

Wrong.

I was 56 when that bike rolled around my personal Something and Elm. For me it wasn't a literal bike on a real-life corner, it was the words of my 13-year-old son, Cody, asking me to take him to the local Harley-Davidson Dealer. We perused the accessories, ogled the bikes, and sat on a couple of beautiful Road Kings. The great debate was launched in my mind. "I can't do this!" "I'm too old!" "I can see myself cruising to Gatlinburg for the weekend." "I can see myself lying in a ditch with the Road King on top of me." Eventually, reason won out. I realized that I wasn't too old, that I could cruise to Gatlinburg, and that there was absolutely no reason I needed to wind up under a Road King in a ditch. Yes, my age brought a few disadvantages. My reflexes and muscle tone had decreased while my waistline had increased. I also realized, however, that I had gained a wealth of wisdom and caution through the years that far exceeded the disadvantages I now experienced. Somewhere on that showroom floor I made up my mind. I was going to ride.

I'm writing this a couple of years and a lot of lessons later. I ride one of the three motorcycles I now own almost every day. (My friends accuse me of suffering from MBD, Multiple Bike Disorder). Sometimes I ride all three. Starting to ride again after 40 years was one of the best decisions I've ever made. I would recommend it to anyone. I would also recommend, however, that others who decide to ride at or after middle age navigate the process a little differently than I did. This book is about what I learned, and am learning, in my still-new adventure. It's written for others like me, folks past 40, 50, 60, or maybe even 70 who want to fire up their bikes and ride to work, to Gatlinburg, or to some beautiful remote destination. If you've heard the call and are considering riding, this book can help you decide. If you've decided but don't quite know what to do next, it can help you plot a course. If you've begun and want to gain from the experience of others you will find it helpful as well.

Oh yeah, and if you aren't over 40, you still get to read this book. They won't ID you at the checkout. If anyone asks, just tell them the Old Man said it is OK. There are things that will benefit new riders of all ages. Also, I've tried not to make gendered references here, so I apologize if any sexist comments or assumptions have slipped in. In years past motorcycles were a boy thing. Men rode bikes. Men sometimes rode bikes with women riding behind. Men who rode behind were riding "bitch". The world is more enlightened these days. Many women ride their own bikes. Some manufacturers produce bikes that are designed specifically with female riders in mind. Some women choose to ride behind and a few men whose masculinity is strong enough to manage it have been known to climb on behind the loves of their lives. Motorcycling is less about how old you are and what your gender is than about the freedom and fun it brings. Old, young, male, female, I hope you enjoy and benefit from this book. I look forward to seeing you on the road.

Chapter 1
Why We Ride

"You are old and you are going to break every old bone in your body." Those encouraging words were among the first I heard from friends when I announced my intention to learn to ride at the age of 56. Although there was a certain amount of wisdom in my friend's warning, I knew when I heard it that she just didn't understand. I wanted to ride. I had wanted to ride for years and had simply never done it. But one day, when I was way past too old and brittle to consider sitting astride 800 pounds of moving metal I decided to do it. Damn the consequences, bring on the benefits. I was going to ride.

In retrospect that probably sounds a tad dramatic. That is, however the way I remember it. I began to mull the idea when my son, Cody, age 13 at the time, swindled me... I mean, persuaded me... to take him to the local Harley Shop to look at a motorcycle ring. The HD signet gleamed and the plastic price tag screamed. $650.00! My son has great taste. His father, unfortunately, has a canoe bank account to go with his battleship fashion inclinations. I didn't buy the ring. I did, however, sit on a Road King, and my decision to ride, percolating somewhere in the back of my brain since adolescence, burst into a full-fledged boil. I left the dealership, went straight to my computer, and found out the options for getting licensed in the state of Tennessee. A couple of days later I was enrolled in a course. A few days later I was sitting on considerably less metal, experiencing considerably more angst, being coached through the exercises of a Motorcycle Safety Foundation course. At 7:14 AM, fourteen minutes after the Department of Highway Safety office opened the day after I finished the course I had my new license in hand.

I love to ride. I loved to ride when I first sat on the Road King in the Harley Dealer. I loved to ride when I coughed up the cash to take the course. I loved to ride as I sweated my way through the asphalt-enhanced heat of a 98 degree Fourth of July weekend to complete the course. I loved to ride as I took my first baby steps, as I bought more bikes, and as I have expanded my range and types of travel. Yep, all the way through I loved to ride. Notice that I did not say that I loved everything about the process, but I did say that I loved to ride. I love to ride now.

Those who forecast certain doom simply do not understand, I cannot expect them to do so. I understand that they are concerned for my safety. They think I am risking life and limb every time I fire up the engine. They are, of course, correct. I also risk life and limb every time I drive my truck out of the driveway, every time I haul my ample backside onto the treadmill, and every time I walk across a busy city street. Some things have less risk, some things have more. Folks have told me that I was doing this because of a mid-life crisis. (Not sure why anyone would see 56 as "mid".) Others have accused me of seeking a "babe magnet". I can assure you that no line of "babes" has formed at my door since I bought my first bike. I ride because I love to ride. If you feel as though you need an explanation, that one is plenty. It's the only explanation you need. We ride because we love to ride. It's something that unites all of us who ride, no matter where or what kind of bike. If you love it you love it. If you don't, you don't. If you don't love it, you probably don't get it.

A scene from the tenth episode of the fourth season of Sons of Anarchy comes to mind. Yes, I watch bike movies and read bike books. No, I am not a member of an outlaw MC club, but yes, I enjoy reading about them. Sonny Barger's books are among my favorites. And yes, although I don't have either the inclination or the testicular composition to live life the way members of the Hell's Angels and other biker gangs live, there is something that we have in common. We all love to ride.

The scene involves Jax, the Vice-President and heir apparent to the presidency of a California outlaw motorcycle club, the Sons of Anarchy. Jax is transporting the love of his life, Tara, to a secure location following threats to her life. Although Jax is struggling with loyalty to the club and is contemplating leaving to begin a life with Tara and his son, his loyalties to the club and the biker lifestyle remain strong. Along the way a state patrolman strikes up a conversation with Jax at a gas stop. The patrolman is unaware that Jax is a member of an MC and is currently on probation for several violent crimes.

The strong bond between bikers is clear in the written dialogue. It is made even more clear in the body language and inflection of the actors. They are both bikers and although their responsibilities and moral perspectives are worlds apart, there is something they both love dearly. They love to ride.

The answer to why we ride is both complex and simple. We ride because we love it. If you're starting to ride, or even contemplating riding, you're one of us. That's the simple part. What's a little more complex is why we love it. This chapter provides some insights.

Ian Chadwick- Why Do We Ride?

Soon after I started what I intended to be the first chapter of this book my brother sent me a link to an essay by Ian Chadwick. I read the essay and began to think. It caused me not only to understand some of the reasons I love to ride. It also caused me to think of others. I decided right then that this topic warranted a chapter of its own. There seemed no better place to put the chapter than at the books beginning. There seemed no better place to begin than Chadwick's essay. I'll include a few of his thoughts here, then add some of my own and those of some others. I highly recommend that you get a copy of the original article and read it yourself. I found it at http://www.ianchadwick.com/motorcycles/whyride.html.

Chadwick writes that *riding is more real*. He says that it places us much more in contact with the world than does a ride in an enclosed vehicle. He says that we are insulated in a car or truck, that we do not experience the wind or the sun or the noise or the smells. On a bike you feel the sun on your back and the wind on your face. You hear the sounds of the traffic and the smell of freshly cut grass. When you ride you are more in touch with the world and less absorbed in the bubble of metal and glass that surrounds you.

Although I wouldn't have chosen the word had I not read Chadwick's essay, real is exactly what struck me soon after I figured out where to find the clutch and throttle. I found it at once invigorating and intimidating. The world was no longer at a distance. It was there and I was in the middle of it. It is a feeling I relished the moment I experienced it, and one I have relished every moment I've spent in the saddle.

Riding is more demanding. Yep, gotta go along with Chadwick on this one. I would have called it more mechanical, but I like his word better. Riding is more demanding than driving in several ways. In an auto or truck you simply slide across the seat and turn the ignition or perhaps press a button. On a bike you turn on the gas, switch on the power, engage the clutch, flick the kill switch, and press the starter button, perhaps stopping to manipulate the choke and shift gears along the way. In an automobile you put the vehicle in gear with a single move, then steer as the vehicle changes gears for you. You brake, allowing the mechanisms to slow and seek the right gear on your behalf. In newer models you don't park, you simply pull alongside another vehicle and allow your car to park itself for you. On a bike you must engage the clutch and manipulate the shift lever at the appropriate speeds, coordinate braking and downshifting, and put your feet on the ground and walk the bike backward in order to park.

Riding is also more demanding because you must learn to counter steer and lean. You have to learn which brakes to hit under what circumstances. As Chadwick points out, you learn to manage the bike, not to just point and steer it.

If all this sounds intimidating, it honestly isn't. It's a part of the freedom and the identification with the road and your environment. Bikers like to be in charge of their rides. They like to engage the clutch and feel the rush of the bike as it races forward. And they love, love, love to lean. Demanding isn't a bad thing. It's a thing bikers love.

Chadwick also points out that *riding is a challenge*. Drivers can ignore squirrels. Riders cannot. An opossum darting into the road is an inconvenience for a driver, a threat to a rider. Riders must be aware of rain, wind, water, ice, and other weather conditions that have far less impact on a driver. Riders need to always plan an escape route, where drivers are usually able to simply make their own.

The challenge is a part of the pleasure and, I think, a part of what some people fear. Yes, you may forget to watch for patches of ice in freezing weather, but it is the act of making yourself remain alert that riders enjoy. A deer may dart from a thicket onto the road in front of a rider. Having developed the skills to manage that challenge is a part of the pleasure. Yes, non-riders, we riders understand the challenge, and even the dangers. Unlike many of you, however, we relish the challenge.

Riding sets us apart. Bikers just don't quite fit the mold. The challenge is a part of that, but bikers are people who choose to be alone. As Chadwick says, we choose not to "run with the pack" of sports cars, SUVs, and monster trucks. We are different, and people recognize the difference. Becoming a biker automatically makes you a part of a distinct group of people. Non-riders look at us with suspicion or pity or puzzlement. Riders look at us as brothers and sisters. We are people who understand. We are people who do what only we do. We are set apart from the rest of the world.

Riding is more socially interactive. Try to ride for an hour, making a few stops along the way. You will find that people talk to you, even if you are decked from head to toe in leather and look like a very poor, aging impersonation of the Wild One. Other bikers will definitely want to chat. They'll wave if they're on the move, say hi if they're in a hurry, and stop to chat about your respective rides, the weather, and good places to eat if they have the time. Non-bikers often also want to chat. They will sometimes compliment your bike or ask questions about it. They may ask questions about where you've been or where you're going. People will chat with you when you ride. It's a very social kind of thing.

For many people driving is something they have to do. It's a way to work or a means to run errands. For riders, *riding is fun*. It really has been a transformational transportation experience for me. I attend faculty meetings once per month at a location about an hour from my house. I used to dread the drive. Now I look forward to the ride. I have a holiday luncheon and meeting at noon this Thursday. I'm already looking forward to the trip while trying to figure out which bike I want to take to manage the large roast chicken I'm bringing.

Riding is passionate. Maybe you can tell I'm passionate about it. It's pretty clear to me that Ian Chadwick is. Just in case we haven't convinced you, here's why some other folks say they ride. The following list includes things other riders have said to me directly.

<u>More reasons we ride</u>

Because it sustains bonds across generations. I know several intergenerational riders: fathers, mothers, sons and daughters all riding together from the time the children are young until the parents approach the end of their riding years. Treasured memories of journeys become the stuff of holiday conversations and the fire that lights the passion of yet another generation. One of my favorite books about intergenerational riding is John K. Newkirk's *The Old Man and the Harley: A Last Ride through Our Father's America*. Newkirk weaves history and adventure into a fascinating yarn about retracing his father's 1930's cross-country ride, his 80-year-old dad riding behind him. (Yep, different old man. I'm still looking forward to some rides at 80.) If you doubt my comments about intergenerational bonding I commend it to your attention.

My son and I have always done lots of things together. Buying him a bike was just a natural progression as we moved from Barney to manga to MMORPGs. I started him at 13 on a Yamaha TTR-125. This was a few months after my first ride. My only regret is that I didn't start him (or me) earlier. These days we ride together, visit dealerships together, watch biker shows and read biker books, and play video games in a computer room decorated with posters and metal replicas of motorcycle signs of ages past. We talk bikes, admire bikes, and talk about the advantages and disadvantages of different kinds of bikes. Biking is an important part of what we do, and is another important stage in our intergenerational bonding.

Another reason folks say they like to ride is that *it deepens and strengthens relationships*. Yep, I know we just talked about biking's effect on father and son relationships. But folks report that biking is a core activity in their romantic relationships, friendships, and social activities.

Several riders I know are married couples. Others are people in romantic relationships. Some of the couples ride individual bikes. Others ride together. I was talking with one of my friends yesterday, who is learning to ride, but who also rides on the seat behind her husband. She spoke at length about how much they enjoy their trips together and how relaxing they both find riding. It's common to hear couples who ride together speak of it as one of the core activities of their relationship. Couples who don't ride may be skeptical. I've heard a couple comment, "Must not be much of a relationship if all they do is ride." Spoken like a true non-rider. Perhaps I can see how a few hours of watching TV and a couple of runs to the fridge is more quality time than riding for hours through beautiful landscape, stopping to take pictures and chat, breaking for lunch at an unknown restaurant, and arriving home with a closeness that elicits some activity other than television would be better. Hmmm, perhaps I can't.

Lots of friendships develop and are formed as a result of riding. As I'll say a couple of times in this book, I usually ride alone. But "usually" is not always. I've made some very good friends at dealerships, gas stops, and rallies. Some of my rider friends of the past are now occasional travel companions. A couple of my friends have figured, "If that old guy can do it, I certainly can." and have gotten their licenses. We don't ride together a lot, but we do ride. We don't talk bikes constantly, but they are a frequent topic of conversation. Bikes are a source of commonality and bonding in many friendships.

Riding also provides a source of social activities for enthusiasts. Anywhere you find a few bikers in reasonably close proximity you will find parties, benefits, and rallies sponsored by bikers and bike-related groups. Even though I don't currently own a Harley, I like to drop by the burger and chili events Brad holds at Boswell's, the local Harley dealer. I also like to participate in the events they host, like the annual Christmas Toy Ride. I like to attend the breakfasts and rides sponsored by Sloan's, the Murfreesboro dealership where I bought my KLR. There are small rallies all over the southeast (and every region of the US) every year. Attending these is an important part of my social calendar. For some, biking becomes the central focus of their social calendar.

Because it is therapeutic. There's a famous saying immortalized in helmet stickers, posters, wall hangings, and the minds of bikers everywhere that emphasizes the therapeutic benefits of riding. It goes something like, "You'll never see a motorcycle parked outside a shrink's office." The accuracy of this statement can be seriously challenged by looking out my office door on Monday mornings, or by chatting with one the many riders around the country who seek better life circumstances through consultation with a therapist. Still, there's something that rings true about it. For many bikers a ride relieves stress, clears the mind, and helps to change perspectives in a very positive and beneficial way.

One of my friends remarked, "I can get on the bike feeling all the pressure of a terrible day. After a couple of miles I feel the stress start to break away, almost like a chunk at a time. By the time I've been riding for maybe 15 minutes I don't even remember most of what I was worried about." Another commented, "I don't know how to explain it. It's not that I'm not paying attention to the ride. I'm focused on everything I should be. It's just that riding is almost like meditating. I get into a "zone" where it's all about the ride and about what I'm doing at that moment. It's very relaxing and therapeutic.

Because it saves money. One of the most frequent things I hear from people who ride to and from work and on household errands is that using their bike saves them money. It's probably pretty hard to make that argument when you invest in a $30,000 bike in order to get 50 miles to the gallon. It's a much easier argument to make if you spend $5,000 to get 65-75 mpg. I ride my KLR 650 to work more than either of my other bikes. I have about $5,500 in it and get somewhere around 60 miles per gallon. I have it decked out with winter wiring, an after-market windshield, and a lot of luggage. I can drive to and from work as well as back and forth to my various appointments on less than $10 per week. My Ford Explorer gets a little over 20 mpg and costs me about

10

$25 per week for the same use. Yes, I did invest $5500 in my bike and it will take a while to recoup that, but my truck is paid for, 11 years old, and I plan to get another 10 years out of it given my current minimal use. It doesn't take much work with a calculator to see that I'll save money under those circumstances.

Because it's good for the environment. I hear this a lot and it sounds reasonable. Motorcycles are smaller, therefore require less metal and other resources to build. They use less gas and rubber per mile than do automobiles. That all makes sense, but I'm not sure it's true. I've seen the argument made, backed by some research, that lower admissions standards and other factors make motorcycles less environmentally friendly than one might think. I'm not sure who's right, but a lot of my friends think it's the bike people. Their arguments make enough sense to that, overall, I'm inclined to agree.

Because it feels good. It just plain feels good to ride. You are both on your way somewhere and are in the middle of nature. You feel the sun and the wind, you hear sounds that you have never heard so clearly. You feel relaxed and at peace. Riding rocks, at least that's what everyone who does it tells me.

Because we can and want to. Fact is, no one has ever said this to me, so if you quote it I get the footnote. We ride because we can and we want to. There's a certain freedom in taking to the road in the way you choose, despite the risk, despite the warnings, despite the fact that people think we're old and crazy. Riding is a form of freedom, a way of saying, "I choose, and I have the right to choose. I choose to ride".

<u>Kickstands down</u>

Every ride ends with a single gesture. You raise your left leg, hook the kickstand with your heel or toe, and swing it down to rest on the pavement. You lean your bike, grasp the handbrake, and step off. That moment of lowering your kickstand is a moment of past, present, and future. With that action you end your ride (past), step back onto your feet (present), and await the moments or hours before your next ride.

Each chapter of this book ends similarly. The sections will be entitled "kickstands down". In those sections we'll look back on what we've talked about in each chapter. We'll consider what that means to our experience as riders in that moment. We'll look toward using what we've learned in our biking future.

In this chapter we've talked about why we ride. We talked about practical reasons and fun reasons and psychological reasons. We also talked about passion. Some readers may think I've been a little too dramatic. If they do, I have a case of V-Twin motor oil that says they don't ride. But then again, those folks probably won't read this book. We love to ride. They might, but may never know

Chapter 2
The Basics of Bikes

One of the difficulties you face when you start to ride is in learning the basics. It would be nice to just hop on a bike and roar off into the sunset, but for most of us that just isn't going to happen. We have to learn to walk before we can run, and in the case of the motorcycle this means simple skills like timing the clutch and the throttle, learning when and how to apply which brake, and remembering to put a foot down at the right moment. In order to learn these things you need to practice. In order to practice you need to have a safe, legal, and accessible site. Unfortunately, little things like a license requirement can make such sites difficult to find. You need a license in order to practice in most places, but you can't get a license until you have been able to practice.

License laws vary from state to state. It's pretty easy to find out how the law works in your state. Usually a quick Internet search or a somewhat (or maybe lots) slower call to your state Department of Motor Vehicles or its equivalent will do the trick.

In Tennessee, where I learned to ride, you get an endorsement (an "M" on your driver's license) that lets the world know you are qualified to ride. You earn the M in one of two ways, either 1) by taking a written exam plus successfully navigating a skills course consisting of a few riding exercises or 2) by taking a weekend course in which you are prepared for the examination and skills course, then receive a certificate for successful completion. You then present the certificate at the driver's license Bureau office and receive the endorsement.

For a skilled rider the first option will probably work. The driver's license folks will furnish a book to read that provides basic information on the law and safe riding. The skills course includes a group of exercises that range from mind-numbing ease to pellet-dropping difficulty. A skilled rider would probably be able to complete them successfully without much difficulty.

Pellet-dropping is an expression some bikers use to refer to "eeek" feeling they sometimes get when a wheel comes just a little too close to the side of the road or they see a deer dart onto the highway in front of them. It is a polite way of referring to the bodily processes of rabbits (dropping pellets) and the way the human body may simulate that response in crisis moments. There, did I say that nicely enough?

Less experienced riders and those who are sheer, raw noobs (newbies, new people) will probably want to take the course. Its advantages include gaining basic riding knowledge, experiencing a few skill development exercises, getting some safety tips, and having the opportunity to take the riding test in a less stressful atmosphere. Its biggest disadvantage is that it really isn't a beginner's course. I don't mean that critically, it's a pretty tall order to show someone how to start a bike for the first time on Saturday afternoon and have them successfully running figure eights in a 20x40 circle by Sunday afternoon. Even though my weathered buttocks had graced a seat years earlier, I struggled to remember FINE-S (the acronym for the starting sequence), then bumbled my way through a pellet-dropping episode of powerwalking (sitting on the motorcycle and moving it forward slowly by twisting the throttle gently and walking it forward). Then, with my stomach barely settled, we were off to run long circles in the lot, weaving between cones as we went. This was hardly a curriculum for noobs, but it was, admittedly, way too slow for the folks (mostly young) who had been on dirt bikes or non-street legal alternatives for many years.

In short, if your skill level is anything like mine was, the new rider's course may not provide enough seat time at very basic skill levels to allow you to progress comfortably. My class was well, planned, well taught, and well supervised. Still, it was a very difficult experience in 95 degree weather. In short, I sucked. I dropped the bike once, accidentally revved it and raced across the parking lot once, and generally performed miserably on several of the exercises. The instructors gently tried to counsel me out, then later assured me that I could take the course again for free if I failed the test the first time. I spent two miserable, hot, frustrating days thinking that I was (dammit) going to learn to ride one way or another. Oddly, when the time came to take the test I aced it, getting one of the highest scores in the class. The instructors smiled proudly and let me lead the pack of grads in three victory circles around the steaming asphalt. There should have been a news flash, "Fat old man aces cycling exam. Film at 11."

I tell this sordid story to underscore the point I made earlier about the need for practice. You may find the course to be enough to prepare you for the exam, or you may not. If you are at the skill level I was at, you will need much more than the course before you are ready to confidently navigate city traffic or speed down a crowded interstate. Further, if you are anywhere near the level I was at when I took the course you are likely to find the course difficult, frustrating, and embarrassing. What you need is experience, seat time. The question, then, is how do you get the seat time.

You could, of course, just ignore highway laws and common sense and ride the streets without either license or skill. This, of course, is a remarkably bad idea adopted by a frightening number of people. Although this alternative would give you the chance to learn, that chance might be short-lived. Hopefully, you would live longer than the chance.

A second possibility would be to purchase a suitable bike and ride in safe, non-public road areas. This is actually a good idea whether or not you have completed the course. Riding in such areas gives you the chance to develop your skills with minimal danger to yourself or other people. There are a couple of key ideas here. The first is the purchase of a suitable bike, The second is the identification of a safe, appropriate practice area.

Let's talk about those ideas individually.

Selecting a suitable bike involves several considerations. These include price, size, weight, weight distribution, and intended use. All are important, particularly for the beginning rider.

Price is, of course, a critical part of the decision for most of us. I renewed my biking career by purchasing absolutely the wrong bike. I bought before I had taken the class, intending to sit on it and roll it around in the driveway for a couple of weeks just to get the feel of it. I had a friend ride it home for me. I walked around it for a couple of days, and then finally decided to get on it. I swung my leg over, and then stood it up. It was a rabbit pellet moment.

The bike I had selected was a Harley Davidson Road King. It was gorgeous. Bright blue trim and fairings, lots of chrome, leather saddle bags, and a plush, comfy seat. It had a huge engine and made gratifying rumbling sounds when I twisted the throttle. It was also way too tall, heavy, and powerful for an old guy who was learning

16

to ride all over again. When I stood it up and it tilted slightly to either side, a bolt of fear shot through me. I knew I was going to drop it. I gingerly put the kickstand down and slowly crawled off it. A couple of days later I tried again. Nope, still too tall and heavy. My legs hadn't grown an inch. I went to the class hoping that a couple of days of instruction would solve the problem. It didn't.

Probably the most significant problem wasn't the bike. It was my inseam length. I have perhaps the shortest legs God ever put on a man. My inseam is 28 and one-half inches. (I claim every millimeter!) A 27 inch seat height sounds reasonable, but you have to allow for the width of the seat. By the time I had straddled that big, wide, comfy pad I couldn't get either foot flat on the ground. It was either tippy-toe on both feet or be a one-foot wonder. There are folks who ride comfortably that way and who will tell you that there is no reason anyone shouldn't be able to ride that way. For me, those people are wrong. I offer two pieces of evidence: safety and terror.

A one-foot wonder is a person who rides a bike that is sufficiently tall that, when he or she is seated in the center of the seat and the bike is upright. Neither foot will touch the floor. In order to ride the bike the wonder has to mount it, then lean the bike to one side or the other in order to balance it when not in motion. These folks are always riding on "one foot", leading the rest of us to believe that they are at best wonders and at worst entirely out of their friggin minds. Most riders like to be able to get at least the balls of both feet on the ground. Many of us (please note the "us') like to be able to get all or almost all of both feet in the ground on any bike we ride. If you're close to my age I recommend a few years of practice before you try to one-foot it, oh, say, 150 years or so.

I found that there were ways to lower the bike. There are ways to lower almost any adult motorcycle. In the case of the RK the method was replacing the rear shocks and purchasing a seat with a dished out front that lowered me in the saddle. When the alterations were complete I was able to get both feet almost completely on the ground. It was then that I discovered the second problem, weight distribution.

The weight of different types of motorcycles is distributed differently on the frame. Some, like the Road King, have a high center of gravity, meaning that when you sit on it you feel the weight right up under your butt. When you shift it to the right or left, a lot of weight moves in that direction. To the novice, it often feels as though it is going to fall. If the novice lets it lean too much, or panics and makes a false move, the novice may be right.

Other bikes, like the Harley Soft Tail and the Yamaha V series have a much lower center of gravity. Some also have a lower seat height and a narrower seat. For example, when I first sat on a Soft Tail, I realized that, although it wasn't the ideal beginner bike, it was one that I could have comfortably managed. Although I rode and enjoyed the Road King, it was a mixed bag. Starting was OK. Riding was wonderful. Stopping, not so much. Plus, every time I put a leg over the seat I was worried that I would drop it. It just wasn't the right match for the noobish me.

What I needed in terms of seat height, weight and weight distribution was a lower, more narrow bike with a lower center of gravity. Now, after an extended period of regular (some of my friends say "compulsive") riding, I'm comfortable on a bigger bike. I'm not sure I would have ever gotten to that point if I had not taken some corrective (read that expensive!) measures early on.

Engine size is yet another factor. You want an engine that is powerful enough to move whatever weight you have but one that will not leave you gasping at its power when you touch the throttle, at least not until you are ready to gasp. For the beginner this often means selecting a bike with a smaller engine for learning, then trading up to a larger engine once your skills are more developed.

Many experts recommend a 250 cc engine for a beginner bike. There are several manufacturers who make such bikes for street use, including Honda, Yamaha, Kawasaki, and Suzuki. Harley doesn't offer a bike in this range at the time of this writing. Their smallest is an 883, and lots of people start on it. It would have been too much bike for me in the beginning, but it seems to work for some other folks just fine. 250 ccs are also available as dual sports and dirt bikes. These bikes may be good options for some and will be discussed in greater detail in later sections of the book.

The 250 with which I am most familiar for beginner use, is the Honda 250. It's what my motorcycle safety class used and what I bought to learn on. There are lots of them around so they tend to be readily available used, and parts are easy to come by. They are also frequently (perhaps most frequently) the bikes used in the new rider courses developed by the Motorcycle Safety Foundation. Until recently Honda manufactured two versions, the Nighthawk and the Rebel. Although they no longer manufacture the Nighthawk 250, the Rebel is still in production. An older version of either can be purchased relatively inexpensively from private individuals, ridden for a few months, and then resold at or near the purchase price. I gave $800 for mine, rode it for a few months, then sold it to a friend of a friend for the purchase price, $800.

Dual purpose and dirt bikes are another starter bike option. Dual purpose bikes are designed to run either on or off-road. Dirt bikes are not street-legal and may only legally be used in off-road settings. Both are offered in smaller engine sizes (250 cc for dual purpose and even lower for dirt bikes). These bikes will work for the new rider who has the opportunity to practice in an off-road setting. If he/she intends to continue to ride on dirt after developing adequate skills for street riding no trade or resale is necessary. Warning: be sure to spend a little stationary seat time on these bikes before buying. They are tall, at least to us short guys. They are made that way to allow lots of ground clearance for rough off-road conditions. They can be tweaked to accommodate the shorter rider, but expert advice is a great idea when lowering a bike. The first time I sat on my Kawasaki KLR 650 I couldn't touch the floor on either side. Brian, the excellent salesman who was assisting me, asked me to stay put then ran off to another room. I wondered if he was going to get a pad to soften my landing. He returned with a tape measure, asked me to put a foot flat on the floor, then measured the distance from the heel of the other foot to the floor on the other side. I crawled gingerly off the bike and we consulted with the service guys. They did some calculations and suggested two inch lowering brackets, a dished seat, some adjustment of the fork, and a shortened kick stand. I still crawl on and off the bike but I sit comfortably and love to ride it on or off-road. By the way, I purchased my 650 after I had learned on a 250. Some folks start successfully on 650s, 750s, and larger bikes, but that wouldn't be my choice.

In summary of engine size, bike height, and bike weight distribution, the old man recommends that you start with a 250cc bike. Also consider the bike's height and weight distribution. Check to see that your toe in your riding boots (see chapter 3) fits smoothly between the left foot peg and the shifter. Spend some time sitting on the bike. Shift it a little to the left then a little to the right beneath you. If you have a friend or loved one who knows bikes, ask him/her to check out your purchase for you. If you don't have a license yet ask him/her to give it a test ride.

In addition to engine size, weight, and weight distribution, you need to give some thought to how you will use the bike you buy. If you just plan to ride a street bike on asphalt or concrete surfaces, your decision is easy. Buy a 250cc street bike. Unless you intend to use a bike of that size permanently, or pass it on to children or grandchildren, I'd consider buying used.

If you plan to ride both on and off-road you'll have other things to consider. If you're going to ride rough paths and single-tracks you will want a light, nimble dirt bike with a relatively small engine. Again, a 250cc will probably be about right. Examples include the Yamaha XT250, the Kawasaki KLX 250, and the Suzuki DR 125. Some of these bikes, such as the XT 250 and the KLX 250 are dual sports and can be used either on or off-road. Others, such as the Yamaha TTR 125 or 230, are strictly for use on dirt.

There are bigger, more powerful bikes for dual purpose use, but they are probably not the best choice for beginners. We'll talk about them in the chapter about off-road riding.

Off-road riding does, by the way, present a safe alternative to streets for learning and beyond. Many areas have dirt roads and trails that are not publicly maintained and are therefore good places to practice while unlicensed. Using them would require a dirt or dual purpose bike (see the section on bike types at the end of this chapter) and a trailer to transport the bike. Inexpensive trailers are available from stores like Lowes and Home Depot. You won't need a larger trailer, just one large enough to accommodate your bike and perhaps a storage box. I would recommend, however, that you consider future bike purchases when you buy. For example, my 6' x 8' trailer works great for my Can-Am or my KLR 650. It also works well for my son's Yamaha XL 250. Putting both the KLR and the XT on at the same time, however, presents some interesting logistical challenges. It can be done, but I wish I had bought a bigger trailer to begin with. I'll probably wind up selling this one eventually and buying something that will more easily accommodate two bikes.

In addition to your trailer you'll need two tie-downs for each bike you intend to transport as well as a wheel chock for each. The tie-downs can be purchased from the store where you purchased the trailer, from many motorcycle dealers, or from the online sources we'll note when we talk about accessories. Make sure you buy the type that use ratchets for tightening and have hooks on each end that will fit around the handlebars. In most cases this will mean fitting around a 3/4 inch bar.

A chock is a tubular rack that holds the front wheel in place when the bike is strapped down. Although a chock isn't strictly necessary, it does help stabilize the bike before and after ratcheting and will hold the bike in place through bumps and sudden turns. Several manufacturers make several types. Some are intended to be permanently mounted to the trailer. Others can be used when the bike is being transported and removed when it is not.

I considered trying to talk you through how to strap

a bike to a trailer in this paragraph. I'd say I thought about it for oh, 4-5 seconds. It really isn't difficult or time-consuming to do, but I really think it's something best learned by doing. Long story short, you roll the bike on, position the front wheel in the center of the chock, put the kickstand down, slip one hook of a strap around the handlebar on the kickstand and the other hook around a suitable spot on the trailer, then repeat that process with the other strap on the other side of the bike. To remove the bike from the trailer, you simply reverse the process. ALWAYS strap the kickstand side down first when trailering the bike, ALWAYS release the non-kickstand side first when preparing to remove the bike from the trailer. My little Nighthawk 250 had a lovely indention on the right side of the gas tank because I tried it in the wrong order the first time I unloaded.

With the trailer discussion out of the way, let's get back to bike selection. As I am writing this my brother, Gary, (who is 18 months younger than I am and not nearly as bright or good looking) is considering a bike purchase. He is also a noob rider and is probably going to disregard some of my suggestions here. I'm telling his story not to publicly humiliate him (although that has a certain appeal). Rather, I'm using his story to illustrate some very good reasons for making bike purchase decisions other than the ones I've recommended. When you buy your bike you may find such factors as previous experience, body size and type, opportunities for practice in a safe area, budget, and time available may cause you to make similar choices.

A modicum of previous motorcycle experience might allow you to start with a bigger, more powerful bike. If you've ridden enough to have the basic motor skills in place and are not intimidated by the size and weight distribution of the bike you intend to ride you may not have to start with a 250. My 650 cc Kawasaki has plenty of power for what I need and a bike of that size would offer a nice alternative. There are lots of nice 750s out there, and Harley makes a 883 cc. My personal recommendation would be that you not start any bigger and heavier than a bike in that range but I know all too well the lure of big chrome and tooled leather. Just remember that you won't enjoy a bike that you are afraid to ride, and you need to be able to ride to gain higher levels of skill.

Your body size and type may also affect your initial motorcycle selection. This is probably going to be a major factor in my brother's decision. I've described my short, heavy body type. Gary is tall and muscular with long legs and an ample frame (read that, some extra pounds). He isn't going to be a one-foot wonder on any bike. Further, he has the upper body strength to support a heavier model. He probably won't choose one of the bigger bikes, (I remember the rabbit pellet look in his eyes when he took a practice sit on an Electra-glide and stood it up for the first time.) but he will probably purchase something in the 750-1100cc range. My personal preference would be that he choose something in the 650-750 cc range but, he, after all, will be the one who rides it. Other factors will also play into his decision. We'll talk about those in the next couple of paragraphs.

The presence of opportunities for safe practice may also factor into bike selection. In Gary's case he lives on a cul-de-sac in a very low-traffic community where the streets are well-paved and privately owned. Because the streets are not government controlled or maintained he can ride there without an operator's license. One of his neighbors is the county sheriff, so he has been able to confirm this option with local law enforcement. Gary has no intentions of roaring up and down the streets. He plans to ease his way out the driveway and spend some serious time power-walking and slow-riding his new bike just mastering motor skills and learning to manage the machinery. I am not recommending this method to him or to anyone else due to some of its inherent dangers, but it is, after all, his choice. Seriously, that's one of the basics of riding a bike. The choice is his, as it is yours. Pick the bike you want to ride.

My brother also has the good fortune of living in the midst of acres of privately owned land with dirt roads and broad trails. The land is undeveloped acreage owned by the developers of his property, and he is free to walk or ride there as he chooses. His location stimulated some conversation about a dual-purpose bike as a starter, but Gary has a very demanding job and didn't want to buy now then be forced into a trade-up situation within a few months. As a result, he's probably going to choose a street bike.

Budget is also an important consideration. You can buy a new 250 dual purpose for as little as $4,000.00. A decked-out trike might run as much as $50,000.00. Obviously, affordability can be an issue. Your starter bike has to be affordable and shouldn't leave you suffering sleepless nights deciding how you will pay for it. Buying used is a good way to make your first purchase more financially friendly. The good news is that a well-maintained motorcycle will run for many more miles than the average first owner will put on it. The bad news for the buyer (good for the seller) is that motorcycles tend to hold their value pretty well. You can save a few dollars by buying used from a dealer. You can expect to find bikes on the sales floor listed at the high end of retail value. You can also expect that the dealer will come off the asking price. You can often save even more money by buying from a private owner. There are risks involved, however. Purchase from a private owner brings no guarantee of condition and no warranty. Some bikes that may appear to be excellent deals (for example, older bikes with extremely low mileage) may not be the bargains they appear to be. Too much sitting around over a period years can cause clogging in the fuel system and deterioration of critical components. Still, there are many careful bike owners who, for an assortment of reasons, decide to sell their beloved, well-cared-for cycles. If you're interested in a used bike from a private owner but are unsure of its condition, take a friend who is an experienced rider along. Let your friend test-ride it and give it the once over. The opinion of a seasoned rider should tell you a lot about your prospective purchase. I should probably add that my 1995 Yamaha Virago is my favorite bike. I bought it used with 7400 miles on it. I got it from an honest guy who had fished it out of another guy's garage. He told me who had done the work to clean up the fuel system. I called the guy, listened to it run, and fell in love. It's almost always my first choice to ride. Used can be a great option.

The amount of time you will have available for bike shopping and swapping may also be an important factor in selection. One of my brother's more important criteria was that his choice of a first bike meet enough of the safety criteria to make him comfortable, yet that the size and power of the bike be adequate to keep him happy for several years to come. This was important to him because he has both a high-demand job and a strong commitment to his time with family. As he so eloquently expressed it, "I don't have time to fool with buying and reselling and trading up." His likely solution I mentioned earlier is a street bike in the mid-range of power with a passenger seat and a minimal cargo capacity. This would allow him to learn comfortably, then ride the bike for pleasure alone and with his wife, on short errands, and commuting to work.

One more factor is very important in your selection of your motorcycle. This, in my opinion, is the most important. Consider what the old man says, consider what your riding friends say, and consider what the salesman says (and, of course, SERIOUSLY consider what your spouse or significant other says) but, in the end, pick the bike you want. I'll never ride it (of course, unless you invite me for wings, beer, and a before-dinner ride), nor will any of the other folks who may offer opinions. Your spouse or significant other may ride with you and worry through your initial ventures, but yours are the buns that will grace it. Pick what you like. Pick what feels good to you. Pick what you will love to ride.

The following checklist is a synthesis of the factors that I've listed as important. You may want to add any additional thoughts you may have to the list and spend some time thinking about it as you do your shopping. After you've had some time to review and tinker with the checklist, we'll talk a bit about the different types of bikes.

Bike Selection Checklist

Cost

____ How much can I afford?

____ How much am I willing to spend?

Bike size

____ How tall is the bike?

____ Can I get on and off it comfortably?

_____ When I sit on it do my feet touch the ground in the way I want them to?

_____ Is the width of the seat comfortable for me?

_____ Can I shift back and forth in the seat easily?

_____ If I can shift back and forth if the height comfortable when I am in the forward position (suggesting that you could shift into that position to start and stop)?

Bike weight

_____ How much does the bike weigh?

_____ Do I think I could sit on it and move it around without worrying about dropping it?

_____ Is the center of gravity high or low?

_____ Do I prefer the center of gravity to be high or low?

_____ Do I think I could pick the bike up alone if I dropped it?

_____ Would I be willing to ask for help if I dropped it and couldn't pick it up alone?

Engine size

_____ Is the engine big enough that it will negotiate the terrain I'll ride?

_____ Is the engine small enough that I will be comfortable and confident when I ride?

Bike use

____ Will I ride on streets only?

____ Will I ride on dirt only?

____ Will I ride on both streets and dirt?

____ Will I ride short or long distances?

____ Will I ride both short and long distances?

Practice bike

____ Do I want to purchase a practice bike for learning?

____ If I want to purchase a practice bike, what are the best places for me to find one?

Kickstands down

This chapter has been primarily about motorcycle selection, although we started with a discussion of the available ways to obtain a license. We've also talked about some safe alternatives for developing basic skills.

The important factors in picking a bike are cost, bike size, weight, engine size, and how you will be using the bike. I've organized these into what should be a helpful checklist at the end of the chapter.

Bike selection isn't a perfect process. You'll probably wind up making some compromises in one category or another. But the object of our love doesn't have to be perfect. As I've said, my Virago is my favorite. The only real compromise is that I wish it had more luggage space for longer trips. Still, I can either make that work by packing carefully or I can take the Can-Am. The Virago isn't perfect, but it's as close as I need, and it's perfect in all the categories that matter. Take your time. Do lots of looking, sitting, and talking. You'll find the bike you love. When you do, buy it and ride it.

Chapter 3

The Five, or Six, or Maybe Twenty Types of Bikes

We talked about picking a bike in chapter 2. In this chapter I'll give you the old man's summary of the different kinds of bikes you can choose from. The order of this chapter might seem a little backwards, but I've given a fair amount of thought to this. If you want to make the right choice in a bike I think you are better off if you know what features and characteristics you are looking for, then narrow your selection to the makes and models that best fit your needs. If you happen to think doing it this way is a remarkably bad idea, no problem. Just forget that you've read chapter 2, read this one, and read chapter 2 again when you finish. I am, after all, a flexible kind of guy.

Fact is, some folks aren't gonna take my recommendations anyway. I'm pretty sure I wouldn't have. I didn't even look at the little 250's I now recommend until I had already rabbit-pelleted my way through enough miles on the Road King to decide that smaller was a better way to begin. I talked to a lot of people about buying motorcycles. I'm not sure why, but I seem to be a magnet for folks who have always wanted to, but never have (about bikes, I mean). I haven't kept track but I'll bet in the last year alone at least 20 people, some known to me and some unknown, have approached me for advice on what bike to buy. I tell them all the same thing. Buy a cheap used 250 to learn on while you figure out what you want to ride forever. A couple of them have taken my advice. A couple of them (literally on the dealership sales floor) have listened to me respectfully, turned away at the end of my spiel, walked directly to a salesperson, and bought a bike of 1300 cc's. (No hard feelings, that's pretty much what I did.) Most have made a decision that fell somewhere in between. Most, listening not just to me but to one of the excellent motorcycle sales professionals I am privileged to know, have honored both their internal call to chrome and pipes and the wisdom of old men past. They've decided what was important to them in their first bike and have chosen accordingly. That, my friends, is as it should be. I won't be riding your bike, nor will your neighbor who rides, nor will the salesperson. Ultimately the choice is yours. For any of us to insist otherwise dishonors the very concepts of individuality and honor on which riding is based.

Although this chapter describes the different types of bikes you might consider, it is, like the last chapter, a way of helping you choose. You've trusted the old man enough to spend a few bucks on this book. Now trust him enough to try a technique that may support you in your decision of what bike to buy. Take the checklist from the end of the last chapter and compare it to the features and characteristics of bikes you find in this chapter. Then go see some dealers and sit on some bikes. Don't be shy when you sit. Never, ever sit on someone's bike when you see it on the street. Never, ever consider buying a bike unless you sit on it. If it's a private owner who wants to sell you his/her used beauty, ask first. If it's a dealer's bike, it's probably polite to ask first, but they want you to sit on it. Sit on it, straighten it up, notice how it feels under you, how much it weighs, where the center of gravity is, and how much of your feet touch the ground. Find all the gizmos you need to turn it on and off. Check out the position your feet will be in when you ride and the level of comfort you will experience when you shift or brake. Try out a few different bikes. Sit and re-sit until you find what you like. There's no reason to make a purchase your first day.

Let me inject another little piece of advice at this

point. This is something I would do differently if I was going to go buy a first bike again. If you are going to take the Motorcycle Foundation Safety Course before you get your license, wait to buy your bike until after you complete the course. A weekend on a bike will tell you a lot about your preferences. If you've never ridden, or if you haven't done much riding, you'll know lots more about how to spend your money after you've taken the course. Who knows, you might even think, "Ya know, those little 250s are pretty good bikes for learning. I wonder where I could find a good used one for oh, say, about 800 bucks.

Although different people may break it down in different ways, there are 6 basic kinds of motorcycles. These include dirt, dual purpose, standard, cruiser, sport, and touring.

Dirt

Dirt bikes are made for off-road use. Having said that, there are lots of different off-road surfaces. There are also different off-road uses. It is also possible to buy accessories that will make some dirt bikes street legal. This usually means lights, turn signals, and a horn.

I've seen dirt bikes with engines as small as 50cc. These are tiny little bikes made for tiny little people, backyard bikes for very young children. This book isn't about arguing whether children should be allowed to ride at an early age, so I won't go there. I will say that the strongest argument against it is safety. I will also say that the strongest argument for it is safety. Those who oppose childhood riding think it's just plain too dangerous for kids. Those who support it argue that the skills kids learn in a controlled environment at lower speeds make them much better riders when they eventually hit the road. In fact, studies have shown that experienced dirt bike riders are involved in fewer motorcycle accidents as adults than are folks who start to ride as teens or adults.

Having said that and perhaps fueled a debate in your household, let's talk about the different kinds of dirt bikes. Again, different experts may break it down different ways. I'm hardly an expert, but I am the author, and I break it down as follows. Among the dirt bikes there are two general categories: trail and competition. Trail bikes are what most of us ride for fun. For adolescents and adults they typically run between 125 and 250 ccs. They are light, nimble, and lots of fun. People ride them on forest trails, through streams, across meadows, and just about anywhere else you can imagine. People who are good on trail bikes do some pretty amazing things. People like me go up and down hills and along winding trails with smiles on their faces.

There are many advantages to learning on dirt. Lots of people start with dirt bikes because they are lots of fun and are relatively inexpensive. If you have a reasonable leg length (unlike, of course, the old man) you will almost never go down if you ride conservatively because all you have to do is put your feet down. If you don't ride conservatively you don't have as far to fall.

Competition off-road bikes are amazing pieces of equipment often ridden by some pretty amazing athletes. While the rest of us mortals content ourselves with runs on paved ridges followed by a round of twelve ounce curls, competition dirt riders fly along dirt tracks at incredible speeds, jump their bikes over deep holes, and corner at breakneck paces. Equally incredible, the bike types include motocross, rally, enduro, trials, and track. These are fun to look at and even more fun to watch in competition. They are not, however, a starter bike, and are unlikely to be a suitable option for many riders.

Dual purpose

Dual purpose bikes are the best of both worlds, so long as you don't expect them to be the best in either world. Dual purpose bikes are made to ride either on dirt or on the highway. They typically have a high ground clearance, a high center of gravity, are light weight, maneuverable, and knobby tires that do better on dirt and sand than do street bike tires. You can literally ride right off the road and onto a trail on a dual purpose bike.

I say that dual purpose bikes are the best of both worlds because they function well on or off the street. I say that they are not the best of either because the design that makes them appropriate for both imposes some limitations for both. I have never seen, for example, a dual purpose bike with 1100 ccs. Why? Because an 1100 cc engine would be both too big and too powerful for most off-road settings. Similarly, dual purpose bikes aren't really made for more difficult trail situations. They're just too big and respond too slowly (compared to a trail bike) for most people to ride on higher-difficulty paths. So, with a dual purpose, you can do most anything any other bike will do, but you will probably not be able to do it as well as some other bikes of their type.

Take, for example, a Yamaha TTR 230 (trail bike, 125 ccs) and compare it to a KLR 650. The Yamaha is taller and more nimble. The KLR is more powerful and adapts to road conditions more readily. People use the TTR for riding in some pretty serious off-road conditions. People are known to make coast-to-coast jaunts on their KLRs.

Nimble is biker slang for how quickly a bike responds to commands, how well it turns, and how easy it is to manage. As a general rule, smaller, taller bikes are more nimble and bigger, heavier bikes are less so. Off-road bikes are usually more nimble than street bikes.

Dual purpose bikes can often be dressed out to make your dual purpose a true multi-purpose. I have, for instance, invested more than a few dollars in my KLR. Stripped down to its basics it is a street bike that will more than hold its own. Add a piece of luggage to the rear rack and it's good to go for commuting or a day trip. Snap on the side rear luggage and I'm ready to ride for a week. Is the weather cold? I swap out the sport windshield for a bigger touring model, plug in my electric vest, turn on the electric hand grips, and I'm ready to go, If I want to travel to a great off-road site I mount all the luggage, ride to the site, stash the luggage in a hotel room, and hit the trail.

Adventure

Some folks count adventure bikes as a kind of dual purpose. I really can't argue that point very much. Adventure bikes are bigger, heavier versions of their dual-purpose cousins and are made for comfortable travel to the places in the world that are not readily reached by any other kind of bike. Biker brethren who are far more talented in the seat than I will ever be, take off on these things to remote areas of the world such as the mountains of rural Mexico or the jungles of Africa. They also hop on them for coast to coast ventures on well-maintained interstates. They are dual purpose, but to my mind they are a class all their own.

The quality and features of adventure bikes comes at a price. Be prepared to spend substantially more for an adventure than you would for a dual purpose. This is also where the truly high-end bikes start. BMW, for example, makes a great 1200 cc, with twice the engine size and four times the price tag of my KLR 650. It's a beauty, and will run just about forever if cared for properly.

Adventure bikes improve on-street performance over that of dirt and dual purpose rides. As they improve street performance, however, their ease of management off the pavement decreases. Adventure bikes are tall and heavy. BMW lists the seat height of the R1200GS at 35.2 inches. Try that with a 28 inch inseam! the weight is listed as 490 pounds dry, 560 pounds wet. Now imagine trying to balance that bike with your 28 inch inseam when a rock slips under the wheel! Adventure bikes are wonderful inventions. They are not a good first bike, however, and are not really for the vertically challenged. I'll content myself with admiring the Beemers and other adventure bikes from a distance.

Here's a little more biker lingo for you. *Dry* weight on a bike refers to what a stock model weighs with no fluids in it. Add gas and oil and you have the wet weight. In case you hadn't noticed, gasoline is heavy and a big tank like the ones on adventure bikes adds to the weight considerably.

Some people like to speak of the progression of dirt to dual purpose to adventure bikes as a continuum from suitability for dirt to suitability for road. I think this pretty much nails it. Small, light, nimble bikes like the TTR are easy to manage in challenging off-road situations. They are really not suited for the road at all. Larger, less nimble, but powerful dual purposes find a place in the middle. The largest, least nimble, and most powerful adventure bikes allow you to get off road, but are best suited for less challenging paths and the open highway.

Standard

The term *standard* is sometimes used to refer to a street bike that is smaller, puts the driver in an upright posture, and has very little in the way of accessories like windshields and fairings. The Honda Nighthawk on which I learned is an example of a standard bike. They tend to be good beginner bikes because they are relatively inexpensive and are easy to ride.

I'm not sure how common the use of the word "standard" actually is. I had never heard it until recently when I came across it in another book. That prompted a check of the gold standard in reference material, Wikipedia. Yep, those guys knew what it meant. At that point I knew the use of the term was legit. Still, I wasn't sure how widespread it was. Trying to get a handle on its commonality, I called a couple of buddies at dealerships. Both knew the term, but both said they rarely used it. Maybe it's because lots of folks start with standards, but most move to something else after they have some miles under their belts.

Naked is an older term sometimes used to refer to bikes with only basic equipment, lacking the fairings, windshields, crash bars, and floorboards that many other types of street bikes have. The term is said to be used almost synonymously with *standard*, but I couldn't swear to it. I've never heard anyone actually use either.

Cruisers

Cruisers are often referred to as a distinctly American bike. They are the bikes of both big and small screens, the stuff of the American legend. Actors and characters from Peter Fonda to the Sons of Anarchy to House (last episode only, please watch as he and Wilson ride off to their final adventure together) have immortalized them. They are the bikes many Americans love to ride.

Cruisers are typically bulky and muscular. Although they are great to ride, they are really more about appearance than performance. Cruisers are designed to allow the rider to lean back comfortably in the seat. Foot position is typically forward. The engines are torqued to promote control and infrequent shifting at slower speeds. They are the most comfortable bike to ride at moderate speeds and in start-stop situations. Although they are still comfortable at higher speeds, extended riding at Interstate speeds can produce fatigue from pulling against the force of the wind while holding the handlebars.

My Virago is a cruiser, albeit a smaller, less bulky version. As I think I've mentioned, it is also my favorite to ride. It is comfortable, has plenty of power, and handles great considering that it isn't really about handling. It is a little short on storage space, as are most cruisers. Some will accommodate saddle bags, although they won't work on my Virago. What does work is a small accessory rack that I purchased and attached above the rear fender. I have a tall, narrow bag with a detachable roll top and backpack straps that serves more than adequately for a few days of travel.

Cruisers are about metal and chrome. They were the original "choppers", bikes originally created by outlaw MCs who despised the "dressing" of post-World War II touring bikes. The MCs chopped off all the fancy stuff, anything the bike really didn't need, in order to make it go faster. The terms have evolved over the years, and today is used to refer to a bike with a long fork, high handlebars, no rear suspension, and minimal accessories. Today's choppers may be created by stripping down a decked out bike in a garage. More often, however, they are purchased from the factory "chopped".

"Dressing" is what you eat with turkey and mashed potatoes. It is also a term used to describe the extra baggage and accessories that are included on larger bikes, particularly touring models. Large touring motorcycles loaded up with luggage and gizmos are often referred to as "full dressers".

The word custom is also applied to some cruisers, even when they are shipped as is from the factory. This practice originated from factory innovations combining parts of different types of bikes. It continues to be used today to indicate a bike for which several options are available from the factory.

A "power cruiser" is exactly what it sounds like: a cruiser built for greater performance, primarily through a bigger engine and increased power. The engines are mostly
V-Twins. They also typically have better brakes, suspensions, and better ground clearance than do traditional cruisers.

A V-Twin Engine has two cylinders that are arranged in a V shape. They are easily recognized by the V shaped columns that contain the cylinders located under the gas tank and/or seat of most power cruisers. A few manufacturers use a different design, but the greater number of cruisers produced today have V-Twins.

Sport bikes are made for speed and handling. They are breathtakingly fast and amazingly nimble on curves. The rider sits in a forward-leaning position, bending low to minimize wind resistance. The sound they make as they accelerate is more like a sewing machine at 100 times the decibel level than anything Singer ever conceived. Very different from the "I'm the boss so back the heck off." rumble of a Harley Cruiser. If you were just passed at 70 mph by a "rrrrrrrrrrrrr" sound and a quick red or blue blur, you were probably just buried by a sport bike.

If you hear someone say *crotch rocket* they are referring to sport bikes. That probably wasn't much of a stretch to figure out. You straddle them on your crotch and they shoot like a Cruise missile. If you've never been on one, talk to guys who usually ride cruisers of touring bikes and ask what they think. You'll hear stories of riding down the highway thinking they're going 70, and then looking down to see the speedometer at 100. Another word you'll hear used for sport bikes is *rice burner*. This is reference to a staple food of many folks where crotch rockets evolved into a force in the market, Japan. Strictly speaking, a crotch rocket is always a rice burner but a rice burner is not always a crotch rocket. Some of the best dual sports are made in Japan and three Japanese manufacturers make very nice lines that include everything from standards to cruisers. My KLR 650 is a dual sport rice burner. My Virago is a cruiser rice burner. By the way, some people think the use of the term "rice burner" is a bit of an ethnic slur. I will admit that some people certainly use it that way. The Japanese are, I think, more polite than many of us Americans. To the best of my knowledge they have not taken revenge by calling Harleys tobacco burners or corn burners.

There's a very old bias against sport bikes and rice burners in particular that suggest that they are not well made. Excuse me, friends, but we are well into the second decade of the second millennium of the Common Era. There was a time that the Japanese bikes were inferior. They were blazing fast but just weren't that well made. Those days are long gone. Japanese sport bikes today are well-made beasts that eat up blacktop with amazing efficiency. If you don't like them, don't ride one, but at least be up-to-date with your bashing materials.

I've probably also created a misconception that only the Japanese make sport bikes. Let me hasten to correct that. There are excellent crotch rockets produced in other part of the world. Some argue that Ducati, an Italian manufacturer, makes the best sport bike. Triumph, Moto Guzzi and others could certainly dispute that claim.

There are sub-categories of sport bikes, including lightweight, middleweight, and supersport. Lightweights are smaller, lighter, and not so fast as the higher-end models. They are considered beginner bikes by some and typically are built in the 500 cc range.

Middleweights are bigger and faster, averaging perhaps 600-750 ccs. Supersports are that 120 mph blur you saw on the highway. These are sometimes referred to as superbikes and are built at 1000cc or better. Some people recognize divisions within this category such as literbike, hypersport, and hyperbike, but we're just going to call it supersport and leave it at that. Letters of outrage should be directed to my bogus email box located somewhere offshore.

Touring

You may see just about any bike of 650 cc or better on the Interstate. You may even see some smaller engines here and there, although I would recommend that only for the actively self-destructive. The bike designed for the Interstate, however, and for any long-distance travel, is the touring bike.

Touring bikes are wonders of technology and comfort. Do you want to ride for eight hours through sun and wind and rain and park it at your motel with energy to spare for some sightseeing, dinner, and dancing? A touring bike is your best bet. Do you want to carry a passenger who enjoys those same benefits? Think touring. Would you like to have a fairly wide selection of clothing and other personal items for your trip? Consider the luggage capacity of a big tourer. Do you want to check the time, listen to satellite radio, and carry a glass of iced tea handy when you ride? Again, touring bikes are your easiest and best bet.

Touring bikes are big, powerful, comfortable, and spacious, spacious at least, compared to other motorcycles. Notice that first word: big. They are tall, broad, and heavy. A great bike for the experienced rider with the skill and strength to manage one, not so much for the new guy or gal who is saddling up for the first time. Harley-Davidson's Road King and Glide series the Honda Gold Wind are probably the best known examples.

There is a class of touring bikes called sort-touring that is lighter and more manageable but still provides many of the benefits of their touring cousin. BMW, Kawasaki, Aprila, Ducati, and Triumph offer models in this category. When you go look at these bikes you may find that some look a lot like the adventure bikes we talked about earlier in the chapter. I would be hard-pressed to disagree with you. Just remember that there is no quiz at the end of the chapter and that the lines between some classes of bikes are more than a little blurry. Should you be overcome with anger at my lack of clarity, I commend that offshore email account to your attention.

Trikes

Trikes are motorcycles with three wheels. They are probably considered a touring bike by most people, but most people aren't sitting at my iPad at this moment. A regular trike has one wheel in the front and two in the back. A reverse trike has two in the front and one in the back. You can buy a manufactured trike of either variety or you can buy an aftermarket kit that will convert touring bikes to trikes. There are also specialty shops that will custom-make a touring bike into a trike.

Trikes are more stable than two-wheelers and are not a bad option for beginners, particularly if you don't care how many wheels are under you. They are big, comfy, powerful, and have lots of storage space. They also have a lot of the gizmos that make pleasurable travel in the electronic age more practical. I love my Can-Am, a reverse trike. I also think the big, tricked out Harleys and Gold Wings are remarkably cool.

You get some interesting reactions from people when you ride a trike. People want to know how you like them, how much they cost, and whether or not they will lean on curves. If you ride a reverse trike people ask the same questions, but also seem to have one of two reactions. They either think your bike is amazing or they think you are an idiot. I've actually had folks tell me that if it has two wheels in the back it is a motorcycle but if it has two in the front it isn't. Never mind that both the federal and state governments and every motorcycle manufacturer in the world disagrees with them. They are right! I enjoy my conversations with everyone else in the world and commend the attention of the detractors to the aforementioned offshore inbox.

Scooters

Scooters are typically designed with comfort and fuel efficiency in mind. They are the transportation of choice for many commuters. When I've visited cities in other countries, Hong Kong, for example, I've been astounded to see the number of riders on the street at rush hour, the vast majority of them on some sort of scooter.

I don't know much about scooters. I've never ridden one, but have sat on a couple of newer models on the dealer floor. The ones I tried out were like sitting on a cloud. They also have lots more storage space than most motorcycles. Folks who commute on them put whatever they need for work in the space under the seat. When they get to work they take that stuff out, stash their helmet and gear in the compartment, and walk through the door. Most smaller motorcycles suitable for commuting just don't have that kind of space. The low cost and high efficiency of scooters makes them an increasing choice for commuters who might not otherwise consider a motorcycle. Oh, did I mention that people also love to ride them?

Scooters are available in a broad range of power options. I understand that some run as low as 50ccs. Suzuki, on the other hand, makes a 400 cc and a 650cc model. I was going to mention that smaller engines usually get better gas mileage, but was intimidated by the resounding "duuuh" it would no doubt produce.

If you're used to the controls on a regular motorcycle you'll find that things work a bit differently on a scooter. I just watched a cool YouTube video where a guy described how he crashed his scooter before he ever got on it because he treated it like a regular bike. He then demonstrated his error for the camera.

You need standard rider gear for a scooter: helmet, gloves, and shoes or boots with anti-slip soles. Protective jackets and pants are also a good idea. Going down at 45 mph on a scooter is no different from going down at the same speed on a cruiser. Hopefully it won't happen, but it's better to be prepared just in case. If you're going to ride in cold or wet weather, you'll also want to take a look at one of the chapters that follow, the one purchasing the gear that you wear.

Rat, survival, and custom

You'll hear lots of other names for different types of bikes. Sometimes they describe subclasses of the manufactured types we just talked about. Sometimes they refer to a category of bike all its own. I'll never be able to cover all of them here. I probably don't even know some of them. Here are a few examples.

Rat bikes are patch-together masterpieces kept operational by years of repair, replacement, and modification using whatever can be found, will work, and is cheap. Rat bikes look unusual because they are. We aren't just talking about replacing a stock air filter with a high performance job. We're talking duct tape on pipes and mufflers, twist ties replacing clutch leveler brackets, and junk yard forks from an entirely different model replacing the old, worn-out versions from the bike being preserved.

"Preserved" is not exactly the right word for a rat bike. Morphed, managed, and coaxed to continue are probably more appropriate. When you preserve something you invest funds in maintaining both function and appearance. With a rat bike the goal is to keep it running as much as you can for as long as you can at the lowest cost possible.

Having trashed rats (pun unintended), let me hasten to add that many of them are very cool. There's a special kind of magic in the grafted metal and borrowed plastic that form a rat. You just have to admire the creative effort that assembled them while you wonder at the courage of the rider who braves them.

Survival bikes are a lot like rat bikes, except that the object is to build a ride in the tradition of the Mad Max movies. In Mad Max survivors in a post-apocalyptic society patch together whatever parts they can find to produce serviceable bikes. In real life people build bikes with similar features: oversized gas tanks, matte black finishes, and parts that don't quite fit borrowed from other models and manufacturers. Rat bikes are made as cheaply as possible. Survivor bikes are made with life after an apocalypse in mind.

Survival bikes are sometimes called *black rats* because they look like rat bikes with a matte black finish. The basic differences between rat and survivor are still present, only the names have been changed to protect the less-than-innocent.

We talked about factory custom bikes earlier in the chapter. These are actually fairly standard but allow the buyer to choose options on things like color, wheel types, exhaust style, and handlebars. An entirely different category of bike, also referred to as *custom*, is created by taking a production bike and tearing into it. Almost anything is game: extended forks, higher handlebars, a bigger engine, a modified frame.

Custom bike manufacturers change appearance, but they often also improve performance. Many custom bikes are faster, more nimble, and quicker off the mark than are their factory counterparts.

If you'd like to get a better idea of what rat, survival, and custom bikes look like, I suggest an Internet search or a trip to a local bike show. I did a Google search a few minutes ago and found cool pictures of bikes in all three categories. I found not only pictures, but links for clubs, blogs, and forums for each. If you hear a type of bike mentioned and don't feel comfortable saying, "Ummm, errrr, what was that again?" Try Googling. I'm betting a little effort will bring some big results.

Sidecars

OK, so sidecars aren't motorcycles. They can, however, be purchased as a part of a motorcycle or as an item that can be added to a motorcycle. They're more like a bike than an aftermarket horn, so I'm discussing them here rather than as an accessory.

The folks I know either hate or love sidecars. I happen to be among the lovers. Nearly everyone who is old enough seems to have some vague association with Colonel Klink (obscure, post 55 television reference). Sidecars have a military origin and are very practical even without a machine gun mounted on the front
Sidecars provide space for a passengers and cargo, often both in the seat and in compartments within

the body. Some have built in drive trains that make a two-wheel bike into an all-terrain vehicle. That's why I want one. I'm dying to take off through a farmer's field on a snowy day.

I know of at least one manufacturer who builds their products with sidecars connected. That company is Ural, a Russian manufacturer. You can view their products on their website. Several companies offer aftermarket versions. An internet search will lead you to them. I particularly like the ones that attach and detach to and from the bike quickly. To me that's the best of both worlds.

Trailers

Yep, you're right. Trailers aren't bikes, either. They are, however, an important part of the riding experience. The type of bike you ride may help determine the kind of trailer you buy.

Lots of experienced riders will tell you that, once you've learned to pack, a trailer really isn't necessary. This is particularly true if you have a trike or a big touring bike. Not everyone agrees, however. Some of us are less willing than others to do without some of our daily niceties. For the nicety lovers among us, trailers are a wonderful thing.

Most trailers attach to a hitch that is manufactured for a specific bike. You get a Harley hitch from the Harley dealer and a Honda hitch for your Gold Wing. The 1 7/8 inch ball on the hitch matches the 1 7/8 inch coupler on the trailer. You then connect the lights on the bike to the lights on the trailer with a standard harness. Most any trailer will work on most any bike, with a couple of exceptions. One exception is the case where a manufacturer makes both the bike and the trailer and want to make sure you use only their products. Can-Am is an example. My Can-Am uses a standard trailer hitch, but the wiring harness is anything but standard. The harness connects not only the lights, but also the bike's rather sophisticated computer system to the trailer. The advantage is that the computer constantly monitors the behavior of the trailer and alerts the driver if issues arise. The downside is that, without severe, warranty-voiding alterations to the lighting harness, you can't pull anything other than a Can-Am trailer. The really bad news? Those puppies retail in the $4,000 range. The other exception to any motorcycle trailer to any motorcycle rule has to do with tongue weight. You need to be sure the weight imposed by the tongue of the trailer when loaded does not exceed the maximum weight rating of the hitch. If your hitch is rated for 40 pounds and the trailer is rated at 50 you shouldn't try to pull it.

Kickstands down

Thus, we end our discussion of the 3 or 4 or 12 categories of motorcycles. As we've learned, there is no official or legal definition of each category, except the legal standards that separate off-road vehicles from on-road. Bikes tend to be grouped by their common characteristics, but some models and certainly many custom bikes blur those lines to the vanishing point.

I recommend that you read this chapter a couple of times, once as a straight-through read and once while doing internet searches. For each type of bike run an Internet search. Read what you find about them, look at the images, and check out any videos you may find. When you've finished your second read, head to a couple of dealerships. Check out what they have on the floor and try to figure out the category of each. Sit on the different types and notice the hand position, foot position, and the general position of your body when you are mounted. Ask a salesperson any questions that come to mind. If the salesperson isn't interested in helping you, find a new salesperson or visit a different shop. A dealer who doesn't want to deal with you isn't much of a dealer at all.

The next chapter is about the basics of riding. It includes information on starting a bike as well as the steps you need to take to master basic riding skills. It won't replace a good riding course, but it will enhance your knowledge and skills in such a way that your early riding experiences will be much more positive and comfortable.

Chapter 4

So I Bought One, Now What?

So you have your bike. If you listened to the old man you have a somewhat used 250 cc of some sort and a safe, legal place to practice. If you listened a little you have a bike in the 600-800 cc range and a safe, legal place to practice. If you didn't listen at all (I didn't when I bought.) you are the proud owner of a half-ton of gleaming metal, chrome, and leather and figure you'll get around to the safe, legal part sometime pretty soon. Regardless of what bike or bikes you have, the next step is the same. It's time to learn to ride.

If you're going to start to ride you're going to need some basic gear. If you've been to a dealer or an accessory shop you've probably already started to collect it. Similarly, if you've signed up for the Motorcycle Safety Dude safety course or have friends who ride, you already know what you need. If you don't have your gear yet, please jump ahead to chapter 6. It's entirely devoted to the gear you'll wear to make your rides safer and more comfortable. After you've read it and gotten your gear, come back here. If you're going to ride now, buy now. If you don't have a helmet, boots, gloves, jeans, and a mesh jacket, now's the time to head back to the dealer or go online and get them. Whichever type of bike you selected you need to protect yourself, and no matter how confident you may be in your own ability to manage that beautiful mass of metal, there's always the "other guy" out there somewhere just waiting to knock you out of the saddle. You may never get knocked, but should it ever happen to you remember that there are two knocks, the one where the guy knocks you and the one where you knock the pavement. Good gear gives you a much better chance of coming through both knocks intact.

There are six foundational steps in learning to ride.

Those steps are what this chapter is about. I strongly suggest that, if you are new to motorcycling, you take these steps seriously and spend enough time on each to assure that you have a reasonable level of mastery. By "reasonable level" I mean several things. First, you need to be comfortable enough with the bike that you don't have to spend a lot of time looking for the controls you need to manage different situations. For example, when you're ready to fire it up, you will want to limit the amount of brain freeze you experience sitting there trying to remember what to pull, twist, or switch next. Similarly the first time you are out riding and run out of gas in your primary tank (notice that I am speaking of this as a "when" not an "if") you will want to minimize the number of panic moments you spend searching for the petcock so you can switch to reserve. Knowing your bike will allow you to respond more quickly and efficiently to any situation you may encounter. It will also save you the embarrassing moment that comes when, after you have cranked the resistant engine to the point of frustration, a grizzled greybeard (or worse, a pimple-faced kid) reaches over and mercifully opens the choke for you.

A *greybeard* is an older, possibly more experienced rider. Although it may sound like a derisive term, in the biker community it is actually a form of respect. Greybeards are respected for their knowledge of biking, but also for the wisdom they have gained though life in general.

A second important factor in deciding how much time to spend on the foundational steps we'll talk about next is muscle memory response. When you are puttering around a parking lot at 15-20 mph it's OK to take the time to think, "Lessee, I want to stop now. First I want to pull on the clutch level and hold it. Then I want to downshift into first while simultaneously applying the rear and front brakes. After that I need to get my left foot in position to set it on the ground while assuring that my right foot can move off the brake to help balance the bike if needed." If you're speeding along at 45 mph and the driver in front of you suddenly slows down you can't afford the time to think all that through. You want muscle memory to do it for you.

Muscles, of course, don't do the remembering. Brains do. But the relationship between your brain and your muscles needs to be such that, when the brake lights in front of you flare you automatically respond. Many folks refer to this as muscle memory.

The surest way to develop muscle memory is through repetition. This means doing whatever it is that you want to do over and over again until it begins to happen automatically. For example, for two of the steps discussed below, getting to know your bike and starting it up, you may want to go through the motions (not actually powering your bike up and down) over and over again until your body does it for you, automatically, without ever having to look. You at least want to be able to find the necessary spots on the bike quickly, even if you're OK with sneaking a peak.

Science also tells us that most muscle memory is best developed in short, incremental practice sessions. This means, for example, that 1/2 hour to 1 hour of practice per day will enhance muscle memory more effectively than a session of several hours on a single day. The key, then, to developing the basic muscle memory to respond appropriately to your bike and to make it respond appropriately to you is frequent short sessions of repeated activity over a period of several days.

Working on your motor skills will help you automatically do the things you need to do, but it will also help you learn not to do some of the things you shouldn't. One example is the automatic separation of movements that roll the throttle and squeeze the front brake level. Your right hand does both of these. Obviously, it is usually important not to do both at the same time. Practice helps you mind and body learn to stop the bike when needed, accelerate it when needed, and avoid trying to do the two simultaneously.

The first steps in learning to ride, then involve doing enough safe space riding to develop your muscle memory and enhance your overall skill level in seven areas. These areas should be developed in steps, including: 1) getting to know your bike, 2) pre-ride inspection, 3) starting it up, 3) power walking, 4) backing, 5) slow riding, 6) turning, and 7) stopping.

<u>Getting to know your bike</u>

When I bought my Road King (a big, beautiful, powerful and heavy model) I had seen lots of bikes before. I had been on a few and had ridden one. My first day at the Harley Dealer was, however, a study in how to act like a noob. Had a major television network been present with cameras rolling I might have had a new career in stand-up (or maybe lay-down) comedy. As it went, however, I learned a lot from Brad and Wayne and the folks at Boswell's in Cookeville. Among the things I learned were where the various devices are located that are used to start the bike, and that, depending on the model of the bike those devices might be located in very different places.

The first step in learning the basics of riding is to know where all those startup devices are and to learn to manage them in the way that starts your bike easily.

There are six primary devices on some bikes, five on others. In this section I'll provide a brief overview of these devices. We'll talk about what each does in later sections of the chapter. For now, just concentrate on learning where they are and what they are called.

We're going to run through the list twice, once with diagrams and once with a more lengthy description of how to use each device. I recommend that you take the book with you to the bike and use the section with diagrams to help you find each one. Then read the sections with the descriptions of how to use them. Some of the information may be a little repetitive, but that should prevent a lot of turning back and forth between pages.

Petcock

The correct name for the fuel valve is the petcock. Most bikes that don't have fuel injection have petcocks. They usually have three positions, open, closed, and reserve.

When open the valve allows gasoline to flow freely from the gas tank to the engine. When set to reserve it switches to the reserve tank, a safeguard against running out of gas. When set to closed gas is trapped in the tank. You should close the petcock when you store the bike and when you transport it. If your bike is fuel injected it won't have a petcock. The electronic system takes care of everything for you.

Ignition switch

The ignition switch will look very familiar. It's the place you put the key in. Insert the key, turn it, and you allow electricity to flow from the battery to the engine.

Clutch lever

The clutch lever is located on the left side of the handlebar just in front of the hand grip. It should be positioned so that you can reach it with the first finger or two of your left hand when you are seated on the bike. To engage the clutch you pull it toward you. This allows you to shift into a higher or lower gear or into neutral. You'll use the clutch lever and the gear shift lever (located in front of the left foot peg) to switch the bike into neutral before starting if.

Shift lever

As I just mentioned the shift lever is immediately in front of the left foot peg. In order to change gears you pull in on the clutch lever and either push down on the shift lever or lift it up with the toe of your boot. First gear is down one notch from neutral. To get to second you lift up one full level to second (one half would put you in neutral), One more lift gets you to third, another to fourth, and so on. Every time you change gears you need to engage and disengage the clutch, I'll say more about managing your clutch and shift lever later in this chapter.

Front brake lever

The front brake lever is located on the right handlebar in the same position as the clutch lever on the left. If you pull in on the front brake lever you engage the front brake only. More on the interesting consequences of doing so at inappropriate times will follow in later chapters.

Rear brake lever

The rear brake lever is a right foot thing. It is

located just in front of the right foot peg. If you push down on it you engage the rear brake. The front and rear brakes should be used strategically. Sometimes you use the front only, sometimes the rear only, and sometimes both of them together. We'll talk more about braking strategies later.

Engine kill switch

The engine kill switch is located on a small instrument panel in front of your right thumb. You have to switch it into the start position in order to start the engine. It's called the kill switch because it's what you use to kill the engine both at the end of the ride or if you need to quickly stop the engine from running.

Choke

Finding the choke can be an interesting adventure. It's generally on the handlebars, the left side of the engine, or the right side of the engine. The best way to find it is to ask the salesman or consult the owner's manual. You use the choke to change the fuel/air mixture when you start the bike. It is particularly important in cold weather. If your bike is fuel injected that search for a choke may take a while. On a fuel injected bike the computer takes care of the fuel/air mix for you. There is no choke.

Pre-ride inspection

The pre-ride inspection (PRI) is something every rider should do before firing the bike up. After years of hopping into a "cage" or automobile without so much as a thought to oil level, tire, pressure, and turn signals it may seem unnecessary to complete this process. Still the Motorcycle Safety Foundation (herein known as the

Motorcycle Safety Dudes or MSD) recommends the PRI for at least a couple of reasons. First, a PRI for an automobile isn't a bad idea at all. Second, the presence of four wheels and walls of steel (OK, and fiberglass) make a cage much more forgiving should one of the basic systems on your means of transportation fail. I've included the Motorcycle Safety Dude's list below, but let's talk about a couple of the items on it and why those items are important.

Cage is a term avid bikers use to describe enclosed vehicles such as cars and trucks. It's a reference to the loss of freedom experienced by taking to the road surrounded by a mass of metal.

The MSDs recommend checking your tire pressure before you ride, every time. This is important because it causes your bike to behave consistently and predictably while moving. On an automobile a low tire may affect your ability to steer effectively, turn efficiently, and could even cause a blowout. If a wheel fails to perform on an automobile the other three will probably provide enough support to allow you to deal with the problem. On a bike, with only one additional wheel, low pressure can lean to incidents that rank somewhere between embarrassing and disastrous.

Another example of the importance of the PRI has to do with turn signals. The MSDs suggest that you make sure your turn signals are working (for that matter, all your lights) each time before you ride. This, of course, is most easily done if you have a second person available to stand in front of and behind the bike while you flip the switches. If no one else is available, however, you can complete the test yourself by turning switches on and walking to the front and rear of the bike. For brakes or switches that don't lock in place try flipping the switch with one hand and cupping the other around the lamp so that you can see the reflection in your hand. You can also direct the front or rear toward a surface that will reflect enough light to allow you to see what's working. I have a friend who has developed his own device for this purpose. Kenny mounted a mirror on the end of a broomstick, allowing him to place a foot on the rear brake pedal and hold the mirror in front of the light he's checking at the same time. Most folks will probably find that they can do the check without walls and mirrors, but these are practical alternatives for those who cannot.

Starting it up

The first few starts on a motorcycle can be an adventure in exploration. You may find that when the dealer explains the layout of the bike and fires it up for you everything seems crystal clear, yet when you start it for the first (and second, and third) time you forget to do some things and do others out of order. Having taken the time to repeatedly review the controls used in startup will be a key to making this process go smoothly.

This section is going to assume that your new bike has electronic start. Most bikes made for the street these days have an electronic ignition system, drawing the necessary start-up power from the battery. In the old days motorcycles were "kick-started", using a lever mounted behind the right foot peg. Older bikes may have a kick-lever, as may certain dirt bikes. Sometimes the kick-lever is the only means of starting the bike. On some models it is a backup in case the electronic system fails. Given the fact that you'll probably be riding a bike with an electronic start system I'll focus my comments on that option.

Motorcycles have historically had a traditional

carburetor system. In order to use this system you have to manipulate a "choke" in order to adjust the flow of gasoline to the carburetor in order to start the engine. This position of the choke is known as "full". In order to move the choke to full you need to either pull out on a knob or move a lever to the correct position. With the knob or lever positioned correctly your bike should start right up. If it doesn't, and you know it has been started in the very recent past, try the steps described below again. There's a good chance you've missed something and can easily remedy the situation. I have found that the uses of certain expletives enhance the process, but your experience may be different.

The choke will adjust the flow of gasoline only if there is gasoline present to flow. Of course you need gasoline in the tank, but you also need to assure that the "petcock" is set to either allow flow from the primary or reserve gas tanks.

As I mentioned above the petcock has three primary functions. The first is to allow gasoline to flow to the engine. If the petcock is closed no fuel will flow. If it is open for either the primary or reserve tank fuel will flow from that tank. I mention this a second time because I am betting most will forget to close or open it at least twice. After you've cranked away for several minutes with the engine steadily refusing to start think about the petcock. That's where my money says the problem is.

You need to know were the petcock is and how to use it so you can adjust it when you store your bike, when you run out of fuel while riding, or when you want to restart your bike after it's been shut down for a while. When you have finished a ride and are going to park your bike you will want to close the petcock. This will prevent gasoline from venting or sloshing out of the fuel system.

When you are going to ride, you will obviously need to open it again. If you have been riding and have neglected to keep tabs on your fuel level, you may need to switch to the reserve tank when you run out of gas. Most folks will tell you that you should be able to find and correctly manipulate the petcock without looking to assure that you can do it quickly and efficiently. This would be particularly important, for example, should you run out of gasoline in the primary tank in heavy traffic.

If you search your bike from fork to rear reflector and can't find your petcock, don't panic, you probably don't have one. If you chose to start with a bigger, more expensive bike and have no petcock you have a fuel injected system. There is no petcock, there is no carburetor, the bike handles this entire process for you. "What," you ask, "Have you just made me spend 153 seconds of my valuable time reading about carburetion systems when I don't even have one?" "Nope," I reply, "time not wasted at all. You will now know that your friends who have chokes and petcocks aren't tweaking their handlebars and scratching their knees when you're firing up your bikes. See, this book really is a very efficient use of time.

One more word about the choke. When your bike is warmed up, that is, able to run smoothly, without the choke being set to full, you want to close the choke. As you might imagine, you do this simply by moving the knob or lever to the closed position. Bikes warm up at different rates, so you need to learn whether yours is quick about it or takes a little time. As you're learning you may want to let it run a bit at full choke, then gradually close it off. If you close it off a bit and the bike stutters or stalls, move it back a bit. When you get the choke fully closed, gently roll the throttle a time or two. If the bike continues to run smoothly you are ready to go.

There is one other component that can affect the way your bike idles, or runs while sitting still, and that is the adjustment screw on the carburetor. The adjustment screw looks like exactly that, a small screw situated on the carburetor, probably up somewhere fairly high and located toward the center of the seat. If your engine refuses to warm up, try adjusting the carburetor. A little turn to the right should make the engine run faster. A turn to the left should make it run slower. Two basic rules: 1) Be sure you notice the starting position of the screw in case you decide that you want to move it back there, and 2) Move the screw a little bit, maybe an eighth turn at a time. If your carburetor does need adjusting, it probably doesn't need much. An eighth or two will probably do it. The carburetor adjustment screw really doesn't belong in a discussion of start-up procedures. You will rarely, maybe never, have to use it. I've mentioned it here because it may affect your ability to start your engine. You probably won't have to use it but, if you do, it will make the starting and riding processes go much more smoothly.

I mentioned the ignition switch earlier. As I also mentioned it is very similar to the one in an automobile. You put the key in and turn it to the right. This supplies the power from the battery that allows your engine to start. On some bikes it may perform additional functions like locking down the front wheel or opening a compartment on the bike. For the purposes of start-up you will only need to insert the key and give it a turn to the right.

Unlike a cage, the key doesn't immediately supply fire to the engine. It does allow power to flow from the battery, but the "kill switch" which should also be called something like the "fire-up switch" is needed to actually crank the engine. We'll talk about the "kill switch in a couple of paragraphs.

When you start your bike you normally want it to be in neutral. I say normally because if you need to start it with a dead battery someday you will have to have it in first gear for a push start. Under normal circumstances, however, you want the bike to be in neutral. You accomplish this by manipulating the clutch lever and the shift lever.

The motorcycle is similar to the automobile in that the clutch should be engaged in order to shift gears. You engage the clutch by pulling the clutch lever, located in front of the hand grip on the left handlebar and holding it in position. You can then shift the gears by either pressing down on the shift lever (located immediately in front of the left foot peg). If you are in neutral and you push down on the shift lever, the bike goes into first gear. If you put your toe under the shift lever and move it up gently you put the bike in neutral again. If you put your toe under the shift lever and move it up firmly the bike goes into second gear. Do it again and you are in third, then fourth and, depending on the bike, fifth then sixth. When bikers speak of "one down, four up" or "one down, five up" this is what they are talking about. "One down" refers to the position of first gear from neutral. "Four up" or "five up" refers to the position above neutral of second and the higher gears. When starting the motorcycle it is best to put it in neutral. Some will start while in gear if the clutch is engaged. Others are designed so they will not. As a rule, put your bike in gear in order to start it.

Most street and dual purpose bikes have a light on the instrument panel to let you know when you are in neutral. Dirt bikes typically do not have such a light. If you don't have or for some reason can't see a neutral light, just put the gear in first by engaging the clutch and pushing and releasing the shift lever repeatedly until it won't push down any more. This will put the bike in first gear. Engage the clutch again and lift slightly on the shift lever. This should put you in neutral.

Some motorcycles, particularly older models with smaller engines, are notoriously difficult to get into neutral. If you try repeatedly to get the bike into neutral but seem to always wind up in first or second, try "rocking" the bike by shifting into first releasing the clutch, and rocking the bike forward and backward. It won't move much in either direction, but a few seconds of this activity should allow you to stop, then shift into neutral. If it doesn't work the first time, try it again. Sometimes those older gears can be a tad stubborn.

The next device you need to use is the "kill" switch. It's called that because a quick flip of this switch will allow you to instantly stop your engine should you need to do so. It's also the way you shut down at the end of the ride. Yep, if you switch it one way to turn your engine off when you're done, you need to switch it the other way when you want to start up. The kill switch is located on the right handlebar.

The final touch to firing up your beauty is pressing the starter-button thingy (SBT), more commonly known as the start button. The SBT is located on the right handlebar at the bottom of the control cluster nearest your thumb. Once everything else is done you simply press it, and your beautiful bike roars or purrs into action.

The MSD has developed an acronym (FINE-C) to help you remember how to start your bike. If you've ridden ATVs in the past or have used much gasoline-driven power equipment you will find it to be somewhat familiar. Still, I strongly recommend that you memorize it and use it. Even with this kind of previous experience you may find yourself proudly stepping over the seat, calmly switching on everything you think you needed to, and getting no reaction when you push the SBT. If this happens chances are you have forgotten to do something in the startup procedure. You can avoid this situation, or can remedy it if it does occur, by using the MSD checklist. Here's what they recommend:

The "F" in FINE-C stands for fuel. This is to remind you to turn on the petcock. If you've done the previous shut-down properly the last thing you will have done is close it. Now you'll need to open it to allow fuel to flow to the engine. If you try to fire the bike up, have lights, but nothing happens, you probably forgot the "F".

"I" is for ignition. This means that you should turn the ignition switch. Of course, in order to do so you'll need to insert the key. Remember that, unlike cages, turning the ignition will not turn the engine. Your bike will continue to sit quietly even after you have completed step 2.

Neutral or "N" is the third step. This is the procedure described above in which you put the bike in neutral. Two things to remember: 1) if you have a light for neutral on your instrument panel it will come on when you have it right, and 2) if you have difficulty getting the bike into neutral, try rocking it.

To complete the Engine ("E") step you need to flip the kill switch from off to on. This puts you two short steps away from your ride.

"C" stands for choke. If you don't have electronic ignition you may need to adjust your choke. After a few runs you'll know about where you need to set it and how quickly you can shut it down based on your bike's preferences and the ambient temperature. The colder the bike's storage temperature has been the more choke it is likely to need for a longer period of time.

As great as FINE-C is as a reminder, I think it could use one more letter. After all, after you adjust the choke there is still one more thing to do. You still have to push the start button. I recommend you add the "S" to make the acronym FINE-CS. (Maybe you could remember the whole thing with a somewhat less than clever phrase like, "May I sail FINE CEAS as I ride." OK, so I will leave clever acronyms to the MSDs and will stick to my day job(s). Regardless, at this point push the "S" and your bike should start. At this point you are ready to go.

FINE-C
Developed by the Motorcycle Safety Foundation

F- Fuel
I- Ignition
N- Neutral
E- Engine

C- Choke
(S)- Start button

You won't need it to start the bike, but we do need to talk about the throttle before you start to power walk, the skill we'll discuss in the next section. Sit on you bike and grip the right hand grip on the handlebar. You are now gripping the throttle. The throttle is the equivalent of the gas pedal on an automobile. If you push down on the pedal in a car the engine speeds up. If you roll the throttle down the engine speeds up. If you take the pressure off the cage's pedal the engine slows down. If you roll the throttle back toward its starting place the engine slows down. The bike won't move unless it's in gear but if it's in gear the more you roll on the throttle the faster the bike will go.

Power walking

Power walking is the easiest way to move your bike forward other than going downhill or loading it on a trailer. Power walking is just what it sounds like, sitting on the bike and moving it forward under the power of the engine using your legs for balance. In order to maintain balance you have to walk along with the bike. If you're on level ground you could always do the same thing without the engine, but it's lots more work. If you're facing much more than a slight slope with a heavy bike walking the bike without power becomes something between a challenge and impossibility. My brother, Gary refers to such circumstances as "a pisser".

Power walking is a great first step to do before you actually try riding. It helps you get accustomed to keeping the bike balanced, to shifting between first and neutral, and to using the hand brake. You can't use the foot brake when power walking because your feet are busy walking. (Well, duuuuh!)

I've tried to think of clever and effective ways to describe this process, but I don't think I can do much better than this. Sit on the bike facing the way you want to go. Start it, put it in first gear, and then ease off the clutch slowly while rolling on the throttle gently. The bike should move slowly forward. As it moves, walk along with it making sure you and the bike stay upright. If you like visual aids you might find a brief Internet excursion helpful. Fire up your computer and let your fingers do the walking. Try a Google search for "power walking a motorcycle". I just took a break to check and there were several hits, many on YouTube. All the videos I watched were short and accurate. As you watch, remember to focus on what the rider is doing as well as what the narrator is saying. Then just get on your bike and do what the rider did.

<u>Backing</u>

So you may have noticed when we talked about gears that I didn't mention reverse. That's because, odds are, your bike doesn't have one. Some bikes, mostly trikes (motorcycles with three wheels) do have a back-up gear. To the best of my knowledge, however, no two-wheel bikes are made with reverse. This situation produces the following formula: you + neutral+ reverse. To back your bike up you sit on it as you would if you were intending to power walk, then walk it backwards by pushing off first with one foot, then with the other. In other words, you walk backwards while sitting on the bike, making sure that when you go the bike goes with you.

Of course, you can also back a motorcycle without sitting on it. Most folks don't in most situations. Backing while sitting gives you greater control and stability, and it probably makes it easier to do in a difficult situation. The only time I don't sit to back is when moving my KLR 650 out of the garage and into the driveway. I do it because it is a quick, easy move with which I am familiar. It also means I don't have to crawl on and off the bike. Two inches of lowering and a dish seat (3 1/2 inches total) are enough to get my feet flat on the ground when I sit, but I still can't swing my leg over the back without substantial effort and a tad of caution. For me, on that bike, backing it up without mounting makes more sense than taking the time and effort to climb on. It has the additional benefit of being an unending source of opportunity for harassment and good-natured mockery from my friends who ride.

The lack of a reverse gear makes the decision of how and where to park much more important than it is in a cage. If you park facing downhill you have to back up when you leave. If it's much of a hill, backing is likely to be more of a job than you want it to be. In some situations it may be impossible without help. Unless you want to stroll into your favorite restaurant and loudly ask the patrons, "Could someone please come help me back up my bike?" you want to be very aware of your parking arrangements.

The simplest answer is to scope out the nature of the slope before you park. Once you're sure of the lay of the land, park it so the front wheel faces uphill. Nose up, you can let the engine pull you up the grade. A second option is to park perpendicular to the grade, that is with the slope to the side of your bike. Just be careful that when you park and when you get off the slope isn't enough to allow gravity to pull the bike over. If it, is, you'll want to find a different spot for your bike.

I stopped writing between swigs of coffee to look for online videos about parking motorcycles. I found a couple. Both were very informative and something I wish I'd watched when I started. You might want to take a look to see what you can find.

Stopping

The process of stopping your bike includes five basic processes: 1) recognition of the need to stop, 2) applying the clutch, 3) rolling off the throttle, 4) applying one or both brakes, and 5) putting one or both feet down to balance the bike. I've called these processes rather than steps because you can't always complete them in the order I mentioned. Hopefully you will recognize many situations that will require stopping well before you actually need to stop. For example, if you approach an area where traffic is slowed and particularly heavy you may want to slow down a bit. In this case you might roll off the throttle in anticipation of that oversized dude with the big biceps and a wife-beater swinging his backhoe out in front of you. You'd actually roll off the throttle before the need to stop became evident and before applying clutch or brake.

Let me mention a couple of very important things about using the brakes. You want to use the rear brake only on certain occasions, the front only on others, and the front and rear brakes together on most. In most situations you want to use both brakes. The two working together provide maximum stopping power when you are traveling in a straight line on pavement or some other solid surface. Whether you want to slow to a stop at an intersection or come to a quick halt in traffic, the two brakes together are your best bet.

You will want to use your rear brake only when you want to slow down on uncertain surfaces such as sand or gravel. You may also use it when you want to hold your bike in place when stopped on an uphill grade. You don't want to use much of the front brake on loose surfaces because it will cause the front wheel to slide and possibly turn. You may want to use the rear brake only when stopped facing uphill to leave your right hand free for the throttle when you start. The other time you may want to use rear only is if you discover that you need to brake during a turn and you can't slow down enough by rolling off the throttle or downshifting. You should make every effort to slow down sufficiently before you enter a turn, but if you can't, use the rear brake only. The rear brake won't disturb your trajectory as much as the front and will slow you with less risk. Using the front would leave you much more vulnerable to undesirable twists or turns of your front wheel.

The front brake gets a lot of use when power walking, slowing the bike while coasting, backing, and while loading or unloading from a trailer. Other than these circumstances use it in conjunction with the rear brake or use it sparingly. One word of warning. By sparingly I don't necessarily mean gently or infrequently. 70% of your stopping power comes from the front brake. When you need to stop quickly, the rear brake alone is no substitute. Just try to stay away from using it on irregular or unstable surfaces.

Stopping is another one of those things you want to leave to muscle memory. Aside from recognizing that you need to stop or may need to stop the rest of the process should become automatic. Again, when you need to react you don't want to have to stop and think, "Lessee, which of these lever-thingies am I supposed to pull on." As with other processes in this chapter, you need to practice. The old man recommends some repetitious riding in a safe place. Ride a short distance, stop, ride again, stop, ride, some more, stop. Do it over and over until your comfort level grows and your muscle memory starts to take over.

<u>Slow riding</u>

There's something magical about "seat time", that is, the time a motorcyclist spends with one butt cheek on each side of the bike's seat. As you sit and gaze at your beauty the bond between the two of you grows. Parts that used to be just wonderful shinies become wonderful shinies that will do things when you pull or push or twist them. The bike becomes easier to balance, more comfortable to dismount, simpler to stop, and more responsive when you ride. Thus, seat time with the bike moving is the key to both muscle memory and skill development. Spend a lot of time riding at moderate speeds. Resist the temptation to make it go as fast as you can. I can assure you there's a limit. No need to find it right away. Also resist the temptation to let the bike sit for days at a time. Practice time is far from the most entertaining time you'll have in that seat, but it is what will lead you to the roads you want to travel. If you can ride for a few minutes every day then do it. If you can only ride three times per week, make it happen. If you need to write your rides into your schedule, do it. Before long your trips to work and the errands you run will become your practice sessions. The only way to learn to ride is to ride.

Turning

You won't have to ride far to discover the need to turn. Even if your safe place includes a long, straight, flat mile you'll eventually need to turn the bike in order to get back home. (That is, assuming you WANT to get back home.) In my experience turning is much easier than most folks think it will be. You just have to make sure you have enough speed and turn the wheel. The bike tends to do the rest for you.

One of the most interesting things for me has been watching my son, Cody, learn to ride. The fact that my oversized backside ever found its way to motorcycle leather is mostly his fault. He's fourteen going on 45 as I write. A couple of years back he decided he wanted to ride a Harley. The first words to form in my head were my mothers, "Those things will kill you." The first words out of my mouth were much more reasonable but substantially less clever. "Ummmm, we'll see." We have seen, and today we both ride. (The voice of my son eventually trumped my mother's post-mortem warning.) I realized after a while that I had never seen or heard of a motorcycle doing bodily damage to anyone. I had heard of accidents in which people's decisions or lack of skill brought them harm while riding. My son and I set out to be safe riders and have loved (almost) every minute of it.

I mention Cody because the process of watching him ride has been in many ways a mirror of my own process. I find this to be particularly true of turns. As he has learned to turn he found that he could turn in a very short radius or a very long one, but he tended to use whatever space he had available. If he didn't have much space, he made it just fine. If he had lots of space he also did well, but whether he had a lot or a little he tended to use almost every inch of the dirt or asphalt out there. I did the same thing. So, by the way, did my brother when he started.

Find places to practice turns in your safe place. Practice turning in tighter spaces and in larger ones. If you have a large enough space pick up some soccer cones and lay out a course. After some practice you'll find that turning becomes another of those muscle memory things. You just do it.

One of the little challenges I experienced during my first couple of months on two wheels was to learn the difference between steering and counter steering. When you steer you do exactly what you expect you should do. You point the front wheel in the direction you want to go and then go there. When you counter steer, you do the exact opposite of what you think you should do.

Steering is done at lower speeds, in my experience at speeds lower than maybe 12-15 miles per hour. I've found that I never need to glance at the speedometer to decide when to steer. I just do it when I'm moving slower. Counter steering can only be done at higher speeds (meaning over 12-15 miles per hour). When you counter steer you pull back lightly on the side of the handlebar opposite the way you want to go. Although you might expect this to steer the bike it doesn't. Instead, it leans the bike in the way you want to go and the bike goes that way all by itself. In steering you point the bike where you want to go. In counter steering you lean the bike and it steers itself.

Fact is, you could steer the bike forever and never master the art of counter steering. If you point the wheel where you want to go at higher speeds it will go there. It will just go there more slowly and with less control than if you counter steer. You'll do fine if you start out steering then learn to counter steer as you gain experience. If your experience is similar to mine you will find that it feels wrong at first, uncertain after a bit of practice, then absolutely right as you begin to master the skill. You don't even have to turn to practice. Just make a run down your safe space and practice pulling gently on the side of a handlebar then letting off. You'll notice the bike start to lean, then move in the opposite direction, then straighten back up as you let off on the pressure. If you want to complete a turn, continue the pressure and lean a little into the turn you want to make. The bike will lean and turn and you will go with it. You may need to learn to handle the throttle a little differently so that you are not pulling against the other hand when you want to turn right, but a little practice will resolve this issue.

Speed management and line of sight are also important. Speed management refers to controlling where you slow down and where you speed up. If you intend to slow down on a turn it is best to do so before you enter the turn. You may do this by braking, rolling off the throttle, or a little of both. As you come out of the turn you may want to accelerate. This will help you to regain the speed you lost and will help balance the bike as you exit the turn.

Line of sight is more important than most people imagine. By line of sight I simply mean where you look. When you turn, be sure to look where you want to go. Sounds simple, yet the tendency for many folks is look either right in front of the wheel (probably being ecologically sensitive and trying not to squash ants) or look where they don't want to go (oh, say the bushes at the side of the road). Looking in front of the wheel won't help you guide the bike. Looking where you don't want to go stands a pretty good chance of getting you familiar with those bushes. Looking where you want to go seems almost magic. You look there, you go there. If you're having trouble with turns try looking where you want to go. Betcha you wind up going there.

We've talked a little about leaning, but I'd like to say a few more words about it. When I say that you lean, I mean that you do just that. You shift your body weight from the top down in the direction of the turn you want to make. This helps the bike make the turn by contributing to rather than resisting the centrifugal force the bike has generated and gives you greater control over where your turn goes. No matter how it feels, it's actually pretty hard to fall over. As long as your speed is fast enough the force generated by the bike will hold you up and you will make the turn much more smoothly than had you fought it by not leaning.

Turn signals

This brief section on turn signals is dedicated to all

the riders too young to remember when no turn signals, even on cars, were self-canceling. This meant that you had to remember not only to switch them on before the turn, but also to switch them off afterwards.

Unless you invested in a high-end bike you probably don't have self-canceling signals. If you're anything like I was, or like almost everyone else I know, it will take a while to consistently remember to turn them off when you've used them. A few things may help.

First it may help to talk about where your turn signals are located. On every modern bike that I'm aware of they are located a thumb's reach from the handgrip at the center of the instrument cluster on the left handlebar. It's a switch that can be moved to the left or right, or pressed straight down toward the handlebar. Toggling it left turns on the left signal. Toggling it right turns on the right signal. Pressing it straight down turns off both signals. You can't turn off the left signal by pushing the switch to the right or the right switch by pushing to the left. You have to push straight down to be sure both lights go off.

If you have trouble remembering to switch off your turn signals, you can improve your performance with practice. Plan a series of turns in your safe place in which you switch on before the turn and off afterwards. Try it repeatedly over a series of sessions. Automatically remembering to switch off the signal isn't quite muscle memory, but repetition will help just the same. I might add that I have tried an assortment of expletives in various orders over the last several years. So far none is more effective than the other.

Kickstands down

This section has been about learning the basics and committing those basics to muscle memory. You don't have to learn this way. If you can pass the license exam you can fire your bike up and head for the horizon without so much as an instant of practice. You will, of course, learn these things along the way. But the old man is telling you from his own experience as well as from the experience of others that a few hours of grinding out the practice sessions described above will make your early days on your bike much safer and more pleasurable, and will provide greater assurance of many years of happy riding.

Chapter 5

Cooler, Safer, and More Comfortable:
Getting Gear for your Bike

No doubt about it. Your bike is cool. It is cool to look at, cool to ride, and even cool to park in the garage. Regardless of its cool factor, however, a betting man like me (heck, I allow myself $25.00 every time I go to Vegas!) would wager the bank that within a week you'll be thinking about adding some accessories. You'll find ways that additional gear can make your bike safer, cooler, more comfortable, and more useful.

I have spent lots of time and a fair amount of money adding things to the bikes I love. My Can-Am has everything from custom floorboards to a new waterproof power source (cigarette lighter). My KLR 650 has after-market headlights, tail lights, grip warmers, luggage, clock, thermometer, and more. Yes, I could have done without those things, but I like my time on my bike even more because of them. I just put some aftermarket lights on the Virago to make those late day winter rides safer and more pleasurable.

If you've spent much time at bike shops or surfing the sites of online retailers, you've seen lots (and I do mean lots) of different gear and lots of alternatives for each type. You can easily spend a small fortune on accessories and you will find that the more expensive the bike the more expensive the accessories. Rider footpegs (the ones the rider's feet go on) for my KLR, for example, top out at about $85. Pegs for my Can-Am run about $150 plus whatever adapters I need. Harley-Davidson accessories retail for prices similar to the Can-Am. Accessories for other bikes may fall anywhere at or between these price ranges. A smart biker who doesn't want to spring for everything at once will lay out a plan for what to purchase when. Others of us (note the emphasis on us) may make wise additions at some points and wildly absurd decisions at others. I do recommend, however, that the first additions to your bike be those that will make your bike safer. Comfort and coolness can come later.

You'll find that I talk about some accessories more than once during the chapter, That's because some serve more than one of the purposes we're discussing here. Headlights, for example, both add safety and enhance appearance. Similarly, seats make a bike more comfortable but can also make it look more cool. When we talk about comfort we'll talk about the effect of seats on a comfy ride. When we talk about appearance we'll talk about what they can do to spiff up your ride.

Making it safer

I was fortunate enough to make some pretty good expenditures when I first got my KLR 650. The first order of business, as I have mentioned elsewhere, was to get my feet on the ground. Yes, there are bikers out there who are perfectly comfortable riding while able to get only one foot down. That would not be me. They are one-foot wonders. I am probably more like a one-foot blunder. My first accessories, therefore, were the Corbin dished seat and the 2 inch lowering brackets.

My next concerns, also handled before I took the bike off the showroom floor, were visibility and bike protection. The KLR has a pretty decent lighting system straight from the factory. I decided I wanted mine to be awesome. It was both about what I wanted to be able to see at night and about how easily I wanted others to be able to see me day or night. I added Denali lights attached to the fork (so I see where my front wheel is going when I turn at night) and an Admore rear lighting system that multiplied the size of my brake, turn signals, and running lights. I had the Denalis wired straight to the battery so that I could use them in places like campsites even with the engine turned off.

I also took a step to assure that my bike would be protected. The KLR comes with a skid plate made of a heavy-duty plastic material. It's pretty good stuff, but it has been known to shatter when hit by rocks or other debris. This isn't much of an issue on the road, but can be huge in an off-road environment. I had the stock plate replaced with an aluminum version before the bike ever left the dealership. In addition to the skid plate I also had a baffle installed on the windshield. The baffle is designed to divert most of the air at highway speeds back over the rider's head. It diverts wind well. It diverts bugs not at all. During my first summer on the KLR I learned to recognize that "oh shit" look in the eyes of several species of bugs just before they smacked into my visor or jaw. I have since added the Cee Bailey touring windshield for the winter and their sport windshield for summer. The bugs of the world are no safer, but my sleep is no longer haunted by their grizzly deaths. Even more important, I haven't felt the "whop" of incoming bugs on and about my chin in months.

Skid plates protect the front underside of the engine from rocks and flying debris. They are made for off-road bikes. You just don't usually hit anything with that part of your engine when you're on the road. It's actually pretty common to do so on dirt.

Height
The height of your bike matters. My apologies to all the grizzled veterans of the road who think baby bikers

should pop out of their cages ready to trust a single foot to balance 400-800 pounds of metal, I'm sorry, but you are out of your friggin minds.

Height may not matter (much) to an experienced rider. Frankly, I think it's just plain old denial for the best of riders to say that the ability to put both feet on the ground never matters. I am equally sure that for the new folks that kind of balance and control means a lot.

There are lots of things you can do to get your feet on the ground on a tall bike. The easier ones involve lowering the suspension, changing the seat, and making your leg longer. Because some or all of these require a compromise of some sort, you may want to get the expert advice of a good mechanic or parts person. Bikes are typically lowered by using lowering brackets or shorter shock absorbers. This works well, but results in a significant compromise: your bike's ground clearance is reduced. In other words, the distance from the bottom of your bike to the ground is decreased. For most new riders this probably won't affect you much. It matters most off-road or on the road when you are making tight turns. Off-road this means you have to be careful on bumps and short hills not to scrape the bottom or high-center your bike, resulting in loss of control. Making tight turns on a lowered bike may cause the foot pegs or floorboards to scrape, preventing you from turning as sharply as you'd like.

Often you can limit the effect of lowering on ground clearance by combining one or more of the strategies available to you. A Harley Road King, for example, can be lowered in both the back and the front, but it is not necessary to lower both at the same time. Replacing the rear shocks with shorter versions lowers your butt a bit, and replacing the front shocks drops it even more. I've already mentioned the technique we used on my KLR: two inch lowering brackets kept me with decent ground clearance. Adding a custom seat got my feet down flat. With high-heeled boots (NOT stillettos!) I can actually bend my knees a little when I stop for a light.

Speaking of seats, there are several manufacturers who make seats for the short-legged. Corbin, Mustang, Russell, and Harley-Davidson are among them. Most of these seats are designed to move you forward and down on the bike, with padding adjusted so that loss of comfort is minimal. My KLR has a Corbin that works great and is comfortable for moderate rides. It isn't bad for a full day if you take enough walk-around breaks. There are also pads that you can add to a seat to make it more comfortable. Remember, however, that more gel under your butt means less ground under your boots.

One other word about seats and bikes. When you saddle up and stretch out your legs it isn't just about height, it's also about width. The wider the bike and the seat, the less leg you'll have available to reach the ground. Touring bikes tend to run a little wider than others. If you're having trouble standing tall on a tourer, try a cruiser or some other model instead. The other option is, of course, a trike, which gives you a nice, comfy, wide seat (convenient for me because my own seat matches that description). The price tag can be a little surprising, but comfort, safety, and convenience are greatly enhanced.

I talk about boots in the chapter about gear that you wear. I'm including a note about them here to talk about a way to lengthen your leg, or at least the distance your leg will reach. When I first started riding the KLR I loved me some boots with 1 7/8 inch heels. There are only a couple of motorcycle boots out there with that kind of height. I also found logging boots that met these specs. The logging boots were comfy, waterproof, and very heavy. They worked well with the bike unencumbered. Adding luggage on the rear racks, however, made mounting an adventure worth of an Olympic gymnast. They were just too heavy and cumbersome. Given my lack of athletic talent and my tendency to have more mounts and dismounts that would earn a "2" than a "10", I decided to stick with motorcycle boots.

There are other options for lowering your bike. I've talked about the most common and probably the least expensive. If you want to buy a bike but need it to be lowered a bit, talk with the folks in the parts and service department at your local dealer. They'll know your alternatives. I have also found these folks to be refreshingly open and honest in their advice. Most motorcycle dealers that I have encountered (unlike the reputation of many auto dealers) are very concerned with customer service and with making you happy with your purchase. I have yet to get poor advice from one.

There are other options for lowering your bike. I've talked about the most common and probably the least expensive. If you want to buy a bike but need it to be lowered a bit, talk with the folks in the parts and service department at your local dealer. They'll know your alternatives. I have also found these folks to be refreshingly open and honest in their advice. Most motorcycle dealers that I have encountered (unlike the reputation of many auto dealers) are very concerned with customer service and with making you happy with your purchase. I have yet to get poor advice from one. (My brother did get poor advice from a salesman, but the dealer quickly rectified the situation.) Ask them for their recommendations and why they are making those choices. Find out if they have any similar bikes that sit a little lower so you can get an idea of what will work for you.

Lights

Lights can do some pretty amazing things for you in terms of visibility. Although headlights on many bikes are very well made and highly illuminating, a good set of after-markets can both intensify and broaden the light you have for night-time driving. They also make you much more visible to oncoming traffic, day or night. My Denalis seem to make the road 2-3 times brighter as I cruise from work to home in the darkness of winter. Branches, deer, and other nocturnal critters appear way before I would see them without these lights. There's no question about my own visibility, either. My neighbors tell me that my KLR looks like an oncoming 18-wheeler with the stock lights and Denalis fired up.

Enhanced tail lights, rear turn signals, and brake lights make you harder to miss from behind and make your intention to change course much clearer. All this translates into greater visibility and safety. Denali and Admore aren't your only option; there are several quality manufacturers of good after-market lighting out there. None of them are cheap but, to my way of thinking, the ability you gain to dodge a deer or alert an oncoming motorist is worth every penny. Spend some time and research your choice carefully. You want high visibility with a minimal draw on your battery. Aftermarket lights also vary considerably in their appearance. I chose the Denalis for my Virago because I liked the performance on my KLR so much. I'm happy with my decision, but would have really preferred them in chrome. I could have gotten chrome for a few more dollars from other manufacturers.

There are also some lighting systems out there for the sides of your bike. Many are neon and certainly make you easier to see. If you like neon they also improve the look of your bike. I don't have them on any of my bikes. Neon just isn't my thing. Some people love it. Neon is available for the Can-Am. I'm not aware of any made specifically for the KLR, although if I looked hard enough I'll bet I could find a set to fit. I won't be looking very hard, however. Those neons wouldn't last very long on anything rougher than a wide dirt road. Besides, the abuse I would take from my dirt bike buddies for lighting up the woods far outweighs any benefits of visibility.

If you add any kind of lights the most important considerations are amount of light actually generated, ease of installation, and amount of power required. If you're going to spend the money you'll want to make sure the lights you buy do what you want them to do.

The lights you add to your bike should light up the road in front of you in a dramatic way. With your after-market lights on a dark night you should be able to see farther ahead of you, have greater peripheral vision, and see things more clearly within the range of your stock lights. There are some cool YouTube videos demonstrating some of the differences. You will also have a decision to make about where you want the lights installed and will probably need to buy a bracket to make the installation. Some people prefer the lights to be placed high on the bike, on the forks up around the fairings or just below the windshield. On the Virago I had to mount them on the crash bars because there was no space on the forks. These placements throw all the light directly in front of you. The brackets you buy from the manufacturer will determine the exact placement, but you want to be sure you are not blinding oncoming traffic. Another alternative for light placement is down on the forks in a position so that when the fork turns the light turns with them. This is my preference because, when you turn, it illuminates the place you are going to go rather that the place you would have gone. This is probably more important for off-road riders than it is on the highway.

You may also wish to consider ease of installation, particularly if you plan to install the lights yourself. My Denalis were super-easy. I told the service manager, "Put 'em down there." a couple of days and a few dollars later, they were right where I wanted them to be. I understand they are actually pretty challenging to install. You have to remove the seat, the gas tank, install an electrical box, and manage the wiring. If you're going to do it yourself ("turn your own wrench" as the gearheads say) you will probably want to read some installation instructions or talk to a manufacturer's salesperson about what will be required to put them on. At a minimum you'll need to take a few things off the bike to run the wiring. Some come with plug and play kits, which make the process much easier.

No matter who does the installation you'll have a basic decision to make: do you want to wire the lights directly to the battery or to some system that fires after the bike is started. The advantage to having your after-markets wired to the battery is they will burn even if the bike is turned off and the key is out of the ignition. The disadvantage to having your after-markets wired to the battery is they will burn even if the bike is turned off and the key is out of the ignition. In other words, you can use the lights in the dark without starting the bike, a real advantage at a remote campsite. However, if you forget to switch the lights off after you switch off the bike, you can drain the battery at a remote campsite. The former is great, the latter really sucks, not that I have personally ever experienced the latter, of course.

A *gearhead* is someone who does all, or almost all, their own work on his or her bike. If some calls you a gearhead, don't hit them. Say thank you. They mean it as a complement!

A final factor to consider when buying after-market lights is amount of power required. Tail light assemblies shouldn't use any more power than the stock versions you replace. Most of the higher-end after-market headlights are designed to draw minimal power. Neon side lighting can be a power hog and can create a real problem by overtaxing your battery, particularly if you add heated grips and garments in the winter. The first bike I ever got my son was a Honda Rebel 250. I bought it used for a song. It was an amazingly cool ride. The previous owner had decked it out like a baby softtail; saddlebags, floorboards, heel-toe shifter, cushy seats, and a ton of after-market lighting. There was so much lighting, in fact, that he had installed a second battery just under the handlebars to run the extra lights. Turns out they drew so much power the bike wouldn't run without the second battery. Make sure you figure out how much power you need for the lights and other electronics you're going to run. If you are a tad electrically-impaired, as am I, ask the light seller or your local service manager.

Windshield
Your bike may or may not come with a windshield. A lot will depend on its purpose and price range. Larger, more expensive bikes tend to have windshields. Smaller, less costly models tend to have none. Choppers, even expensive models, tend not to have them because of the design of the bike. Bikes made for commuting or touring

have them, off-road and dual-purpose do not, or at least they have very small wind deflectors rather than full sized shields.

Windshields are great for many reasons. They protect you from moving air, rain, cold, bugs, and assorted flying objects. Mine have saved my face and helmet from insects, rocks, rain, soft drinks, limbs, and a sailing deer. I will ride without one in the winter, but the sacrifice I make in comfort even on a still day is significant. 35 degrees may feel chilly, but a 45 mile per hour breeze at 35 degrees ambient temperature is just plain cold.

The height of your windshield is important. Many manufacturers recommend that the top of the windshield rise to a point somewhere between the bottom of your chin and the tip of your nose when you are sitting on the bike in a relaxed position. This, of course, will vary between riders, and even for the same rider depending on where you are in the seat and how relaxed you feel. Resting propped in a seated position in the safety of your garage will probably place you in a somewhat different position than will sliding down the road in a pellet-inducing experience.

If the windshield height is very far below your chin you will probably experience more wind turbulence to your head than you would prefer. If it is within an inch or so over the top of your nose the top may partially obstruct your vision. Some people prefer their windshields to extend over the tops of their heads. I usually ride my Can-Am, which has an electric height adjustment, with the windshield fully extended. I'm very comfortable in this position and experience very little wind turbulence.

It may seem a little surprising that experts

recommend looking out over the top of the shield. When I was learning about this stuff it seemed reasonable to me that a covered face was better than an exposed forehead. In some ways this is probably true. If your face is covered the turbulence is reduced and the chance of taking a bug or rock shot to the forehead is substantially lowered. Fact of the matter is, however, a windshield that tops out around the tip of the nose diverts nearly all the turbulence and along with it many bugs, pebbles, and other flying objects. Air moving upward along the windshield from bottom to top carries the turbulence and objects with it upward over the top of your helmet. The result is, even with the windshield centered fairly low on the face, you experience very little turbulence.

My trial run with deer turbulence was unintentional. I swear it was. I was riding home late on a chilly winter evening, thinking more about the work I had left behind at the office than about things that might be standing in the road before me. It gets dark early in the winter in my part of middle Tennessee. In December everything goes dark about 4:30 to 5:00 PM. With a good cloud cover it's pitch black by 5:30. I live out in the sticks. As the world grows dark deer and other wildlife start to move around in search of water, food and perhaps a chance to get frisky. I rounded a sharp curve and found myself looking into the eyes of a young buck clearly thinking he was about to experience an alien abduction. I clutched, braked, and tightened my sphincter for the collision. I heard the deer hit the front of the bike. I grimaced at the sound of flexing fiberglass, and watched as the deer took a 35 mile per hour slide up and over my windshield. To the credit of my amazing machine I was totally unscathed. The bike never swerved or wavered. I was delighted when I arrived home (about two miles) to see that the bike was unscathed as well. I was pretty sure that the deer hadn't faired as well in the scathing department as I had, so I rode back in my pickup truck to see if I could render assistance. On a dark, cloudless night on a windy country road free of other traffic, the deer was gone. I wasn't sure he was unscathed, but I was pretty sure he had clearly lived to tell the tale. As a matter of fact, I'm sure I saw him a few weeks later standing 50 or so yards out in the field beside the road where we collided. He heard me coming, gave me an OMG look, and bolted for cover. The deer and I now have a pact. I drive more carefully on dark, windy country roads and he heads for the woods whenever he hears the roar of the Can-Am.

I was very fortunate (as was the deer, as was the bike) to escape harm in that situation. Please don't try this at home, folks. Still, the deer story illustrates the value of a windshield. The deer, like the wind and smaller, more common objects, was diverted up and over my head. Without the windshield I would have had a face full of venison. With a lower windshield he might have clipped the top of my helmet. With the windshield positioned as it was he just sailed over my head.

I should point out that my fate on two wheels would have been very different than it was on three. There is no doubt that I would have gone down with probable injury to me, the deer, and the bike. I learned some lessons about caution and speed that day, at the same time that I was learning about the value of windshields and appropriate height.

If you want your windshield to be a different height you may have several options. I say "may" because for certain bikes, such as dirt bikes, there may be no stock windshield and no aftermarket available. Frankly, you wouldn't want one on a strictly off-road bike anyway. Dual purpose bikes and crotch rockets often have a very small wind screen just above the handlebars. These screens do deflect a bit of the wind but not very much. They do even less to stop the onslaught of bugs and road debris.

If you ride a crotch rocket you probably do so for its speed and handling. If you ride for speed and handling you probably don't want a big piece of plastic blocking even more air flow that your body and the bike are already blocking. If you ride a dual purpose bike, however, you probably use it both on and off-road and may ride in all sorts of temperatures. This is the case for me with my KLR 650. Here's what I do.

The KLR came from the factory with a small wind deflector. Riding at high speeds is fun and fast but it makes you appreciate the full-face helmets for more than just their safety value. As we discussed earlier, a big bug to the bare chin won't knock you off your bike but it is enough to elicit a fair number of expletives. The same bug doing a kamikaze into a windshield or visor makes a distinct ping, but leaves you with the expletives deleted. Temperatures are also a factor. As we discussed earlier moving at speed on a cold day can be bone-chilling.

Fortunately there are solutions for those of us who want to ride our dual purpose machines at higher speeds and in all kinds of weather. My first attempt at an add-on shield was an adjustable baffle that screws to the stock shield and snaps into 5 positions to allow the flow of air to be adjusted. It doesn't stop heavier flying objects and doesn't divert much rain, but it does do a pretty decent job of reducing turbulence. I have found, however, that I still get enough wind on cold winter days and encounter enough visibility issues when it rains that other alternatives are desirable. The variety of conditions I experience when I ride my KLR lead me to the conclusion that a variety of solutions were the way for me to go. I now have three windshields plus the stock screen. They are easily interchangeable with the removal of a few screws and bolts. I use the stock version or stock plus baffle if I'm going off-road, a touring shield for the road and for the cold months, and a sport shield for commuting and recreational rides. Yes, I have invested a few hundred dollars, but, for me, the comfort and pleasure easily justify the investment.

If your bike is made for the street and is not a crotch rocket it may or may not have a windshield. If it doesn't have one you can probably get one. If it does have one that doesn't fit you it can be replaced with an alternative either from the dealer or from one of several online sources. Some come with an adjustable windshield, allowing you to raise or lower it to suit your height and riding position. My Virago, for example, came with an adjustable stock windshield. It comes to about the tip of my nose and has done everything I wanted it to do so far. If you choose to buy one from an online source be sure to read instructions about how to make your selection. In my experience the chances are you will get it right when you order, but check the vendor's return policy just in case.

Windshield width is also important. Width determines how much of your trunk is protected. It's often harder to adjust width than height, but there are manufacturers who make windshields broader at the top than at the bottom (accommodating the breadth of shoulders). Some of us sport a little extra breadth around the waist as well. The good news is that the fairings on many bikes do a good job of shielding love handles.

If you replace your windshield you may find several tint options available. Blue or red tints may match the color of your fairings. Smoke or green may look cool.

The wrong color or too heavy a tint, however, can earn you a ticket if you ride at night in some jurisdictions. Be sure you know the laws about tinting in your area and others in which you may ride before you buy.

Motorcycle windshields get dirty and require regular cleaning. It's tempting to use a window cleaner made for glass or to swipe it with the blue stuff in the bucket at the gas pump. Don't do it! Your motorcycles windshield is not glass. Cleaners made for glass surfaces often have chemicals that will gradually erode the material. Be sure to care for your windshield with products made specifically for motorcycles.

A final thought on windshields. I've probably gotten more advice and experienced more collective scorn from other bikers about my windshield collection than about anything else in my biking experience. Some think I should just suck it up and deal with the bugs and the wind. Others wonder why I have that funny shaped thing on my handlebars. Most, of course, have nice things to say and ask very good questions about why I do what I do. The comment I have for those who tend to criticize my bike-related decisions, "I don't recall that I bought the bike for you to ride. I'm very happy with my decision." If you are a wind in your hair, bugs in the teeth kinda person, just ignore this section. If you want to make your bike safer, more comfortable, and more practical all with some minor modification, however, you may want to give some serious thought to your windshield.

Mirrors

If you are small, skinny mirrors are not likely to be an issue for you. Even if your physique resembles that of either the incredible hulk or the incredible bulk, your rear view mirrors are likely to be adequate on a larger, more expensive bike. Broad shoulders on a small bike, however, may mean that you see more of you in your mirrors than you see of the road behind you. Not only is an obstructed view annoying, but it can also be very dangerous.

There are at least two options for dealing with this problem on a bike. One is to buy replacement mirrors that are long enough to extend beyond your shoulders. The other is to buy an extension that lifts the stock mirrors up and out enough to allow you a clear view of the road. Depending on the model of the bike you have you may have either both options available to you or you may have only one. To find out what may work for you check with the dealer and online part houses that specialize in your model. I bought the extensions for my KLR from Twisted Throttle (www.twistedthrottle.com). Similar products are also available from other vendors.

Handlebars

Handlebar spacers are both a comfort and a safety feature. You install them by removing your handlebars and placing the spacers between them and the points where they bolt to the bike. This raises the handlebars by the width of the spacers. Higher handlebars make riding more comfortable for many, particularly for taller riders who have to stretch down to reach the grips. They're also a safety factor, however, particularly for long rides where extended stretching can be exhausting. They aren't just a luxury for the Paul and Paulette Bunyons of the world, either. I've been seriously considering adding a pair to my KLR. The longer the ride, the harder I think.

The pressure on your hands, arms, and shoulders can also be improved with a good pair of hand grips.

There are lots of options. My favorite is gel grips, which include pockets of gel around the grip so that they pad the palm of your hand and your fingers. Grips are pretty easy to add and remove, and actually do a lot for riding comfort. The old ones are a breeze to remove. Just grab something sharp and slice them off. Clean up the handlebar and dab it with grip glue. Slide the new grip on and let the glue cure. Viola, you have new gel grips! If you are removing or adding heated grips you may need to be a little more cautious. You'll want to be aware of live wires, charged surfaces, and other such electrical land mines. No, a 12-volt charge won't kill you, but it will get your attention and might make you squeal like a little girl. That will be fine to do in the presence of your biker buddies if you happen to be a little girl. If not, the impact on your bad-assed biker image can be tragic, indeed.

Cramp busters and similar products are worth every penny of the ten bucks or so that you'll invest in one. You just open their factory packaging, slip them around the throttle, and off you go. Cramp busters transfer some of the responsibility for rolling the throttle from your fingers and palm to the heel of your hand. You don't have to grip as hard. Anyone who has ever had pain or cramps in their throttle hand during a long ride will appreciate the value of these simple little devices. I'm also convinced they are a safety factor as well. I've never seen anyone pull a spontaneous Evil Knievel while trying to shake out a cramp, but I can easily see it happening.

Cruise control

Many higher-end bikes come with cruise control. You can add it to just about anything, and will find it to be a good thing to have for long ride on the interstate. I say good because I find that I am rarely able to use the cruise control on my Can-Am because of the relatively high volume of traffic on many interstates. I use it a lot at night and early morning, but just find it too annoying to constantly set and reset it when dodging between slow drivers in the right lane and flying human-faced anal cavities in the left.

There are several different kinds of after-market cruise controls, most of which lock down your throttle in some way. I haven't used any of them, so I can't make a recommendation. If you want to add one you might talk with your dealer, check out some of the online forums for your motorcycle, or chat with someone at one of the online accessory suppliers.

Hand guards

Hand guards protect your hands from limbs and other debris when you are off-road. In my experience they can also protect you from diving sparrows and moving frigid air on road. You don't usually see them on street bikes, but they are common on dual purpose and adventure models. Hand guards attach to the handlebars near the inner end of the grip. The shields extend back over the hands to provide a protective barrier between them and whatever might be in front of them. There are several kinds by several manufacturers. If you pair them with grip warmers your hands may me the warmest part of your body on a cold winter's ride.

Hand guards can be difficult to install. Some actually require cutting off the end of your handlebars. If you aren't a gearhead you may want to leave the task to a mechanic or professional installer.

Bike protection and operation

Some accessories protect or enhance the operation of your bike. Some will benefit nearly any bike.

These include things like engine guards and foot rests. Others are important for specific models. These include things like skid plates, extended shift or brake levers, and protectors for various components such as the brake master cylinder or fuel pump. These accessories are very model-specific and are beyond the scope of both this book and my brain. They are most frequently purchased for off-roading. I've included a discussion of the most important protective accessories in the chapter on off-road riding.

Battery chargers and bike covers: protection while your bike is stored

Two accessories are critical for the times your bike won't be moving: battery chargers and motorcycle covers. If you are a seasonal rider or if there are extended periods of time when you don't ride you will want to get a battery maintainer or trickle charger. Trickle chargers plug into the wall on one end and attach to the terminals of the battery on the other. Somewhere close to the terminals but far enough away to hang out from under the seat of your bike there is a weather-protected quick-detach bracket. When you want to ride you pop it off and go. When you get back you plug it in and walk away with no worries about battery maintenance.

A motorcycle cover is also a good investment even if your bike is typically garage kept. I have one for each of my pampered garage babies. They come in handy for occasions like travel and when you need garage space for something else for a couple of days. For example, I recently installed luggage racks and a new windshield on my KLR. I managed to use up every corner of the garage and two extra days in the process. During that process I parked the Can-Am outside, all snug and protected by its Official Can-Am factory cover.

The bike was safe from sun and weather and I got to enjoy the comments of friends about how remarkably cool that sport cover looked on the Can-Am.

Engine guards

Engine guards are also important. "Engine guard" is, by the way, the optimistic term for these twisting tubes of metal. Other names, in descending order of optimism, include nerf bars and crash bars. Engine guards do all three. They guard your engine against possible crashes effectively nerfing any damage the working parts of your bike might receive. They attach to the front of the frame and loop outward so that if your bike falls over they break the fall. Some manufacturers and vendors will deny that they are useful in a crash. I beg to differ. I can tell you from personal experience that crash bars protect the rest of your bikes in drops, slow on-road crashes, and off-road crashes moving along at a pretty good clip. They are not perfect, but they will save you some scratches and dings on your bike, as well as some possible major damage, at least at slower speeds.

I think engine guards are a remarkably good idea even if you are sure you ride like a pro. For one thing you never know what the other guy is gonna do. If you ever drop the bike because some dude forced you off the road you will be delighted you made the investment. Engine guards offer some protection against freaks of nature. Lowering my KLR meant that its kickstand (also called a side stand) was too long. I couldn't park the bike with the kickstand side turned toward the slightest incline without risking a drop while or shortly after dismounting. I had the stock stand shortened twice (a cut and weld thing done at the dealer) but still wasn't happy with the results. Of course I loved the opportunity to amuse anyone within gaping distance by crawling off my too-tall bike while holding the kickstand down with my foot, but I was concerned that it would eventually find its way to the ground. "Eventually" happened one day when I backed the bike out of the garage, dismounted, and walked back to close the garage door. I had gone maybe 15-20 steps when I heard it crash behind me. A combination of an overbalanced rear bag and a strong gust of wind had knocked my baby over. Today my KLR sports a shorter kickstand and a healthy tilt to the left when it is parked. On the day of the crash my engine guards got a little scuffed, but everything else on the bike remained pristine. I commend engine/nerf/crash guards to your attention and consideration.

Footrests

There are three general categories of footrests that may be on your bike. The first, the rider footrest, is on every bike. It's the place you put your feet when the bike is moving. If they are short pegs that protrude a tad more than a foots-width from the side of the bike they are cleverly called foot pegs. Some bikes have long, flat footrests that allow you to put most or all of your foot on them while moving. These are known as rider floorboards. Floorboards are generally more comfortable for longer rides and often look remarkably cool. If your bike doesn't come with them you may be able to add them as an after-market accessory. I added them to my Can-Am, for example, but I've never seen them offered for a KLR. Frankly, I'm not sure why anyone would want them on a bike that gets used off-road for any more than a 20 second scoot to a backyard parking space. I do recommend floorboards highly if you plan to be on the bike for hours at a time.

Rider floorboards sometimes require a switch in the shifter. Even when the change isn't required, some folks prefer a heel-toe shifter rather than the kind you shift with your toe only. If your bike came with floorboards it probably also came with a heel-toe shifter. If not, you can add one. When you use a heel-toe shifter you rest your foot on top of the shifter, pressing downward with your toe to go into first or to downshift and pressing down with your heel to shift into higher gears. You use the clutch just as you would with a toe-only shifter. There's a small learning curve when you switch shifters, but many maybe most folks who have floorboards, much prefer the heel-toe version.

If your bike was made to carry a passenger in addition to the rider, it will have either passenger pegs or passenger floorboards. Either are fixed to the frame at a distance behind the rider versions. Pegs are standard on most bikes. Passenger floorboards are typically available only on larger bikes.

Highway pegs are foot pegs that attach near the front of the bike either to the frame or to the engine guards. They are generally used for longer rides, allowing the rider to stretch his/her legs out from the more confining rider position. Some bikes come with them. For others they are available as accessories. For still others they are no more than a wish and a prayer. You'll need to check with your favorite accessories retailers and perhaps try a Google search to see whether you'll be stretching your legs toward the fork or your prayers toward heaven.

Performance enhancement

There are accessories that can make your bike run faster, leaner, and louder (or more quietly). These tend to be very model specific and are probably best learned about through the online forums, or a mechanic who knows your model. At this point I haven't found the need to make any such modifications to any of my bikes. I have thought about an exhaust for the KLR that makes it roar like a Harley (OK, maybe not quite like a Harley). When an insert is removed and putter quietly for off-road use when it is attached. So far I just haven't been able to justify the expense with the possibility of a louder vroom-vroom.

You can improve the performance of some bikes with a combination of an after-market exhaust and a kit that alters the performance of the carburetor or fuel injector. You use a jet kit for a bike with a carburetor and a fuel processor for a fuel injector. Be sure you get the right pipes for the right exhaust or the performance of your bike will decline rather than improve. Information about what combinations you need are usually available from the folks who sell them. The following information won't help you choose what you need but should save you a multitude of "duuhhh" moments when talking with a salesperson.

Changing the muffler is the simplest, cheapest performance modification for most bikes. "Slip-on" versions (a tad of an exaggeration in some cases) can raise or lower the volume of your system. On the street some folks prefer their bikes loud and rumbly. Hearing a well-tuned bike with the right exhaust system installed is a truly beautiful experience. Off-road bikes not designed for racing are usually much more quiet. This is by design, an attempt by the manufacturers to minimize noise pollution in the woods and to comply with the standards many states set for off-road riding. As I mentioned earlier, you can get more vroom out of these bikes, but most will never sound like a hawg made for the streets.

If a muffler just isn't enough, you may want to

consider a "full-system" alteration. These modifications are so named because you change more than just the muffler. You remove and replace the entire exhaust system. This includes the heads and pipes, as well as the fuel delivery system as mentioned earlier. There are two general categories of full-system alterations. One is designed to increase performance. The other is intended to enhance appearance.

Just as its name would suggest the full system alteration for performance is intended to improve a motorcycle's speed and efficiency. They do this by increasing the horsepower and torque of the engine. Performance exhausts are most frequently installed on racing or touring bikes, although kits are available for other types. There are several performance improving systems for some dual-purpose bikes, for example. I keep looking at my KLR and thinking, "Hmmmmm." I found out most of what I know about performance exhausts (I think I've exhausted my wealth of knowledge in these few paragraphs.) by reading online forums and talking to mechanics at the dealers. I'd recommend that you check those places first if you're looking for ways to improve your bike's performance.

The second type of full-system exhaust is purely for appearance. It makes your bike look purty. These systems may perk up the performance a tad, offering greater improvement than a muffler, but nearly always less than a performance system. They also tend to be the most expensive systems, in large part due to thicker heat shields and cooler twists and turns in the pipe. They also are usually heavier than the other types of systems.

Yep, I agree, you probably aren't going to sink a portion of your 401K into pipes for your learning bike, but if you can't resist the call of the big chrome and metal you may do what I originally did and buy a big cruiser or touring model. If you decide to keep it (unlike what I did with my Road King) you may want to think about either improving performance or enhancing appearance. These paragraphs should provide good foundational information for beginning your quest.

If your bike has a chain drive system you can change its performance by changing out one or both of the sprockets. It's easy to recognize a chain drive system. You just look for a chain running from the area near the engine to the back axle. Sprockets are wheels with teeth on their outer rim. The teeth pass through the chain so that when the engine runs with the bike in gear, the front sprocket chain turns the back one. By changing the size of the sprockets you can make changes in some aspects of the bike's performance. "How might this gem of knowledge be useful to the new rider", you ask? I'm glad you're paying attention. Perhaps a personal story will be useful here.

As we discussed in the chapter on bike selection my first bike was a Road King, but I really did most of my learning on a Honda Nighthawk 250 and a Honda Rebel 250. Those were great little bikes, picked up used for a song and resold a few months later for approximately the same tune. They weren't very fast but they were comfy and handled well. People use them all over the place. I even talked with a guy about my age who decided to deck his Rebel out like mine and take it on a backroads, cross-country trip. 75 mpg and cheap hotels will get you through most of North America on one of those things. For me, the only rub was power in the lower gears. I have, perhaps, mentioned the ampleness of my backside. I'm carrying a substantial number of extra pounds. I don't particularly like carrying those pounds up steep inclines. The Rebel liked it even less than I did. My house sits at the bottom of the Cumberland Plateau. Take a right out my driveway and a left at the corner and you start a 400+ foot climb in about 3/4 mile of road. Even with a running start in high gear on that little 250, I'd have to downshift into third gear to make the climb. The bike as geared from the factory just wasn't enough to make the climb in fourth.

I never changed the sprockets on my bike, but I met two other people of similar girth with the same model of bike. They had put on a different set of sprockets, giving their bikes enough power to make the climb without downshifting. I keep calling the Rebel "my bike". It was actually my son's, purchased for the day he would get his permit and shamelessly ridden by me while he was waiting to get older. Had we kept it I would have considered changing out the sprockets for him. He isn't heavy at all, but those bikes aren't really made to take big folks up steep inclines. It is also relatively easy to change out the sprockets on many bikes (check YouTube for demo videos), or relatively inexpensive if you want your mechanic to do it. A couple of words of warning are in order, however. First, be sure you get the right sprockets and the right combination of sprockets. If you are a gearhead or an astrophysicist there are sites online that will walk you through the selection process with a series of formulae and diagrams. If you are a mere mortal like me you may just want to call the parts folks and ask, or leave it to the mechanic at your local dealer. The other word of warning is that if you change the behavior at the bike in first gear you are also going to change it in the other gears. Giving it more torque in first will limit its performance in fourth, for example. Too many folks, the trade-off is worth it. If you won't be using the bike on the interstate but need more get up and go at lower speeds, a sprocket swap may be a good thing to consider. And, by the way, just in case you have been inspired by this section and have raced to your bike to check out your sprockets but, alas, have not found any, you probably have a belt drive or a shaft drive bike rather than a chain drive. No chains, no sprockets.

There are three different types of drives: *chain*, *belt*, and *shaft*. Each has its own set of advantages and disadvantages. Your selection of bike, however, will determine your type of drive system. You won't be able to just sully up to the bar and say, "Give me a red hot Suzuki crotch rocket with a shaft drive". The drive system is determined by the model. If you have a very strong preference for a particular type of drive, however, that may affect the model you choose.

There are several other modifications you can make to enhance your bike's performance, but most of these are probably outside the realm of interest for the beginning rider. We'll leave the discussion of performance ignition, ECU remapping, clutch springs, piston size, and air filter preference to other books and authors.

Hopefully, this section will give you what you need to confidently make decisions or seek additional information about possible performance-enhancing accessories for your new bike.

Making it cooler

There are lots of things you can do to make your ride look cooler. Some of them are relatively inexpensive. Others will make your checkbook shriek. If you're a beginning rider you may not want to sink big bucks into making your first bike shiny. On the other hand, my son's Honda Rebel is decked out with all kinds of after-market accessories. With custom pipes, added lighting, saddlebags, floorboards, a broad windshield, and a set of floorboards it looked like a baby Heritage Softtail. In short, it was cool. I bought it for him to learn on (I swear it was for him!) He called it his pimp daddy ride. Although we both loved the bike we found he really needed the XT-250 so he could use it both on and off the road. The Rebel went to the dealer as a part of a trade for the XT-250. I think it lasted 2.5 seconds on the showroom floor. It was VERY cool.

To find out what you can get that will make your bike look cooler try talking to your dealer, asking around in the online forums, and running an Internet search for images of your model. I recently acquired my 1995 Yamaha Virago 1100 (notice how I casually worked it into the conversation) and, although I'm pretty happy (nope, I love its look!) I ran a Google search to see what pictures were out there. The Virago is no longer in production, having been replaced by the V-Star, but it is a kind of a cult classic. I found nearly a thousand images posted by proud owners. Most were pretty close to the stock version, but there were some with pretty cool mods as well.

Things that can make your bike look cooler include pipes, luggage, windshields, custom handlebars, chrome replacement parts, floorboards, seats, and lighting. You'll need to make the decision about how much you want to sink into the bike you'll be using to learn on. My brother Gary has added a new windshield, saddlebags, and mirrors to his V-Star 650. I'm going to try to get him to spring for a set of Denali's, and then I think he'll be done. He'll hear the call of the full dresser before long and will want to move on to bigger things. I doubt he'll want to invest much more in a bike he won't have for long. Remember, however, that when you sell the bike you don't necessarily have to sell all the accessories. With the purchase of a new bracket he'll be able to fit those

Denalis on whatever bike he buys next. Local money is on either a Yamaha Royal Star or a Harley Davidson Heritage Softtail. Stay tuned for updates!

Some accessories are likely to remain on your bike when you sell it. Given that appearance will be a part of what attracts a buyer, you are probably not going to remove an exhaust system modification. They are often well worth the investment, however, for appearance, check out such names as Vance and Hines, Bassani, Milwaukee Twins, Rush, and Rinehart. Be sure the sets you like will fit your bike. If you decide to spring for one you may want to decide in advance whether you or someone else will do the installation. The chances are good that the pipes themselves will install pretty easily. The chances are equally good that the carburetor or fuel injector kit will require some pretty good wrench-turning skills.

Luggage

Luggage also does a lot for your bike, both in terms of its appearance and its utility.

There are several different categories of bags. These categories vary in size and placement on the bike. Working from front to end, there are tool bags that fit in front of or immediately behind your windshield. Often they are a couple of inches wide, a few inches deep, and run the width of your handlebars. They won't hold a lot of tools, but will readily accommodate the screwdriver, pliers, and adjustable wrench you need for many minor repairs.

Moving toward the rear of the bike the next stop is the handlebar bag. Handlebar bags have attachments that wrap around the center of the bars to hold the rest of the bag in place. They are long and slender, and are often just the right size to hold some essentials like chapstick, a disc lock, a GPS, your cell phone, and other small items that are nice to have readily available. I've been asked whether these bags should face front or back. I'm not sure there is a correct answer other than to suggest that you consider both ease of access and mobility of your handlebars when you place one. If you have a hard time getting into it or it blocks the movement of your handlebars you may want to turn it around.

The next stop is the tank bag. Being the insightful individual you are, you have probably already concluded that tank bags sit on top of your bike's gas tank. It's really a very handy spot to fit anything from a small to a mid-sized bag, and may allow you to incorporate a number of gadgets that will enhance your riding experience.

When you get to tank bags it becomes useful to start talking in terms of liters. No, this isn't because you will need to calculate the amount of your favorite brew it will hold. It's because the size of bags made from the tank to the rear can vary greatly in shape, size, and composition. These factors affect all kinds of things like price, available space, and positioning of the bag.

The smallest tank bags tend to run in the 5-7 liter size. That's not much space but it can hold the things already mentioned as well as some larger items. They are handy for snacks, paperwork, maps, and additional tools.

Mid-sized tank bags are often between 7 and 12 liters. In my opinion they start to get really handy at this point. I have used bags of this size to carry all the items listed above plus lunch, bug repellant, sunscreen, and a small drink or two.

The largest tank bag I have seen holds at about 20 liters. These bags have lots of space for small items.

They aren't quite to the point to allow you to carry a change of clothes (unless a change of clothes means your t-shirt, undies, and socks), but they are great for day trips and short overnight jaunts. Lots of folks also use them for commuting.

If you can't find an official reference to the size breakdown I mentioned, that's because I made it up. I couldn't find an official reference either. I do think these sizes I mentioned will help you get some idea of the size bag you'll want to look for.

You should think about other limitations when you think about bag size, For example, if you can't step over your bike, but instead have to do as I do and sort of lay down on the front of the seat while swinging your leg over the back, too much bag may snag on too much belly.

Tank bags fasten to your bike in one or more of several ways. All of them work, although some are more convenient and perhaps a tad more reliable than others. There are three primary attachment systems: strap down, magnetic, and gas cap. Strap systems use two or more straps that attach to different points under or around your tank. Somewhere between the two ends of each strap there's a clip that allows you to release the bag easily. Strap systems work really well. They are relatively easy to install, easy to remove, and when pulled down tight they fit snugly and securely.

Magnetic attachment systems use several magnets sewn into the bottom of the bag. The attraction of these magnets is great enough that the bag will stay on through any kind of wind, bump, turn or tip over that I've ever experienced. I've never tried them in a high-speed crash and have no intentions of ever doing so. Please note, magnetic bags attach to metal, but just kinda ignore plastic. If your tank is plastic (Pay attention dirt bike and dual-purpose guys!) or if you swap the stock tank out for plastic (Ahem, listen up, dual-purpose guys) this is not the bag attachment type for you.

A couple of manufacturers make a bag that uses a special attachment to fasten to your gas cap. I love these bags. They are easy-on, easy-off. They stay snugly on the bike through all kinds of riding experiences. They are easy to install. Oh yeah, one downfall, they are expensive. I probably should have written that in all caps: EXPENSIVE. A large gas cap mount tank bag (at the time of this writing) will set you back as much as a piece of high-end luggage for the back of your bike. No, I am not too old to recognize the value of having certain items readily available to you in a secure spot that is easily removed when you dismount. I said I love these bags. When it comes to price, however, I am just sayin!

If you don't mind parting with some of the aforementioned Dollars, Euros, Pounds, Pesos, or Yen you can also get tank bags that are loaded with cool accessories. Some have such devices as map holders, internal dry bags, phone and GPS chargers, GPS space or brackets, document pouches and other remarkably cool gizmos. If you're gonna spring for a high-dollar tank bag, I recommend serious shopping. Chances are your local dealer or retail shop won't stock all the variety you'll want to consider. Ask them to drag out their catalogues, surf the Web, call online supply houses, check out return policies. If you do a lot of day rides or even frugally-packed 2-3 day trips, a good tank bag may be the best onboard luggage investment you make.

The next stop on our front to back luggage tour is the rear wheel. OK, so you won't really tack a suitcase onto the wheel itself, but the frame above and around the wheel is the prime spot for attaching larger luggage. This spot will accommodate incredible things. I have actually seen two bicycles and a large airplane luggage-sized trunk strapped on the back of a speeding BMW motorcycle. Please don't try this at home, folks! The old man recommends that you stay with luggage options designed specifically for motorcycles. These include saddlebags, side cases, and top cases.

Saddlebags are probably what you'll want for cruisers and touring bikes. They also work on dual purpose bikes, but the side and top cases we'll talk about may be a better way to go. Saddle bags aren't common on crotch rockets or dirt bikes. They can defeat the goals of speed and mobility. Some will fit, however, and if saddle are the bags you want you can probably find a way to make them work.

Saddle bags are large containers, usually rectangular or oval-shaped. They either hang across the bike behind the driver (often secured by a strap under the seat) or attach to brackets that are fastened to the frame. They come in a variety of sizes and with a fairly wide set of options in trim. Saddle bags can transform your day-trip cruiser into comfortable transportation for a weekend jaunt or more. Several folks I know have done coast-to-coast vacations on cruisers with saddlebags and a tank bag. They are standard equipment for touring bikes and can be found to fit many different models. You won't usually find saddlebags on adventure bikes because they are usually factory equipped with rear luggage.

Speaking of rear luggage, two general types are available, side cases and top cases. Within these broad categories there are a number of different types. Many can be purchased with quick-release brackets. The brackets are mounted to the frame and, with special adapters, allow you to quickly snap your luggage on and

112

off. This is handy for many reasons. I can, for example, transform my KLR from a dirt bike (OK, a really big dirt bike!) to an adventure touring bike in less than 60 seconds. Similarly, if I'm traveling for an extended period, I have three substantial pieces of luggage that I can simply snap off the bike and carry to a tent or hotel room at night, then snap back onto the bike in the morning. When I'm commuting I leave the side cases in the garage and throw the stuff I need for the office in the top case. I then lock it up and head for work.

Side cases are like mid-sized pieces of luggage in assorted sizes, shapes, and colors. They typically include some sort of retractable handle, a lock, and a system for fastening them to the sides of the bike. The interior may be padded or bare and they may or may not have internal straps to help retain your personal items. Many can be purchased with removable interior bags. I have such a bag for my top case and use it specifically for commuting. When I get to the office I pop the lock, remove the bag, then lock the case back up. I didn't bother with the bags for the side cases. When I travel I just pop them on and off and carry them wherever I'm going just like I would with any piece of luggage.

Top cases are similar to side cases except that they fit on the tail section of the bike. Most will require a modification to the stock tail piece as well as an adapter bracket for the specific kind of luggage you acquire. The cases are made to clip on and off easily. Some have internal lighting systems and can be rigged to work in concert with the running lights and turn signals.

Most bikes have another cluster of luggage options available for the rear of the seat or the space just behind it. Possibilities include tail bags, passenger seat bags, and sissy bar bags. Tail bags are strapped on behind the seat to some sort of bracket or luggage rack. Some such brackets are stock; others must be purchased separately. My KLR came with a rear platform that worked great for a tail bag but had to be replaced to add rear luggage. The Virago is a stripped down model with nothing behind the passenger seat. The previous owner had added a sissy bar and a passenger back rest. I added a rear rack that attaches behind the sissy bar. I also bought a tail bag with a rigid base and a steel frame. The tall, narrow bag is built like a backpack with nice shoulder straps. It isn't really made for hiking, but it's great for lugging the bag for short distances. It straps nicely onto the rack behind the sissy bar seat.

When thinking of luggage on the tail of your bike you are less restricted by its size and dimensions than you are on other areas. Tail bags and luggage that hang out on both sides are common, as are pieces that extend well beyond the tail. It is important to keep oversized pieces balanced, within reasonable boundaries, and clear of the rear lighting. A word of warning: the choice you make when you strap any kind of gear to a bracket or rack on your bike is very important. Bungie cords are cool and versatile. They also stretch, sometimes sever, and are overly responsive to the vibrations any bike makes. You're usually better off with strap made specifically for use on bikes. They won't shake loose, don't stretch, and are easy to use.

You are not, of course, restricted to bags and luggage made for motorcycles. Folks use all kinds of creative alternatives to gain a little extra storage space. I've seen backpacks, tractor bags, ATV luggage, ammo cases, milk crates, and several other things strapped to motorcycles. If you can find a way to attach it securely, if it will keep your stuff safe and dry, and if it's legal it's probably something you can use.

As with many motorcycle accessories, the array of alternatives can be dazzling. There are some questions you can ask yourself to help guide your purchase.

When Buying Luggage Ask Yourself

1) How much space do I need?

2) What kinds of bags or luggage are available for my bike?

3) How much am I willing to spend?

4) How important is it to be able to quickly and easily add or remove the item from the bike?

5) Do I need it to be waterproof?

6) Do I need it to provide anything other than storage?

7) How easy is it to transport after I take it off the bike?

We talked about windshields earlier, but they also deserve a mention here in the "cool" section. If you surf the web a bit you will find several different manufacturers of windshields and windscreens. Some are identical to the original shield and are intended to replace damaged stock equipment. Others offer an alternative choice of size, shape, and composition. Some are very short. Others are very tall and are intended to cover most or all of the rider's body. I have a stock windshield on both the Can-Am and the Virago. I went all ape-poop on the KLR, however. For it I have the stock shield with an after-market deflector. With a moderate amount of effort I can swap that out for my winter shield (head-tall Cee Bailey's aircraft grade) or my touring shield (also Cee Baily's, but smaller to allow greater air flow on and around my body). My bike looks very different depending on which shield I have mounted. I like all three, but have seen a few models that to me just don't look like they belong on anything two-wheelish. Preference is, of course, the right of the owner. If you change out your windshield pick one that you like and, of course, that does what you want it to do for the way you plan to ride.

Handlebars

Handlebars also make a big difference in the way your ride looks. Depending on your bike model the manufacturer may offer alternatives, or you may need to check with your favorite suppliers. There are several different types. The type you'll use will depend to some extent on your choice of bike and to some extent on your aesthetic preference. Let's talk about a few of the alternatives.

Cruisers are the long, standard height handlebars that you see from the factory on most cruiser motorcycles. They tend to be relatively long and slope toward the rear to allow the rider to sit in an upright, comfortable position. Since some bikes are also called cruisers it's important to be clear about which you are talking about.

Ape hangers sport the high grips of chopper fame. They typically extend outward a few inches from the place where they fasten to the bike, then bend away from the ground, continuing upward for as much as 20 inches. Using ape hangers requires the rider to reach up to grasp the grips. Riding on a big chopper with tall ape hangers some guys look just like a big chimp in a helmet and leather. Just don't tell any of them I said so.

Mini-apes, sometimes called buckhorn bars, are shorter versions of the ape hanger.

The grips are still well above the base, but well under the height of full ape hangers. They also typically curve back toward the rider just before the grip, providing a very natural, comfortable riding position. I have mini-apes on the Virago and love the way they look and feel, particularly for long rides.

Clip-ons are actually two separate short bars. One connects to the fork tube on each side of the bike. They are most frequently seen on sport bikes.

You can buy custom handlebars or stick with the ones that come on your bike. Look at the models on the sales floor. Watch the streets to see what others are riding. Attend some bike shows or rallies and see what is out there, and don't forget your good friend Google. If you change your handlebars it may substantially change the way your bike looks.`

Chrome and black

Many of the chrome parts on your bike can be swapped out for black. Many of the black parts can be replaced with chrome. In every case I can think this is purely a matter of preference. Some people like more chrome. Some like more black. There are too many potential changes and the possibilities vary too much between bike models to allow much discussion here. Surfing the web is probably your best option for finding these accessories. When I started looking for alternative colors for my bikes I assumed that the manufacturer would have some version of almost anything available. Wrong guess! I found that, for most manufacturers, there are specialty parts houses that carry things the manufacturer doesn't. (The possible exception to this is Harley Davidson, which carries a ton of parts for each of its models of bikes.) I found the parts places with Google using the bike model name along with the name of a part. For example, using KLR 650 and skid plate produced the names of several good sources.

Floorboards

Floorboards can replace both rider pegs and passenger pegs, at least on some models. They also look very cool. If you do buy floorboards make sure what you're getting will fit. Confirm the year and model of the bike and, if possible, eyeball both the connecting point on your bike and the picture of the boards you'll be adding. Make sure they look like they'll work. Also make sure that, if they don't, the vendor has a decent return policy. I have $400 worth of Honda Rebel floorboards sitting quietly in my basement. They didn't fit and the exchange-only policy of the vendor was no help. I didn't need a second set that wouldn't fit any better than the first.

Seat

The seat can make an amazing difference in the appearance of your bike. I love, for example, the plush, cushy, old-timey look of the seat on my Virago. The KLR would look a little strange with so much cush, however. If you go seat shopping for appearance you need to think about the way a change will affect the model of bike you own as well as your own preference. I looked at several alternatives for the KLR before setting on a Corbin because of the sleek look. Remember that the other, most important, consideration was its effect on seat height. The second runner up was a Russell, a great looking seat that just looked to me more like a distance seat than off-road. Had I planned to spend more time on the highway than on the dirt I might have chosen it instead.

Lighting

We discussed the effect of additional lighting on safety, but it can also have a big effect on the appearance of your bike. Some of the biggest appearance changes are from light bars, neon add-ons, and larger, flashier taillights. We talked about most of these earlier so I'll just mention a few things about how each may affect the appearance of your bike.

Light bars and other after-market lighting systems can trick out (my son would say "pimp out") your bike in some pretty incredible ways. Light bars attach to the front of the bike, typically at the top of the forks, and provide additional headlight power. They are usually chrome and hold between 2 and 4 additional bulbs. They can be wired to your ignition switch so they shut on and off when you switch the bike on and off. Your dimmer switch is another option. This allows you to dim the light bar when you dim your headlights. You can, of course, wire directly to the battery, placing some sort of switch in the line so that the light bar operates independently of the ignition. Light bars probably do more for the appearance of your bike than most other add-on lighting systems because they add chrome as well as lighting. They are popular on cruisers and touring models. Many are model-specific, meaning that you order the one made to fit your bike.

We also discussed neon in the section of safety. For folks who like neon it also makes a bike look just plain cool, particularly at night. My son's Rebel 250 had it, and I must admit it kind of grew on me over time. The set drew a lot of power and required a second battery that the previous owner had attached to the top of the fork and enclosed in a water-resistant bag. It had an on-off switch all its own so that you could either fire it up or leave it off. Given that it was wired straight to the second battery it also posed the danger of a forgotten shut-off, but frankly, glowing neon is flat-out hard to miss. I can't remember a time when either of us failed to turn it off.

Taillights present some additional options and may be purchased as a bar, similar to the headlight bar, that incorporates the entire rear system into a single unit or as larger, more stylish individual lights. Appearance on tail lights is purely a matter of individual preference. If you add tail lights you'll want to consider both style and visibility. The light bar I put on the rear of my KLR 650 looks great with the rear luggage attached but makes the rear look wider than I would prefer when I strip the bike down for street or off-road use.

Making it more comfortable

If you love to ride, you'll find yourself spending lots of time in the saddle. I find reasons to ride just about every day, unless the storms are severe or the temperatures are very low. There are also folks who ride even more than I do. Many of us who ride a lot like our bikes to be as comfortable as possible. Here or some of the ways you can make that happen.

Seats

We've discussed seats in a couple of places. You can use them to lower your position on the bike. You can use them to improve your ride's appearance. A third, and very compelling reason if you ride a lot, is to make your bike more comfortable. You can do this in several ways. One, of course, is to buy a new seat with more padding in more of the places you like it. A second is to buy one of the pads that can be strapped to the top of the seat. The third is to have your seat itself altered to make it more comfortable. I've tried all three options, and have found that each of the three is useful depending on the bike and how you fit it.

A new seat is the easiest and most expensive way to go. We've already talked about a few of the manufacturers and ways to find them. There are other good ones out there. Finding the manufacturers isn't hard. It's a little more challenging to find out how the seats feel before you buy one.

You can get an idea about how seat's feel understanding its purpose and looking at its style. A lean, narrow, straight seat is usually less comfortable than a wide, heavily padded, contoured design. The lean, narrow models are usually made for off-road, dual-purpose, and sport bikes. The emphasis is on providing mobility and control. The wider, cushier types are more often designed for street bikes, particularly cruisers and touring models. There are exceptions; however. Looking at two seat alternatives for my KLR provides an example. The Corbin seat I selected places more emphasis on mobility and control. It's OK for long rides, but its emphasis is on off-road applications. The Russell has a padded, seat-shaped rear, making it more difficult to move around on but much more comfy for the long haul. The wider and cushier the seat, generally the softer the ride. Take a look at Harley all-day seats or the Mustang after-market for excellent examples.

If you live near a major city, or need an excuse to ride to one, you might be able to find some examples of after-market seats among the used bikes at the local dealers. I took a ride around recently to the six dealers located within an 80 mile radius of my house. I found three after-market seats made by independent manufacturers and three made by Harley-Davidson. I rested my posterior on all of them for several minutes and came away with some clear preferences. I'm not saying which seat I liked best because your toosh is different from my toosh, and the level of toosh-satisfaction is bound to vary. I do encourage you, however, to toosh-test as many after-market seats as you can before you buy one.

Another good source of information about after-market seats is online reviews. They won't tell you for sure which you'll like best, but they will tell you what others like and will provide some insight into how the seat will affect your ride. Make your selection wisely. You'll be sitting on that seat a lot.

Add-on pads are another way to enhance seat comfort. There are several kinds out there. The most popular at this time are probably constructed of gel surrounded by a fabric exterior. They usually strap down to the seat. Add-on pads make quite a bit of difference in feel of the seat. I use one on my KLR and find it to make rides of more than a couple of hours much more comfortable.

A third option for making your seat more comfortable is having a skilled professional reupholster the whole thing, incorporating the right types and quantities of padding into the seat itself. Sciatica is not my friend. It obvious thinks differently, because it visits me on almost every ride of more than 10 minutes. The Virago has that magical combination of height, padding and position that makes my friend easy to manage with some very slight shifts on the seat. The KLR is a bit more of a challenge, but with more extensive shifting, an occasional use of the highway pegs, and a pad, I ride without much pain. The Can-Am, however, was another matter. Although the seat and peg combination seem to work well for most people, they required constant shifting for me to stave off persistent ache in my hip and lower back. I found that if I shifted backward and upward, onto the passenger seat, I could ride with no pain whatsoever. This worked pretty well when I was riding alone, but could produce more intimate arrangements than were appropriate when I was carrying a passenger. The answer came from Bill, the owner/operator of a local furniture store. Bill worked with me patiently through several appointments and trial pads, helping me select the right layering of firm foam and soft as well as the right height. When we found the right size, he built it into the seat. I ride the Can-Am with total comfort these days, thanks to Bill's diligent effort.

I should add that I could probably have solved the problem with the right set of floorboards as well. Problem was, the right set wasn't available. I scoured the internet and talked to lots of folks. The only thing that would have moved my feet enough was a set from Rivco that would have lowered my feet a couple of inches while moving them forward about four. That sounded like a great idea, but it was available only for the sport version of the Can-Am. I had the touring. Rich Colano, the owner of Rivco, spent a substantial amount of time with me on the phone and assured me that they would have a model for my bike within a few months. Problem was, my hip wanted relief right away and I wasn't sure the new boards would solve the problem when they were done. I sought Bill's help and am glad I did. I really appreciated Rich's time and input and will probably try out his boards when they are ready. He and his business are obviously a class act.

Highway pegs can also make your bike more comfortable. It's great to be able to move your legs around or to stretch them out after a long ride in the saddle (or a short bout with sciatica). They typically fit on crash bars, which may or may not come stock. One word of warning. If you can find a way to do it you may want to try out highway pegs on a bike like yours before you invest. I added them to both my KLR and my Virago. The position of the crash bar puts the pegs very close to the driver on both. This means feet on the highway pegs are a minimal improvement for me on the KLR and not much of an improvement at all on the Virago, at least for me. In the case of the Virago, the highway pegs wouldn't be much of an improvement anyway. The rider pegs are situated well forward, meaning that added pegs really don't give you much extension. They lift your legs a bit, but really don't stretch them out much more. If I were buying again, I'd probably get them for the KLR but not for the Virago.

Some folks really like to have backrests for long trips. Back rests both provide something to lean against to rest your back and help provide a little assurance to a rider that he or she will not slip off the back. Depending on the model of your bike you may be able to get them for the passenger only or for the rider and passenger. They are usually relatively inexpensive and easy to install. They do make mounting the bike more challenging for a short-legged folks. I, for example, can lift, twist, and turn my body onto most bikes with a passenger bike rest. On the other hand, I need to drop from an overhanging limb or hire a crane to lift me onto most bikes with rider backrests.

Other items we discussed earlier include padded grips and a cramp buster. Padded grips replace the stock grips on your handlebars and incorporate some sort of cushy substance like a gel to make the surface easier on your hands.

Music and voice

Lots of folks like to add music to their rides. There are several ways to do this, some of which work very well in almost any setting. Others are much more effective on serene country roads than they are at high speeds on crowded interstates. We'll talk about a couple of options here just to give you an idea.

If you spend enough money on your bike, or if you spring for enough after-market dollars, you can have the best of the sound system world, at least on some models. Higher-end bikes often come equipped with a system. These are often very good and are probably the easiest systems to use. I have a built-in on my Can-Am Spyder. I had a faculty meeting in Nashville yesterday. Given that I like faculty meetings about as much as I like slamming my fingers with an 8-pound sledge hammer, I rode the Spyder. I figured if I had to go I could at least enjoy the hour's ride each direction. I listened to the sounds of my two favorite stations all the way there and back without headphones and with minimal effort to switch between them. Yes, the sound of the rushing wind and the noise of surrounding traffic took the listening experience well below concert hall quality, but I was able to listen happily, understand the dialogue, and rock out to my favorite tunes all the way there and back. In my opinion built-ins offer the most hassle-free music experience.

For sheer sound quality I think it's hard to beat the Bluetooth headsets made either to fit inside some helmets or to fit your head under the helmet. I have a higher-end Vega helmet with built-in earphones and a microphone. It's great for listening to music, chatting on

125

the phone, and communicating with riding companions. It sounds good and doesn't get in the way. I haven't found it to interfere with my ability to hear the things I need to hear from the road around me. The sound quality is very good and it's the only alternative I've found that really works well for audio books. The one downside is a relatively short battery life and long recharge period. If you are going to be using it extensively you need to either be very attentive to charging when you aren't riding or keep it wired to power all the time.

Some folks also use wired earphones that plug into a jack on their built-in systems or into an iDevice or mp3 player. These work well for built-ins and somewhat less well for portable devices. The issue is amplification. Built-ins usually provide enough power to let you hear as much as you want. Portable devices are often simply not strong enough. There are mini-amplifiers that you can place in-line to boost the power. I haven't tried all of them. The ones I've tried help a little, but just not enough to make me happy. Other people seem to like them just fine. My son has an earphone and mini-amp combination that he likes just fine. I've struggled to hear enough to enjoy many songs when I've used it. I'm quite sure my struggle is because my refined musical taste demands a higher level listening experience. He' pretty sure I'm just old and can't hear as well as I used to.

There are also systems that are intended to be strapped and wired to your bike. I've heard a couple of these and they both sound fine and are easy to use. My biggest concern about them is the ease with which they might be stolen. I also have a friend who wired up a small, outdoor sound system and strapped it to his front end (well, his bike's front end). He added a waterproof case to hold the power inverter he needed to convert DC power to AC. It cost him about six bucks to install. It isn't the choice I'd make, but I don't think he much cares what I think. I agree with him. It really is none of my business.

There are also a couple of ways to add satellite radio to your bike. Some sound systems come with it built in. You can also buy add-on systems that include it. My personal favorite is the Garmin Zumo GPS with built-in satellite. It works great with Bluetooth headsets. I don't have one, but am definitely putting it on my Christmas wish list. Why do I like satellite? The main reason is that I just don't like changing stations at 90, oops, I mean 70... miles per hour. Yes, it's easy to do with the flick of a thumb, but that thumb's flick can put you remarkably closer to the rear-end of a semi. Yes, you can stop to change stations, but that just isn't my cup of tea. I can plan a stop like that when going to Nashville. I know about where the Cookeville station drops off and the Nashville station gets strong. If I'm riding in a place I don't know, however, it's cross your fingers and scan. This isn't the greatest idea on unfamiliar asphalt. If music is important to you when you ride you may want to consider some sort of satellite system.

Making it more useful and convenient

There is a pretty incredible array of things you can add to your bike to make it more useful and convenient. I can't even begin to cover them in the space available here. I'm sure I don't even know about some of them. Browse the Internet and visit accessory stores to check out cup holders, GPS devices, clocks, thermometers, compasses, racks, tie-downs, spare fuel tanks, and other options. You may not find anything you can use, but it's nice to know what's out there.

Kickstands down

In this chapter we've discussed accessories for your bike. The right add-ons can make your riding experience safer, more comfortable, and more enjoyable. They can also make it more useful. Your bike will doubtless run and look great right off the showroom floor. The right accessories can make it even better. Shop wisely. Not all accessories are made equal. Nor are they priced equally. The good news is that there's a large community of other bikers out there who are willing to tell you what they know. Don't be afraid to ask about the changes you can make in your bike. I've asked lots of questions about mine. Looking back, I can't think of a single time I was sorry I did.

Chapter 6

All Dressed Up with Anywhere to Go:
Picking the Gear You'll Wear

You've chosen your bike. You love it. You stare at it. You sit on it. You are ready to ride it. First, however, you need the gear that will help you be safe and comfortable on your journeys. You need gear. Gear is used to include several types of accessories: what you wear, what you use to carry things when you ride, and equipment that enhances the bike itself. In this chapter when we talk about gear we'll be referring helmets, clothing, and eye protection: the stuff you wear.

The stuff you wear has different purposes, and for different purposes you need different stuff. You start with a basic set of gear, designed to provide protection and comfort in a variety of conditions. You'll need rain gear, cold weather gear, warm weather gear, and off road gear if you ever plan to ride off the asphalt. You don't need it all to start but if you plan to ride under different conditions you'll want to get the gear that will help you be protected and comfortable on those occasions.

Buying gear provides a bewildering array of wonderful and dazzling choices. You can wrap yourself in the leather and silver of an MC club, don the flashy togs of a motocross racer, or dress in the no-nonsense style of a fashionable weekend warrior. Given the choice you'll face, it will be helpful to know a little bit about each before you walk in the door of a shop. We'll talk about those choices here. First we'll discuss the choice of where to buy. Next we'll talk about the selection of basic gear, Third, we'll review the types of specialized street gear, including rain, cold weather, and warm weather. Finally, we'll briefly summarize the choices you can make when you select off road gear.

Where should you buy?

One of the first choices you'll make isn't about the gear, it's about where you'll acquire it. The easiest source to access will probably be the local dealers who sell motorcycles. If you shop there you'll also have the advantage of getting expert advice from people who know and use the equipment. The downside is that the cost of each piece of gear is likely to be higher than it would be from other sources. Brand names, in particular, will be expensive. Go to the Harley Dealer, for example, and you'll get good quality and good advice, but you'll pay higher prices. You'll find a similar situation places like Can-Am and KTM. At dealers like Suzuki, Yamaha, Kawasaki, Honda, and other multiple-line dealers you will find a greater range of product price and quality with a similarly high level of quality advice.

If you live in or near a major metropolitan area there may be chain or privately owned gear shops available. These kinds of shops often have the advantage of offering high levels of expertise at more reasonable prices than many dealers. Cycle Gear is a retail chain that has a shop within an hour of my rural home. They carry their own line of products that tend to be a relatively high quality at a substantially lower price. They also do an excellent job of standing behind their product. In my experience if there's a problem with the way it's made, they make it right.

Another of my personal favorites for gear is the local mom and pop shop. Small, individually or family owned businesses often offer a very high level of expertise and a reasonable price. In my community, that means Brownie's place, more commonly known as Leather Worx. Folks like Brownie are ideal for helping you find exactly what you need in their area of specialty. No one can cut a chap to fit or help you pick the right leather jacket like Brownie can. He just laughs at me when I describe my attempts to get a fit from Internet sources. Like many motorcycle folks in retail stores, he is genuinely concerned that his customers make the right selection. He is, however, also the consummate salesperson. I recently asked him about a gel pad for my Can-Am. He slipped one out of the box and with a friendly smile and offered, "Take it outside and lay it on the seat. Try it out." I grabbed it and headed out the door unaware that Brownie was trailing along behind me, mounting straps in hand. I laid the pad down, sat on it, then chatted with Brownie as he adjusted the straps and secured them to my bike. When he was finished he said, "Let's go back inside where it's cool." I realized what he had been doing and asked, "Brownie, you were planning on me taking that home with me, weren't you." Brownie just smiled and headed for the door. After a thousand miles I have moved my gel pad to the KLR, but I love it no less.

The Internet is another option for the purchase of gear. You will probably find the best prices here. You will also find that most of the Internet gear retailers are friendly, helpful, and more than eager to provide competent customer service. I've only found a couple of exceptions and I simply don't buy from them any more. A couple have made it clear that they weren't interested in receiving phone calls or in helping me investigate alternatives. I've made it clear to them that I am not interested in making purchases from them. Most offer free shipping for reasonable minimum purchases.

The two downsides I've experienced from my Internet purchases are an occasional long delay in receiving an order and frequent sizing issues. If you need something in a hurry, call or email the merchant and ask about the projected day your purchase will arrive. If you want to be sure something will fit read the sizing charts, read the customer reviews about how the sizes run, call or email the merchant and, if you order, cross your fingers. Most of the Internet retailers I've used are pretty good about taking non-custom returns, but beware of return shipping costs and restocking fees. These kinds of costs can quickly eat up any savings you might have experienced at the time of purchase. There's also time and aggravation to consider. I just don't like packaging things up and taking them to the post office, UPS, or Fed Ex. After a few purchases of helmets, jackets, and pants online I have grudgingly conceded that, for me. Brownie is right (again!). Sized purchases are best made locally.

Picking your basic gear

Basic gear consists of head protection (helmet), eye protection (visor, goggles, or safety glasses), hand protection (gloves), torso protection (long sleeved shirt or riding jacket), lower body protection (jeans or riding trousers), and foot protection (boots). You could spend a small fortune on the basics if you so desired. You can get what you need for a moderate investment with some careful shopping, however. Whether you spend a fortune or a pittance on quality stuff, the basic gear is worth every penny you invest.

Your helmet

The helmet is perhaps the single most important piece of equipment you will buy. It is also mandatory in most states. Based on a substantial amount of research the MSDs will tell you that folks involved in accidents while wearing helmets experience substantially fewer head injuries and deaths than do folks who do not wear them.

There are four types of on road helmets and one made for dirt. You can actually wear any of these either on or off road as long as they are approved by the inspecting agency required by your state. At the time of this writing that is the US Department of Transportation. There are other inspecting authorities out there, some with more stringent requirements than the DOT, so you might want to ask a trustworthy salesperson or run a quick Google on motorcycle safety laws in your state before you buy. If you take the MSD class they'll give you updated information on the laws.

You probably won't be riding (or perusing motorcycle gear) long before some sage rider who thinks he's Buggsy Malone sidles up to you in a gear aisle and whispers conspiratorially, "Don't spend all that money, just buy a cheap helmet and an imitation DOT sticker. Put the sticker on the back in the right place and the cops will never know the difference." Fake DOT stickers might get you past a law enforcement officer at a traffic stop but they won't get you past a fall to the pavement at 70 miles per hour. A tremendous amount of research and technology goes into the development of even the least expensive DOT-approved helmet. The money you spend on that helmet may well save your life, or perhaps even more importantly, may protect you from a devastating traumatic brain injury. Invest the money to get a quality helmet with a genuine DOT approval. You may never need it, but if you ever do you will be grateful for every penny.

By the way, in all the states I'm aware of that DOT sticker is the final word on whether or not a helmet is road-worthy. I mention that because of an experience my son and I had in Houston, MS on a trip this past summer down the Natchez Trace. We were staying at the Bridges-Hall Manor, a bed and breakfast in Houston, MS. Carol, the wonderful proprietor, was not only graciously hospitable but also incredibly helpful to a biker in a jam. As my son and I were unloading the trailer of my Can-Am Spyder in the Mississippi summer swelter the barrel lock for the trailer jammed with the lid shut. No matter what we tried twisting, turning, swearing, and raging, the trailer remained locked. We sat down to assess the damage. The biggest issue was that there was no locksmith who could open it within a couple of hours and no Can-Am dealer within several hours.

We decided to wing it. The trailer would move, so no problem there. We had already unpacked too many things to be able to fit into the motorcycle's compartments, we decided we could ship them. Carol wound up shipping them for us, just a part of her gracious assistance. Being tough, macho kinda guys we could rough it on whatever we could cram in the bike (along with the emergency equipment we had stashed there. The only real problem was that we had locked our helmets in the trailer. (Lesson learned, don't do that!). We couldn't legally make the run to Natchez the next day.

I used my cell phone to make a quick Internet search. Turns out there was one motorcycle shop in Houston, a great little place that doubled and tripled as an ATV and farm equipment dealer. They had two helmets, both DOT approved and, amazingly enough, in sizes that would fit us. (My XXL head took a little cramming into a XL helmet.) Carol furnished us with a ride to the dealer where I was surprised to find that the one that would fit Cody was a dirt bike helmet and mine was actually made for ATVs. I checked the Mississippi state website. Both were OK for the road so long as we had adequate eye protection. We both wear prescription safety glasses that not only look stylish but met the state requirements for eye protection. The next morning we were off and running in our unconventional but perfectly legal DOT approved helmets. A couple of days later a rather eccentric (read that, obnoxious) locksmith in College Station, TX opened the lock for us and we retrieved our usual helmets.

That story should be enough to establish that as long as the helmet has a legitimate DOT sticker it is fine for highway use. This is important because there are several different types of motorcycle helmets. The most basic is also the most fun and least protective, the shell helmet.

The shell helmet fits over the top of your head only. While others may cover the back of the head and neck, the sides, and your face, the shell leaves these exposed to the wind and elements. This leaves you free to enjoy the rush of the wind and the unencumbered sounds of the highway. It also means that if you whack your head you need to be very selective about what part you whack. Unfortunately, selectivity may not be an option when you are doing spontaneous tumbling at 45-50 miles per hour.

With the shell helmet, as with the other types of helmet, you face a trade-off. The more you cover your head with helmet, the more protected you are. The more you cover your head with helmet, however, the less you feel the ride and the more encumbered you may feel. This isn't a call the old man can help you make, other than to tell you about it. I tend to select according to the type of riding I'll be doing and the kind of bike I'll be on. If I'm riding country roads to the store for some bread and beverage I'll usually throw on my dish helmet sporting a manly graphic of the Mighty Thor (OK, so "the Mighty" comes from Marvel Comics). If I'm going to make a long Interstate ride I'll probably wear a modular (whole head coverage that we'll discuss in a paragraph or two). I also vary my choices by bike (more protection for the KLR, less for the Can-Am) and mood. Your helmet choice will need to be one you need to make. Just be sure that when you buy, you buy the real thing.

A second type of helmet covers the top of your head, the back of your neck, and the sides of your head. This type is known as the half helmet. This tends to protect most of your head (defends against most things short of a face plant) and still allows the free flow of air on your face and neck. This is my personal favorite and tends to be the one I grab most if the time when I head out the door.

The third type of helmet is called whole-head, so named very cleverly because that's what it covers. The helmet surrounds the head and extends down the jaw and across the chin as a moulded, single piece. A clear visor drops out of the helmet to cover the face and cheeks, offering protection and allowing visibility.

The first time i put a whole head helmet on I noticed a couple of things. First, I damn near broke my unbreakable safety glasses because you really can't put the helmet on while wearing glasses. Second, I noticed that the helmet gave the illusion of impaired vision. I say illusion because it seemed to me that my peripheral vision was limited. After I had worn it for a bit I found that my vision was really pretty good and any slight vision loss I might have experienced was more than compensated for by the protection it provided.

I actually don't own a whole-head helmet. I own two modulars, however. Modulars offer a set of compromises that at least partially overcome the limitations of the other types. When properly positioned modulars cover the entire head. The front piece is a clear visor that slides up and down. It is also attached to a hinged chin piece so that you can swing the entire front of the helmet up and out of the way when you put it on, then down when you're ready to go. Because the visor hinges independently of the chin piece, you can crack it open a bit to allow air flow when you ride. Most quality modulars also have built in vents that can be closed or opened to adjust the internal temperature. Whole-head helmets also usually have vents.

Helmets also offer various types of accommodation for headphones or ear beads. Shell helmets may allow you to stuff mini-microphones into the chin strap or buy an entirely separate Bluetooth device that fits under or around the helmet. Other types may have inserts for speakers, included compartments to hold separately-purchased devices, or built in sound systems that allow you to listen to music, catch the latest chatter on the CB radio, chat on the phone, or converse with a buddy as you travel together. Of course, the more you get, the more you pay for. My favorite modular is a safety green (read that intensely bright) Vega with a pull down internal sun visor and built-in Bluetooth. Combine that with a bright green mesh jacket and the likelihood that even inattentive cagers will see me coming is great indeed.

Off-road helmets have some distinctive features that distinguish them from their asphalt brethren. We'll talk about them in the chapter on off-road riding. ATV helmets will also work. Just be sure they are DOT approved.

Helmet color is a matter of personal preference.

For those who are concerned with maximum visibility a bright color is the most desirable. For the fashion-conscious it may be most important to match your bike or outfit. To the budget-minded it may simply be a matter of cost.

A brief word about visors and visor fogging may be helpful. One of the few disadvantages of whole-head and modular helmets is their tendency to fog in wet or cold weather. Once you're moving it isn't much of an issue. Air moving through the vents in the helmet will keep it clear. While sitting still, however, the visor can fog up in a hurry. Visors on partial helmets are not immune. I've never had one fog up while in the down position, but I have experienced interesting seconds when I dropped one to the down position on a cold, damp morning. Expecting a clear field of vision suddenly saw a wall of white. Fortunately, I had just started moving and was able to flip it back up in a pellet-free moment. After a few minutes of riding it cleared on its own.

You can usually deal with fogging visors by simply cracking them until you're moving enough for the air to clear them. There are products available that will retard or eliminate fogging, just be sure that when you get one, it's suitable for plastics rather than glass. Many anti-fog lens products are made for glass and, like ammonia, will gradually erode or abrade the surface of a plastic visor.

Sound is important in helmet selection. You want to be able to hear the sounds of the road like honking horns and approaching traffic, but you want wind sound to be minimized. If you plan to listen to music or talk on the phone you want the external sound to be contained enough to allow you to hear what comes through the speakers clearly. Chat with your local salesperson, email your online retailer, and chat with your biking buddies about this issue. Generally, I have found that the more helmet you have and the more expensive the helmet you have the less the wind and road noise.

When you venture beyond your safe space on a ride where you will park your bike you will face a minor decision that has important ramifications. You don't need your helmet when you aren't on the bike. What are you going to do with it? Lot of folks perch it on the handlebars or leave it on the seat. I've never known a helmet to be stolen from one of these places, but I'm rarely willing to take a chance with mine. After all, if someone swipes it I'm stuck. I can't legally ride without one, at least in my state. Some bikes have a built-in holder that swings down at the twist of a key then allows you to hook the buckle through it before locking it back. If your bike doesn't have one of these you can purchase accessories that can be secured to the bike to lock your helmet down. Of course, you can always take it with you, something you'll want to do anyway if there's rain in the forecast.

One other thing about helmets, no matter how expensive the helmet, if you drop it from more than about 3 feet onto a hard surface, it's time for a new one. Motorcycle helmets are built to protect your head through one good hit. After that one hit they are likely to have invisible cracks that will cause them to fail at the next hit. If you drop it hard, buy a new one. Yes, that's expensive, but helmets can be replaced. Heads can't.

Eye protection

Eye protection is another important piece of basic gear. If you've ever been smacked in the forehead by a June bug (big ole green thing with a hard shell) at 70 miles per hour you can appreciate the value of having something to shield your eyes from flying objects. The importance of quality eye protection gets raised a notch if you don't have a windshield. A windshield can't guarantee that you won't stop a foreign object with your eye socket, but it will considerably improve your chances. If you don't believe me, come mourn the passing of the bugs plastered on my windshield of a summer evening ride down a river road.

Many helmets include a shield that is designed to protect the eyes and upper part of the face from flying objects. They are often interchangeable and can be purchased in a variety of colors. Some of those colors are legal for night riding and others may not be, so be sure to ask or to know the law in your area before you buy.

Face shields, more commonly called visors, typically either drop down from somewhere inside the helmet or swing up off the chin guard using hinges at the side. Some helmets also feature inner sun shields, a second drop-down visor that is tinted to ease the glare of the sun. Sun shields are great to have but are not rated for high impact collisions with flying gravel or similar materials. They should be used with the face shield, not instead of it.

Goggles are a good option for those whose helmets don't have visors. This is most likely to be true for shell and off-road helmets. Not all goggles are created equal, however. You want the lens material to be shatter-resistant and anti-fog. You want padded foam to line the rim so that any place the goggles touch your face it is the foam that touches. The foam makes the goggles more comfortable to wear, helps assure a snug fit, and blocks dust that might otherwise sneak between the goggles and your skin. If you wear glasses you also want to make sure they will fit comfortably under the goggles. One more piece of advice on goggles. Don't skimp on the price. You can't ride safely if you can't see where you're going.

Some states allow riders to use safety glasses, that is, glasses that have been approved for use on construction sites and in work environments where danger from flying objects is present. These glasses protect the eyes from objects flying at them from directly ahead or at a slight angle. With side panels (which may be either fixed or removable) they also protect from objects approaching from greater angles. Safety glasses can be purchased in designer styles and with all the latest lens developments. Mine, for example, change from clear to tinted when I move from darker to lighter areas. They also transition nicely from riding distance to reading distance without one of those old-fashioned bifocal lines.

Prescription safety glasses are convenient. I originally bought mine to use while cutting the grass or while attempting to imitate a handyman somewhere on my property. It was a nice bonus when I learned that they were also useful on a bike.

Prescription safety glasses also have their limits, however. Most notably, if you don't put on the little side panels they offer no side protection at all. Because I wear them to correct my vision I have them on all the time. I'd like to say that I snap those little side panels in place on the sides of my glasses, drop the helmet visor, and climb on the bike behind a big windshield. That would offer maximum protection and would be the old man's advice. In reality, however, I typically use some mixture of the eye protection available to me depending on where I'm riding and what the conditions are. For a short ride on country roads behind my Can-Am's windshield I sometimes go with just my prescription safety glasses. If

I'm on the Virago where the windshield is very low I always drop the visor. For long Interstate rides on any bike I always wear at least a half-helmet with the visor down. On the days that wisdom overtakes my desire for the sensation of freedom (think of it as going commando with your head) I wear my bright-green modular and travel with the visor opened a crack so at least me teeth can enjoy the freedom of the open road. Oh yeah, if I think it's gonna rain (notice I did not say if www.weather.com says it might rain), I wear the modular. We'll talk about rain gear shortly, but even the best gear won't stop rainwater from running down your chin and neck inside the collar of your shirt. A good helmet that covers your entire head will put a stop to that.

Hand protection

A good pair of leather gloves offer excellent protection for your hands when you mount up, ride, and dismount (Many bikers refer to dismounting as "unassing", a word that surely deserves a place in Webster's.) You may have noticed that the summary at the end of each chapter is entitled "kickstands down". I dearly wanted to name it "unassing" but some friends counseled me that potential readers might find that offensive. Motivated more by potential sales than my right of literary freedom I decided to flip a coin. "Kickstands down" was heads. "Unassing was tails." The flip came up heads and, as far as I am concerned, the chapter summary got the ass end of the deal.

The greatest danger to your hands probably comes from trying to break a fall, as one might have when mounting or dismounting a bike. If you misjudge the balance and drop it, you may go down as well. If you do, you will probably extend your hand to prevent your body from hitting the ground. While this will protect your torso and legs, it can result in some very uncomfortable abrasions, particularly to the fingertips and palm of the hand. Good quality gloves, particularly leather or abrasion-resistant textile, prevent most such injuries.

Basic riding gloves are typically leather and may or may not have fingers. Those with fingers are more protective, but make certain tasks, such as pushing a small button or picking up a coin more difficult. If they are a poor fit they may actually interfere with your ability to operate some of the controls on your motorcycle. Those without fingers expose a lot of skin to potential injury. I have a pair with and a pair without. I use the fingerless for leisurely rides on the Can-Am. I use the gloves with fingers for the Interstate on the Can-Am and for most any ride I make on the KLR. Your first pair should have fingers, probably what will be required for the course anyway. As with all gear, check to see whether your state has more specific requirements.

Torso protection

Torso protection is designed to protect your arms and trunk. Usually this means something between the low-end protection of a long-sleeved shirt and the higher-end protection of a textile jacket with strategically-placed armor. If you're going off-road there is special armor that we'll discuss in the off-road chapter.

The traditional torso protection is the iconic leather jacket. Leather is tough stuff. It holds up through lots of abuse and keeps what's inside safe from lots of scrapes, cuts, and abrasions, as well as the dreaded road rash. Besides, it looks just plain cool. It's the stuff from James Dean, MC clubs, and Sons of Anarchy. With the right leather jacket and shell helmet you can feel bad to the bone even if you're really only mildly disagreeable at the subcutaneous level. Textile jackets provide the abrasion protection of leather and often include internal pockets at the shoulders and elbows for light armor. Some also have features that allow you to adapt them for changes in weather, such as a pocket on the back to hold a water-retaining device (cooling in hot weather) or liners allowing water-proofing or insulation against the cold. I preferred leather when I started for primarily two reasons: 1) I had a nice leather jacket already, and 2) the BTTB (Bad to the Bone) effect.

Road rash is the abrasion a biker receives on unprotected or underprotected skin when he or she slides along the highway surface. There is always damage to a patch of skin and often imbedded gravel. Leather or textile clothing does an excellent job of protecting against road rash.

Over time, as I have learned about textiles, my preference has shifted away from leather. Textiles are remarkable and versatile pieces of equipment. I now have an unlined Harley jacket for warm weather. The wide mesh allows great ventilation and it has removable elbow and shoulder armor. It doesn't look BTTB cool, but it does look motocross cool. The Harley saw me through a parking lot incident in which I braked to avoid a backing vehicle, not noticing that my front tire was about to hit an uneven space in the lot. I was moving slowly and the bike went down. I tried to step away from it and, instead, pitched face-first across the pavement. Instinctively, probably dating back to my days as a high school wrestler, I tucked my head and did a neat Batman flip, rolling on my shoulders and back, pushing with my arms and hands, then finishing by using my momentum to stand at the end. Not bad for an old guy. A guy and his female companion, obviously bikers, at first showed concern, then burst into a round of applause when I took a bow. I stood the bike up (no way I was gonna ask for help!), parked it, and went in the store to buy my french fries. When I got home I inspected my skin and the jacket. Both were immaculate. No harm, no foul, thank you Harley-Davidson!

In cooler weather I wear a TourMaster that is water proof, vented, and has a couple of liners, I'll say more about these jackets later but they are amazing pieces of gear. Some people find them comfortable in 80-90 degree weather and higher. Not me. I use the TourMaster for cold to warm weather, the Harley for warm to hot weather, and frankly sometimes just wear a shirt when the temps climb above 90. You'll need to decide what works for you depending on your tolerance for weather extremes and your desire for protection.

Lower body protection

Jeans are the traditional lower body protection. They are comfortable, inexpensive, and offer a relatively high level of protection against abrasion. They don't typically have armor, but they will protect you from road rash in many situations. They also have the advantage of being acceptable wear for many work environments. You can just step off your bike, walk right into the office, and go to work.

Some gear manufacturers offer jeans and cargo pants with removable armor, particularly for the knees. Your knees are one of the more vulnerable spots on your body, so the added protection can be a real plus. Prices tend to be reasonable and the few extra dollars is probably well worth the money. One word of warning. The armored jeans and cargo pants that I have tried on have been cut very small, one manufacturer to the tune of three sizes. I'm not sure whether the manufacturers are trying to save money or whether they aren't interested in clothing old, fat guys, but watch the sizing carefully. My money says that if you order a pair of these online you need to order up in size or be prepared for at least one return. The other likely issue is inseam length, but every pair of jeans and cargo pants I've ever encountered can be shortened if needed.

There are lots of other alternatives out there for lower body protection. Textile trousers offer excellent abrasion protection, good armor, and often have ventilation systems that make them cooler to wear than jeans or cargo pants. Some have liners for cold weather. Many bikers buy textile a size or two up so they can wear them over another pair of slacks. This allows them to wear shorts, dress slacks, or jeans that they can slip off after unassing (oops, I mean dismounting). You may have difficulty finding the inseam length that's right for you. The more reasonably priced textiles are made in one length per waist size. Most of us stubby-legged folk just pull them up, strap them down, and ignore the extra inches hanging around our ankles. If you want to spend the extra bucks you can get tailored lengths from higher-end manufacturers. Aerostitch is an excellent example. Textile trousers are a definite step up financially from jeans and cargo pants, but they are worth every penny when it comes to protection.

Leather chaps are also protective, and offer some protection against the cold. Lined versions are available. I find these cumbersome, but many riders like the extra warmth on a cold day. A word about chaps. They are made in standard lengths and don't bunch up well at the bottom like textile trousers. If you want your chaps to fit you will probably need to cut them. I rarely wear my chaps, only dragging them out when it's cold and I want to look all Easy Riderish, but mine were custom cut by Brownie. I was way too scared to do it myself, although I

146

suppose knee length chaps might start a new fashion trend. Brownie sold me my chaps, measured them out, snickered at my leg length, and cut them to perfection. If you buy chaps, make sure the person doing the cutting is skilled and experienced.

Foot protection

If you're going to ride you need a good pair of boots. You'll need a pair to learn with because the course instructors and Department of Motor Vehicles people won't let you anywhere near their courses without them. And yes, you will see people riding everything from sewing machines to crotch rockets in flip-flops and running shoes but DON"T DO IT!!! There are four main reasons.

One reason a good pair of boots is essential is the stability they provide. Unlike flip-flops, sandals, and many types of shoes, a good pair of boots offers a solid foundation that helps assure that your foot will stay where you put it. Your foot will not shift on the ground or inside the shoe. Don't believe me? Consider the adrenaline rush of a quick stop, then consider the extra adrenaline (and perhaps pellets) produced by stopping several hundred pounds of moving metal with a plastic strip sandwiched between your toes. I think you'll agree that the stability of a good pair of boots is essential to safe and comfortable riding.

A well-chosen pair of boots is also slip resistant. I've had sales folks at bike shops tell me that motorcycle boots are more slip-resistant than a good pair of hiking boots. They may be right, but I've gone out several times in both and tried to slip. You can definitely slip in either, whether you are trying to or not, but both seem to offer substantially more slip resistance than most other shoes.

(No, I haven't tried flip-flops!) I haven't done a lot of on-purpose slipping on oil, but on every street surface I've ever tried I don't see much difference.

Slip resistance is important. We've all seen cages slip and slide on wet streets. Bikes and feet also slide. When you're on two wheels any additional stability you can get is very welcome. Somewhere during my first couple of months on the street I decided to ride my little Nighthawk 250 to work after a brief rain. The ride was pretty non-eventful until I rolled to a stop at an intersection in a neighborhood near the office. I had stopped near the painted center line to give myself a little extra room to swing around the corner because I knew the streets were wet. When I placed my left foot, it slipped away from me. The bike was stable, so it was a pellet-free moment, but when I looked at my foot to see where the banana peel had gone I saw only a wet line of paint. I tried to plant my foot again and then a third time. That line was slick! I learned that day that some very unexpected spots can be very slick, and that the slip resistance of a good pair of boots is mandatory.

Riding boots also help protect your ankles against potential burns and unexpected knocks. Burn protection is particularly important if your bike has exposed pipes or engine parts that you may inadvertently touch with your leg or ankle. Pipes and engine parts get hot after riding. They certainly get hot enough to make touching them uncomfortable and can actually cause first or second degree burns. Boots that cover the ankle and lower legs help protect against them. You may also experience unexpected knocks while mounting, riding, or while walking around your bike admiring it. One of my all-time favorites is walking too close to the foot peg and whacking my ankle on it. A good pair of boots helps defend your ankle against flying debris as well as noobrelated clumsiness.

Some other things to think about are waterproofing, heel height, and where you'll be riding. I strongly recommend waterproof boots. I'm not just talking about materials that prevent water from penetrating. I'm also referring to inner flaps and covers that prevent water from seeping through zippers and seams. Zipping along the highway in a rainstorm is an open invitation for water to seep through cracks and crevices to pocket under your arches and between your toes. Wet socks on a cold day suck. So does sloshing your way into a restaurant after dismount. Tall, water-proof boots tucked inside quality rain gear will make your rainy day rides much more enjoyable.

The other thing you need to consider is where you'll be riding. Street boots are fine for any street use I know about and for gentle off-road use. If you decide to ride more rugged trails you will need the extra stability and protection of off-road boots. I'd buy these from a knowledgable salesperson. We'll talk more about dirt boots in chapter 9.

I have two pairs of boots that I use for the street. One is a motorcycle boot, the other is a hiking boot. My Gates waterproof boots are tall, comfortable, and are my usual choice for the KLR. I typically select a pair of Vasque hikers for the Can-Am. Both are quality, stable choices. I prefer the extra protection of the Gates boots on the more exposed KLR and the comfort and freedom of the Vasques on the more stable Can-Am.

Picking your rain gear

"If you ride long enough you're gonna get wet." Sage wisdom shared by many the Greybeard and novice.

Why? Because it's true. So if sooner or later it's gonna happen to you, you might as well be ready for it.

Riders approach rain differently. Some try to avoid it, citing the very understandable concerns of slippery roads, limited visibility, and cumbersome gear. Some ignore it, blazing ahead in their street clothes through most anything short of a tornado. Most of us will fall somewhere in between, gauging our travel by the severity of the storm, it's likely duration, and the ways in which we are prepared to deal with it.

For me, and for many other bikers, rain gear makes the difference in whether we will go or stay. Unless the winds are high and the rain is driving I'll don my favorite gear and keep on riding. It took some effort to find the rain gear I liked, however, and a while longer to find the right size.

The central piece of rain gear is a full-body covering that is either one or two pieces. A one-piece suit covers torso, arms, and legs, kind of a jumpsuit. A two piece has a top and bottom, similar to a jacket and slacks or a sweatshirt and sweatpants. To be effective the neck must include a hood that can be pulled up under the helmet in the back and can be pulled tight (for example, with a drawstring) in the front.

There are lots of wet weather suits out there, and most will do a good job of keeping you dry. For me, four characteristics are critical. The first, of course, is that it must actually be waterproof. The material must prevent water from penetrating and any seams must be adequately sealed. Openings for the head, arms, and legs must have an effective way of closing tight against the body. I much prefer a material that breathes, which helps you avoid becoming overheated. Some synthetics do this very well. A good suit also has either access to pockets or built-in pockets and will fold or compact into a small pile. When not being worn your rain suit should require as little bike storage space as possible. The other possible consideration has to do with the location of heat sources on your bike. If a pipe or some engine part is likely to melt a hole in your rain suit, you want something that is heat resistant.

I have an expensive brand name wet weather suit. It's nice and comfortable but takes up lots of luggage space. As a result, I rarely use it. My favorite for hot weather is an inexpensive Frog Togg outfit. In colder weather I tend to use a my TourMaster jacket and a pair of textile pants. If the rain is fairly light and doesn't promise to get much harder I often just go with the jacket and a pair of jeans.

Water proof gloves are an essential both to keep your hands dry and to help assure that water does not run up your wrists and into the arms of your suit. You can get pretty wet both above and below your armpits if you have a steady flow of water running up your arm. Leather is great, but it has the annoying habit of soaking through pretty quickly. When they're new, they may also leave a lovely black stain on your hands after you take them off. The best waterproof gloves I've used are Goretex, although there are other alternatives as well. There are two important considerations for your rain gloves. First, will they leave you with enough digital dexterity to manage your clutch, brakes, turn signals, horn, and other controls. Second, do they combine with the sleeves of your rain suit in a way that prevents water from flowing in? If they do both you have a pretty fair pair of gloves.

We talked about boots in the last section. Your rain boots should be tall enough to fit well up inside your rain suit and should have inner tabs and covers to assure that water doesn't seep through zippers or around the tongue. There are spray-on waterproofing products that can be used to bolster or refresh the outer seal.

We also discussed helmets in the last section. I'm not a big fan of helmets that cover your whole head. Aside from keeping you alive and keeping road rash off your pearly whites, I really can't see the advantage, except in the rain. One of my least favorite rides down windy country roads featured my favorite set of Frog Toggs and my favorite half-helmet. I was just about out of state and finishing up a gravelly switchback when storm clouds popped over the nearest mountain. (OK, in the Rockies that would have been a really big hill.) I found a place to pull over, suited up, and replaced my helmet. Within minutes the rain was flying. Yes, I had put up my hood. Yes, I had drawn the string tight. But the monsoon blew into my face with such force that by the time I had found a safe place to weather the storm I had rainwater puddling around my navel. In the interest of appropriate decorum we will not discuss its post-naval path. It was a cool day and a cold ride home. In the old man's (somewhat experienced) opinion proper rain gear requires a good whole-head helmet.

Picking your cold weather gear

People talk about riding season. Honestly, I'm not sure when that isn't. I won't ride in severe thunderstorms and I won't ride when the temperatures are near freezing (I don't want the last thing I see in life to be some jerk... errr, fine individual's diet coke that he threw out the window at 32 degrees Fahrenheit.) In the right gear, layered appropriately, you can be downright toasty, even when the winds are frigid. I know guys who ride no matter what the temperature. They are further proof that with the right gear the idea of riding season is a myth.

For me successful cold weather gear begins with a warm torso. I can handle cold most anywhere else, but when body heat starts to leach away from my chest and abdomen the cold begins to become difficult to tolerate. For cold weather I like foundation undergarments, heavy shirts, an electric vest, and my TourMatser jacket with a liner or two zipped in.

Foundation undergarments are the same 1st generation long undies that hunters and fishermen (and police and rescue workers) use daily when in the field. There are several brands, but mine are Under Armor's ColdGear. I wear Base 3.0s for almost any ride below about 40 degrees. They also make a 4.0, but I have yet to experience a temperature for which the 3.0 was not adequate.

I wear a thick shirt over the base layer for two reasons. This helps provide an additional layer of insulation. A heavy shirt also goes a long way toward covering up those body imperfections (read that "love handles") displayed so graphically by foundation undergarments.

I wear an electric vest over my shirt. The vest is like an electric blanket with armholes. It plugs into a harness that wire to the battery. You plug it in, adjust the thermostat, and hit the road. The thermostat is important. A quality electric vest can make you want to strip in a blizzard when set at full power. By the way, you can also get other electric apparel. There are electric jackets, slacks, gloves, and socks. I find them to be more than I need for Tennessee's moderate winters but some folks in harsher climates swear by them.

If the weather is very cold I zip a liner or two into my TourMaster and put it on over the vest. I've tried jackets made by other manufacturers and they worked equally well. I should probably add that we aren't talking mesh jacket here. The outer shell is a textile of some sort, but if there is a weave it is indistinguishable and impenetrable to winter winds. I can tell you that I've been comfy at speeds up to 70 miles per hour in temperatures down to 33 degrees in the outfit I've described above.

The importance of layers in the lower body varies according to ambient temperature and the amount of protection the fairings on your bike provide. On my Can-Am I frequently make do very well with just a pair of jeans. When the temperature drops and, particularly on the KLR, I'll put on my base layer bottoms. I occasionally use a pair of chaps, but have never needed their liners. I don't own electric trousers, although I can see why folks might want them if they ride below 32 degrees.

Warm hands are more important than you might imagine. In the chapter about gear for your bike we talked about thermal grips, but let me say here that I strongly recommend them. You might also consider base layer liners and lined Goretex or leather gloves. I have great thermal grips, so I generally do very well with a pair of fleeced lined leather gloves. For rain or sleet I switch to a pair of Goretex, but do so only if I have to because I lose a fair amount of digital dexterity when I do.

Leather boots are great, but when the leather gets cold feet are not far behind. Base layer socks or heavy hunting socks can be very helpful. Some manufacturers make battery-powered electric socks. I've had little luck with these. The battery compartments tend to be cumbersome and, in my experience, the socks often fail. The old man likes his base layer socks, and feels comfy in them on cold days.

If you aren't wearing a helmet that covers your

entire head you will also find that your face, particularly where there is no visor, can get very cold. There are lots of alternatives that slip comfortably over your head and under your helmet. Motorcycle supply retailers may carry wide bands designed to fit around your head to cover your mouth, cheeks, and nose. Outdoor gear providers have base layer hoods that cover the entire head, leaving only a gap for the eyes or eyes and nose. Either will help keep your face warm on a cold winter's ride.

Picking your hot weather gear

Hot weather presents an entirely different set of challenges. The trick is to maintain maximum protection while minimizing the tendency of that protection to increase the ambient temperature of the body. The temptation is to strip to a tank top, shorts, and sandals, a great alternative so long as you don't so much as have a tricky stop or catch a flying chunk of gravel.

Honestly, lots of folks ride in t-shirts or long-sleeved cotton button-downs in hot weather. My son and I made a 2200 mile trip through Tennessee, Alabama, Mississippi, Louisiana, Texas, and Arkansas during the summer of 2012. The temperature in east Texas topped 112 degrees on two of those days. During our 8 days of travel we didn't have a single day with a high less than 108. Honestly, we wore t-shirts until we discovered the Columbia outlet near College Station, TX. I am now a big fan of the Columbia long-sleeved sun shirts, as well as of the products of their competitors. These shirts were as more comfortable than the t-shirts, offered some sun shield for our forearms, and would have offered a smidgen of road rash protection had we needed it. Yes, it was a compromise. Had we been involved in an accident we would have been much less protected than in textile or leather jacket. On the other hand, we would have been exposed to miserable temperatures in punishing levels of sunlight. We opted for the more comfortable alternative. I think many people would have done the same.

The best option I know of for maximum protection in very hot weather is textile mesh. The material on this clothing is similar or identical to the textile materials made for colder weather except that the gaps between the threads are much larger. This allows for very free flow of air through the clothing and makes it very cool to wear, particularly when moving. These garments also have internal pockets for armor and may have other pouches that allow you to include cooling gear. Earlier, for example, I mentioned the pouch on my Harley-Davidson mesh jacket. Located at the middle of my upper back the pouch holds an absorbent pad that can be soaked in water prior to its insertion into the pouch. Air flowing across the back, through the mesh, and across the absorbent pad provides some very nice cooling during a hot ride. Textile mesh trousers are also very comfortable, particularly when moving. I find my mesh pants much cooler than jeans, even when I'm wearing shorts under them.

A word about color. It's great to be cool, that is, to look hot, but if you want to stay cool you may not be able to wear the hottest colors. Hmmm, I'm not sure I'm communicating this well. What I'm trying to say is that you need to consider colors when you buy for hot weather. Dark colors may be fashionable but will heat you up very quickly as compared to lighter colors. The same is true for all your gear, particularly helmets. For hot weather chose light colors and reflective surfaces. The difference will be well worth any sacrifice you may make in terms of fashion.

Different styles of gloves also offer different levels

of protection for hot weather. Full-finger leather gloves do get hot, particularly when the sun is beating down on them. Many manufacturers offer fingerless gloves. These are much cooler, but don't do much to protect your fingers if you go down or even slip on a dismount. My favorites for hot weather are a stretchable glove with leather palm and finger pads. These are really designed for off-road use, but I have yet to have a highway tell, me, "Go away, bud, those gloves are for dirt." These gloves provide pretty good air flow and reasonably good protection. They also dry quickly so if you happen to soak them through with perspiration or rain they aren't soggy when you put them on the next day. Mine were also inexpensive. I bought them online from Cycle Gear on sale for about ten bucks. I do, by the way, often wear my fingerless gloves when I'm on the Can-Am.

Once again, there's a decision to make between comfort and protection. Ultimately, you'll have to decide what you want to wear and what kind of trade-off you'll accept. In the interest of liability, the old man advises leather. The choice, however, is up to you.

Helmets are hot, no matter what choice you make. Obviously, a helmet that covers your entire head is going to hold more heat than a shell. Head protection is so critical to motorcycle safety, however, that you may be reluctant to wear shells or half helmets. The good news is that most helmets offer excellent ventilation systems that can be closed and opened with the flick of a finger. Manipulating these vents along with cracking the visor at more open settings can make a whole-head or modular helmet quite comfortable even at extreme temperatures.

Be sure the internal padding of your helmet is removable and washable. You will perspire inside it and after a few rides it will develop a very distinct aroma. Yep, if you don't wash it your helmet will stink. Most pads either snap or velcro (is that a verb?) into place. Some use both snaps and velcro. Be sure the padding will come out and that a degree in engineering isn't required to remove it. The padding will have instructions for washing and drying just as clothing does. Be sure to follow the instructions carefully. That stuff will last a long time if handled properly, keeping your head safe, comfortable, and sometimes a little too warm.

You'll want to wear thick socks when you ride, even when the weather is hot. Thick, absorbent socks help keep your feet dry and protect against friction and blisters. Several manufacturers make good thick hot-weather socks. Mine are UnderArmor, but sporting goods stores, outdoor establishments, bike shops, and even larger discount stores often stock several alternatives. A good pair of socks will cost you a few dollars, but the dollars will be well spent. As with other items of clothing, investment in safe, comfortable socks will return great dividends in pleasure when you ride.

Boots are boots. You can buy them longer or shorter. You can get lighter and darker colors. But boots just don't offer many alternatives for internal temperature management. I've rarely found this to be a problem. The one exception has been high temperatures (say over about 110 degrees) and a cloudless sky. Hot sun beating down on a black boot with high atmospheric temperature and even higher temperatures radiating from the road and engines can make your feet hot! I distinctly recall sitting at traffic lights in an east Texas town with the sun beating down on my right side. The thermometer on the bank at the side of the road read 112 degrees. The thermometer on the Can-Am bolstered by bubbling blacktop and the idling engine, read 119. It was early afternoon and the sun was baking my southbound right foot in its black biker boot. I actually decided to make a boot change. I pulled to the side of the road, unpacked my brown Vasque hikers, and slipped them on. The switch didn't exactly refrigerate my toesies, but it did make my ride much more comfortable. Lighter colors and shorter boots may help in very hot weather. Some of my biker buddies have pointed out, however, that a reasonable man would have taken any color of boot complete with its foot into an air-conditioned building and waited out the afternoon in a more comfortable environment.

Educating yourself for your decisions

Speaking of checking out the shops, let's talk a bit about some additional ways to educate yourself about your gear decisions. Yes, the old man has shared incredible pearls of wisdom and the sales folks at your local retail outlets are eager to expound moto-truth as well. My guess is, however, that you'll want to explore a little bit on your own. If you do, here are some ways and places to go about it for the gear you wear.

The temptation for many is to buy a bunch of gear right away, thinking that having everything on hand will prepare you for any situation. Although this might, indeed, prepare you, you will probably find that you don't need to be prepared for everything immediately. For example, when you first start, you probably won't want to ride in the rain. Slick streets, limited visibility, and added discomfort will probably make you a dry weather rider for at least the first few weeks. Similarly, unless you live in a climate that's frigid all the time you probably won't need electric vests and base layer materials right away. What you do need the first time you get on your bike is a good set of basic gear. You'll also need this gear for the MSD class if you take it. So either purchase the gear when you buy the bike, do a little shopping before you take delivery, or show incredible restraint by letting the bike sit undisturbed in your garage for a few days until you have gotten your stuff.

If you do shop around before you buy basic gear, visit several shops, try on different gear, and discuss the alternatives with the salesperson. Although this chapter has provided you with good basic information about general gear choices, each manufacturer does some things in different ways. Learn about those differences before you buy.

Fit is also an important factor. Lots of folks you see on bikes wear baggy gear. Why? Because they bought a size or two larger than they actually need to allow other clothing to be worn under the gear for different occasions and types of weather. If you buy a tight, form-fitting jacket when you're wearing a t-shirt you may be in for a lot of frustration when you try to put it on over a sweatshirt. When it comes to your helmet, definitely seek expert advice a least for the first one. Fit is critical to headgear effectiveness. If it doesn't fit right it won't protect you properly.

There are also lots of things available to read about the gear that you wear. Most of these will be very helpful. I've included a list of books I recommend in the first appendix of this volume. Many of them have sections on gear selection. If you want to know which include gear information check amazon.com or barnesandnoble.com to see if you can access a table of contents for the book. If not, try the publisher's website. I've also found the manufacturer's brochures and sales literature to be very helpful. Of course, they all claim to make the best, but they highlight the features of their products in ways that you will probably find very instructive.

One of the best sources of information about gear is other bikers. Folks who have tried it know what it does and doesn't do. Ask friends who ride. Join clubs and organizations in your area and talk with the members (see Appendix II). Join online forums and read threads about gear.

Online forums brings up the Internet. I find the Web to be an invaluable source of information about almost everything to do with motorcycling. If you want to know about it, fix it, or rig it, there's usually a video, article, or forum that can tell you what you need to know. I belong to several forums and am an avid viewer of youtube. I also scan multiple manufacturer's sites before I make a gear purchase. This is true not only of the gear you wear, but also of the gear you put on your bike. We'll be talking about that kind of gear in the next chapter.

Kickstands down

In this chapter we've discussed the gear you wear. We talked about the basic stuff you need, as well as what you'll need for wet, cold, and hot weather. We also took a quick look at some of the gear you wear for off-road purposes. Finally, we discussed ways of educating yourself to make good decisions about the gear you'll buy.

The next chapter makes a little leap forward in time. It's my reflection on the process of learning to ride. When I started the MSD class I just couldn't bring myself to think of me as a rider. I had way too much to learn. As time went on and I developed skills and tried new things, I came more and more to think of myself as a rider. I'm not sure how you'll react to the process, but I'm thinking it will be similar for you. If so, you may find chapter 7 very interesting.

Chapter 7

Progressing from Learner to Rider

Maybe it's just me. But I don't think so. Maybe it isn't as big for others as it was for me, but for me this mattered a lot. For me there was a definite psychological progression in taking the mental steps from thinking of myself as a learner to thinking of myself as a rider. Looking back I can see several events that moved me along that mental pathway. Each step was important because each improved my confidence and helped me to be prepared to accept new challenges, both in terms of the skills I developed and in terms of the psychological resources form which I could draw.

I think this may be a process that few kids experience. I am a firm believer that kids should be put on a bike as soon as their little buns will fit the saddle of one of the undersized models that are now available at very reasonable prices. Obviously they should stick to dirt until they're legal and obviously parental supervision is a must. Still kids seem to make that learner to rider transition in a couple of hours. Wait until that same kid is the old man's age and the transition gets lots, lots longer.

Admittedly, some folks don't seem to experience this process. An acquaintance of mine talks openly of love for biking, of all the bikes he has owned, and of all the guys from the motorcycle clubs that he has talked to over the years. Yet for him it is a big deal to do anything other than ride a single specific route on a specific country road near his home. Now don't get me wrong, as far as I am concerned the guy is a rider. He rides as much or as little as he wants and it is really none of my damn business. My point is, however, that he clearly thinks of himself as a rider. When I was limiting my own rides that much, I just didn't think of myself that way.

Looking back, I wish I had been more like him. I think I was ready to do some things way before I actually did them. I think I was more self-conscious and less adventurous than I might have been. What I want to do in this chapter is talk about the process of moving from learner to rider. I hope that, if you find it to be a journey for you, you will find my story and my experiences helpful.

<u>Learning to check things out, mount up, and turn things on</u>

There's a certain amount of comfort in being able to get on a bike smoothly, snap the kickstand up, turn all the right switches, push all the right buttons, and push smoothly off for the start of a ride. Being able to do that is a great start and a serious confidence-builder. Tripping over the seat when mounting, forgetting to turn on the petcock, overlooking the kill switch, and/or stalling the engine 2-3 times can be a little unsettling. Yes, I know because I did back when I was starting. I think most of us do. What you may be surprised to hear is that most of us do one or more of those things occasionally even after we have a few thousand miles under our belts.

After a few months (yes, months) in the saddle I began to realize that no one was sitting around watching to see whether or not I hit all the right buttons. As a matter of fact, usually there was no one around. If I stalled it, I started it up again. If I forgot a part of the start-up protocol, I started at the beginning and made sure I got everything FINE-CS right. No one seemed to be watching. No one seemed to care. No one (except my son) ever burst out laughing and called me a noob. (He gets permission to do that, particularly because he was behind me on the bike at the time.)

164

If you have anxiety about getting started on your first few rides you may find the following four things helpful.

1. Make sure you know where everything is and, which switch does what. If I ever have occasion to ride or even sit on someone else's bike (by invitation only, of course) I always look to see if I know where such key components as the ignition and the choke are located. I learned this when I first sat astride a used Harley Davidson Sportster that I was considering as a purchase. I turned on the fuel confidently (F) then reached for the ignition. It wasn't there. The owner, a kind woman, pointed gently to the right side of the bike. I murmured something clever like, "Oh yeah." and quickly switched it on (I). I put it in (N)uetral and flipped the kill switch (E for engine not K for kill. I guess FINE sounds better than FINK.) Confidently, I reached for the choke. It wasn't there. The bike's owner still kind, wanting to save the deal, and probably seriously reconsidering her decision to allow me to sit on it, carefully pointed it out. Since my explanation of my limited knowledge had worked so well before, I tried it again. "Oh yeah," I said.

Since that time I have ridden and sat on several bikes from various manufacturers. I have learned that things are usually in the same place. I have learned that they sometimes are not. My Virago, for example, doesn't have a petcock. Instead it has a switch that allows you to switch between the main and reserve tanks, but no option to shut down the vent. The Can-Am is really tricky. It had no petcock (fuel injection), so after you switch on the ignition you have to push a button on the right handlebar console to tell the computer that you have read the safety statement (yeah, right) and are ready to go. If you don't know where something is don't be shy about asking. The manufacturer just may have thrown you a curve with its placement.

It also helps to understand what the likely reaction is if you forget a startup step. If, for example, your bike starts successfully, warms up for a couple of minutes, then sputters to a stop within a few hundred feet, you probably forgot to turn on the petcock. If you are set to go and push the starter button but nothing happens you probably forgot either the ignition or the kill switch. If you did, just fix it. The decision to explain your behavior with a clever "oh yeah" is entirely optional.

2. Realize that even experienced riders make mistakes from time to time.
I usually ride alone, but sometimes join up with some other folks. The first few times I did so I was surprised to learn that even the grizzled veterans of the asphalt sometimes stalled their bikes. Strange but true. I also noticed that no one really paid any attention when they did. When I did it, probably a little more often than the others, no one seemed to notice.

It's also important to realize that every bike rides differently. My son's XT250 needs lots of gas to get it started. The Virago, on the other hand, seems to want to start down the road as soon as I touch the throttle. When I ride his bike I will invariably stall it if I don't think about what I am doing in advance. The Virago also performs differently in cold weather than it does in warm weather. Fact is, I sometimes just mess up. We all do. No need to be embarrassed or self-conscious.

3. Practice until you don't mess up (very often). If it makes you more comfortable spend some time on the bike switching things on and off in mock starts. I'll bet you have an unconscious routine you go through when you start your automobile. I get into mine, close the door, put

the key in the ignition, lift my rear off the seat to free the seat belt, sit back down, buckle it up, put my foot on the brake, give the gas pedal a pump or two, and switch it on. I do it almost invariably. Why is this so automatic? Years and years of repetition. If you are insecure about your motorcycle startup process, try a little repetition.

4. Stop giving a rat's rump about what people think. I admit it, I'm guilty. I remember one day early in my riding career when I stalled my bike in the driveway because I forgot to switch on the fuel. I was sitting in my driveway behind my very rural, very secluded house and caught myself looking around to see if anyone had noticed. I was amazed to discover that none of my neighbors had made their way along forest trails from their homes at least 1/2 mile away to see if I was going to stall my bike.

Seriously, there are lots of things you can disdain rats rumps about when it comes to riding. Most riders are friendly, supportive folks who will be very encouraging to you about your bike, accessory choice, helmet, etc. A few seem to think their opinion is better than anyone else's and that everyone else should ride, wear, and use exactly what they do. These folks will be very surprised if you point out to them that this is not the case.

5. Get on and off the bike in the way that works for you. The height and width of the seat and the length and width of your legs may make mounting and dismounting a very different experience for some than it is for others. I want to say more about this, but please allow me a brief explanation of terminology before I continue this discussion.

I've done a fair amount of thinking about the use of the term "unassing" to describe dismounting form your motorcycle. As I said in an earlier chapter, I love the term. There are two significant problems with using it in the book, however. One, also discussed earlier, is the possibility that someone might be offended by the use of the word "ass". If the presence of that word here puts anyone off I sincerely apologize. I'll do my best to use the terms booty, derrierre, buns, hips, and seat in every other place in this book. Here, however, I think it appropriate to discuss the commonly used term "unassing" in its literary context. My biggest reason for not using that term in the book isn't its potential for offense. My biggest reason is its logical consequences for the term used to describe getting onto the seat. If, when one dismounts, one unasses the bike, does that mean when one mounts, one asses the bike? Something about that just sounds wrong. I love my bike. It and I share many hours of pleasure on highways and dirt trails around the country. Really, why would I want to ass it? That conjures thoughts and visuals that just don't belong in the relationship between me and my bike. Consequently, I will forgo the use of either term here, reluctantly settling for the words mount and dismount. If you are unhappy about it you'll just have to kick my seat.

I actually envy people whose legs are long enough to allow them to stand with one foot on the ground while they lift the other casually over the seat. I've described the way I nearly lay down on the KLR to get on and off it. The Virago and the Can-Am are much easier. The Virago has a very low seat. I still can't step over it but I am able to swing my leg over to the rear comfortably. The Can-Am is higher, but it is sufficiently stable to allow me to step on a rider peg and swing my leg over "horsey style".

The fact of the matter is, most bikes with decent kickstands are very stable on the ground. One exception occurs if you've had your bike lowered. Another may be if you are mounting on sand or in mud. Otherwise if you face the challenge of the short-legged you can probably stand on the left side of the bike, place your left foot on the rider peg, and extend your left leg, and swing your right over the seat. If you are afraid the bike isn't stable enough try putting a little weight on the left foot peg with your left foot. If the bike stays stable try standing one-footed on it. If it still doesn't move lift your leg and swing away. With the right kickstand in the right place and on a solid surface the bike isn't going anywhere.

Learning the basic skills of riding

We had a fairly lengthy discussion of learning the basics in chapter 4. As a result, we won't spend much time on it here. I refer you, instead, to the brilliant summation made in that early section.

Here I'd like to talk a little bit about the psychology of learning the basics. I think it's something you'll find helpful. These were important lessons I learned through trying.

Be respectful but not fearful. I think this is a hard balance to reach for some people. It was for me. Riding a big touring motorcycle at 70 mph on a crowded freeway has several inherent dangers. Riding a small bike at 25 mph on a deserted country road or in an empty parking lot has distinctly fewer. Lots of folks who start riding a little later in life seem to be a little bit overly cautious. Relax and enjoy your ride. Try some new things but spend some time enjoying the old. Make some turns. Make some stops, both easy and hard. If balance becomes an issue ease off the throttle and put your feet down. At slower speeds and safer conditions you can handle almost anything by stopping and putting your feet down. At slow speeds you can also bounce along (your feet, not the bike) until you have stabilized, then rev it, put your feet up, and move on.

Practice makes (almost) perfect. Have we talked about this more than 10 or 12 times? It is so important and so true. You can look at your bike all you want, watch Sons of Anarchy over and over, read the great motorcycle literature of all time (Mine and Sonny Barger's, I don't make any money off his but I'm skeered not to mention it.). You won't get better without seat time and you will progress amazingly quickly when you spend some time in the saddle as close to every day as possible. I can remember times that my confidence in what I could do grew every day. That growth didn't come from knowing mental cruises with the gang from Charming, CA. It came from puttering down solitary country roads on my little Honda.

For me it was important to realize that my head was better than my heart at telling me what my bike and I could do. I couldn't trust my feelings to tell me what was safe. My feelings didn't know, and seemed to assume the worst. My head was able to look at various situations and say, "Hmmm, maybe you'd better reconsider." or "Yep, you can do that, remember back when you did that similar thing a couple of days ago?"

I first learned about head over heart riding in my Motorcycle Safety class. It wasn't something the instructors told me. Rather, it was something they made me do. I don't think this was something in the curriculum, but I learned it nonetheless.

During the riding portion of the Motorcycle Safety Course you have to successfully complete a series of maneuvers that the instructors first describe, then demonstrate. Some are pretty simple, like weaving in and out through a line of cones. Others are more complex.

For most of the folks in my class the most challenging was running a slow-speed figure 8 inside a 20' by 40' box. There were yellow lines that you were not allowed to cross. The guys who had been riding for years were pretty casual about it, although nobody just breezed right through it. Most folk had done some riding, and were able to limp their way through it. I, the only true noob in the group, looked at it and thought I'd never be able to do it. I sucked during the practice rounds. I made it through the figure eights, but probably swung outside the yellow lines on 2 out of every 4 tries. I made it through the practice sessions pretty well and was feeling OK about it until the instructors mentioned that we might see any of the maneuvers on the exam. Sure enough, when exam time came around the figure eight was a part of it.

Running the figure eight in the exam was an enlightening experience for me. My heart said, "Are you friggin kidding me? I am going to dump the bike right out here in front of God and everybody." My head quickly stepped in, "Excuse me," it responded, "We just did this yesterday. We ran over the lines a little bit, although we stayed inside at least half of them. Neither God nor anyone saw us lay the bike down cuz we didn't. I think we can do this respectably and maybe even successfully. Just calm down and point the front wheel where you want to go." I nailed it. Didn't cross a single line. Didn't lay the bike down. Didn't even put my foot down to steady the bike on the turns. I just plain nailed it. I thought everyone (except God) was gonna faint. I managed to play it off like it was no big deal, like I ran a couple of hundred of those every morning before breakfast. How did I manage that? I'm pretty sure a big part of it was that I listened to my mind instead of my heart. My brain knew what was doable. My heart was afraid we would fail. My brain remembered past successes. My heart was just plain skeered. (And yes, for all the neurophysiologists in the group, I do know that this was, at its essence, the calming of the emotionally reactive part of the brain by the rational part. I am, however, gonna ignore every neural network and say it the way I wanna because it's my book!)

The need for head over heart riding shows up pretty frequently when you're learning the basics. One example happens when you make turns. A very interesting thing about making turns is that lots of us noobs tend to use every millimeter of available space when we turn. We could turn tighter, but we don't. We swing as wide as we possibly can. Early on, we also often to manage to work a butt-cheek tightening fear reaction into the turn. We may have just made a much tighter turn with less space a few minutes ago, but we manage to work all that reaction into a bigger, broader space when somewhere down inside we know full well that we could do it with ease. In such cases I have found it helpful to listen to my head. My head knows what I have done before. It can tell me what I can do successfully. My past experience instructs me. I can turn tighter and complete maneuvers more easily, and my formerly clenched butt cheeks are forever grateful.

I'm sure I need to add that head over heart riding may not work for adrenaline junkies and risk takers. It is probably also less useful for young learners than it is for us older folks. But if you find yourself stiffening up when you need to perform easy maneuvers or becoming fearful about a turn you have made successfully in the past, it may be time to pay a little more attention to your head and a little less to your heart.

As you gain confidence and skills, you should gradually expand your rides. What started as a few laps up and down the driveway should turn into a few around the block. Gradually expand your rides, adding new challenges. Give purpose to your rides, a trip to the grocery, a jaunt to pick up something from the hardware store. Spend some time on your bike almost every day, trying new things and exploring new vistas.

One of the main goals of all this practice is to develop a repertoire of "right responses". It's pretty cool the first time you recognize the need to swerve and do it all on your own. It's equally cool when at some later point you swoop from the curb in a beautiful arc and realize that you just looked like a scene from Sons of Anarchy. These things happen because your mind and body have learned to do the "right things". You now do them without conscious thought. The more right things you learn, the more relaxed and enjoyable your ride.

<u>First days on the road</u>

As you become more comfortable on your practice runs you will probably begin to ride to specific places. I think it was on a trip to the grocery that I started to feel the sense of being more of a rider than a learner. It was, of course, a fairly sparse grocery run. I was on the Nighthawk 250 with nary a saddlebag in sight. My trunk was an orange backpack with space for a two liter bottle of soda along with meat and veggies for dinner. As I was rounding one of the curves on the ridge between my home and the little town where the grocery waited it occurred to me that I was doing more than just preparing. I was riding.

After that I began to ride to more things. The post office is a few miles south. There's an ATM about 10 miles east. If you go either north or west 15ish miles there are some beautiful views and some nice little restaurants. At one time I would have taken the truck to those. As I became a rider I began more and more to take a bike.

For me it was important to do a little route planning. Things like the inherent challenges of the route, the time of day, the weather conditions, and who my companions might be became important.

I found planning my route is important for a couple of reasons. First, I wanted to get as many miles out of the trip as I reasonably could. I also tried to take one route to my destination and another to get back home. This maximized my learning opportunities on each ride while helping to assure that I didn't get bored by too much repetition. Fact is, I have yet to ever feel bored getting on a bike. There have been cold days that I didn't want to go out, but once I had fired it up and gotten out of the driveway, I was delighted to be on the road.

The second thing I tried to remember when planning those early rides was selecting routes that matched my skill and comfort levels. Out in the sticks where I live there are great curvy roads just made for leaning, gravel roads with fierce switchbacks, and steep hills on both. On those roads there are people who drive reasonably, and other folks who seem to think they are competing in a NASCAR run. In my earliest trips I wanted to get as many miles and curves in as possible without having an idiot pushing my rear bumper or having to manage my clutch and throttle after a stop on a steep incline. I also figured switchbacks on gravel roads weren't the best idea for a noob. Thinking about where I was going to ride helped me to avoid some tight spots in my early going.

It was also important to think about the time of day I rode. Ambient light, traffic, temperature, and the angle of the sun all affected my decisions. When I say ambient light I'm mostly talking about daylight, night, and all the gradations of light in between. Obviously, the darker it gets the more help you need from your headlights and taillights. The more you rely on your bike's lights, the less your opportunity to see road hazards, moving creatures, and even other motorists. If you're riding an older, lower-end bike like I was, your lighting system is likely to leave a lot to be desired. Riding a dark county road on a moonless night with a strong lighting system has plenty of risks, but with a puny headlight it can be downright scary. When learning to ride I tried to stay out of those kinds of situations. I was, after all, the owner of a cage, and was able to exercise the option to drive it at any time I chose.

Traffic was another important consideration. Apart from those derriere-holes who think driving 80 mph on windy country roads is cool, I also tried to avoid going to town during rush hour or toward the lake on Friday or Sunday afternoons. The other big thing was staying away from school zones when their days were beginning and ending. The underlying thought behind these choices was limiting the variables until I had some of the muscle memory under control. Riding alone along a well-lit country road at a moderate speed, limits the things that can go wrong. Add a school zone with moving buses, distracted parents in cages, oblivious kids, and harried crossing guards and you add countless opportunities for both your skill level and muscle memory to be overtaxed.

While learning to ride, as a matter of fact, all during my riding history, I've tried to be very aware of the weather. Wet weather means both rain gear and extra caution. Cold weather means bundling up. Cold weather when it is raining is colder (OK, I know it just feels that way) than cold weather when it is not. Overcast cold weather feels colder than sunny weather of the same temperature. If you're wet or cold and miserable it's hard to focus on what you need to do to be safe.

Most of my rides are solo. I do, however, occasionally hook up with friends and organizations for group rides. This was particularly helpful to me in the earliest stages. I didn't do it very often, but having someone riding behind me, particularly when I was pushing my comfort zone, was very helpful. I'm not sure what I expected or thought they might do. I guess I thought it would nice to have someone around to tell the story if I missed a turn and crashed off into the woods or a cow pasture. That never happened and I never needed a rescue, but something about having an experienced rider back there made me feel better.

Speed was an issue for me on my early rides. I was worried that I was going too slow and that someone approaching behind me might be annoyed. Truth be told, I think I was afraid they would believe me to be a noob. The truth, of course, can hurt! In retrospect there was no real problem. I always moved at a reasonable speed for the roads I was on. I wasn't blocking traffic. If someone behind me got a little overeager I could always pull over in a safe spot and let them pass. Pick your roads and routes carefully. Know the traffic patterns and plan to accommodate them. Be aware of the weather. You'll feel yourself moving from learner to rider before you know it.

<u>Picking routes for fun rides</u>

Shortly after starting to run errands on my bike I started to do fun rides. For many riders I know this is just about all they do. Most of the trips aren't particularly long, maybe 25 to 50 miles, but they are both great recreation and provide lots of opportunities for skill development.

I have several ways of planning local fun rides. My favorite is to ask friends who ride. The best routes I have found were recommended to me by other bikers. If I want to include some dirt, I ask the off-road guys. If I'm thinking asphalt only, I talk to the street guys. They can help you find the best views and curves. They can also usually give you a good idea of the level of difficulty of the trip.

I've also been known to use Google Earth, MapQuest, and physical maps to plan my routes. When I'm feeling particularly bold I just ride out to a new area and switch on my GPS. I let it find my location or pick a town or place of interest that is within a reasonable distance. This is a great way to find new roads and new places. I've also met some very nice people who carefully clarified the intent of both maps and GPS devices for me. The one downside is that it is sometimes difficult to gauge the difficulty of some segments of rides picked in this manner. One trip in particular comes to mind. I was exploring central Tennessee by following a GPS route to one of our wonderful state parks, Fall Creek Falls. The GPS told me to take Highway 111 south from Cookeville, then head east on County Route 30 (referred to somewhat smugly by the locals as "scenic route 30"). I dutifully followed its lead and shortly found myself mystically transported to the Tail of the Dragon, a road famous for its turns and switchbacks in East Tennessee. It turns out that scenic route 30 is a shorter, perhaps even twistier version of that fabled road. I had no trouble making the trip, but went through most of those switchbacks much more slowly than the line of local cars behind me would have liked. It would have been a great ride if it had been the one I had planned for. If I had prodded the GPS a bit when I planned my ride I would have found an alternate route, equally beautiful a few miles south.

I love my GPS. I wish, however, it was a little more

explicit about the kinds of roads it recommends. If you ask it to take you to a house about 8 miles north of mine it will take you by the shortest route, one which takes you across ridges and down ravines on a dizzying combination of gravel and dirt roads with a tiny bit of asphalt thrown in here and there. The closest route tells you probably 15 minutes longer than going 15 miles out of your way on asphalt. This really isn't a big deal on the KLR. It's another matter entirely to navigate those trails on a big street bike. If you decide to use your GPS for exploring you may want to ask some locals about the route it recommends for you.

The tricks and traps of commuting

Another step on the path from learning to riding for me was commuting to and from work. I started with trips to sites near my home near Cookeville, TN, then expanded to include faculty functions in Knoxville and Nashville. Although I usually ride country roads on my way to Cookeville, I purposely chose a little Interstate time on my way there several times to prepare for Nashville and Knoxville. Nashville and Knoxville trips ultimately prepared me for the longer vacation trips I now take by helping me log Interstate time.

Some of you will swear that I am still a noob when I tell you that I don't like to take the KLR on the Interstate. Yes, I do it from time to time, but it isn't my preference. Big trucks and buses are my concern. I love the bike but its light weight and high center of gravity make the turbulence from those large vehicles an experience to be remembered (if you live through it!). Seriously, lots of people ride dual purpose bikes like the KLR and the Suzuki DR on the Interstate and like it just fine. I'm just not one of them. I'm much happier on the Virago, which is lower and heavier. Put me on a trike or the Can-Am and I am ready to roll through as many lanes as you can offer

178

me. When I commute I try to stay with the bike I am comfortable with and choose my routes accordingly.

There are some important things to keep in mind when you begin to commute on your bike. You have to be aware of the times of day you will be traveling. Conditions may be very different when you leave and when you return. You will have some different restrictions on what you can do during the day when riding. For example, you may find it difficult to pick up your dry cleaning or carry a cup of coffee on your bike. Unless you are very selective about the days you ride you will need waterproof storage for the things you carry between home to work. You will also need more time to prepare to ride than to drive and may need more time to park. Let's take a closer look at each of these special requirements.

Weather and light conditions may vary widely depending on where you live and the time of year. If your job is from 9 to 5 you may have sun on the morning and rain for the ride home. During the winter you might have bright sunlight in the morning and pitch dark on the way home. My area is blessed (?) with an interesting combination of close proximity to the Eastern Time Zone and a very odd configuration of the Daylight Savings Time line. If you drive two hours straight north it is one hour later than it is at home. These two factors combine to mean that dusk is after 9 PM at the summer solstice and shortly after 4 PM in the dead of winter. A cage provides some margin of protection against a variety of conditions. You stay dry regardless of the weather. You have adequate vehicle lighting because your vehicle is designed to drive at night. On a bike you are much more affected by Mother Nature. Be aware of the conditions you may face when you plan your bike commute.

I should add a quick disclaimer here. Getting wet in warm weather on a bike isn't a terribly big deal. As a matter of fact, if you ride long enough it will happen to you. God will surprise you with a shower at some point. It's no fun, however, to be trapped in a cloudburst or drenched when the temperatures have dropped. So be prepared, think ahead, and act all macho like you meant it to happen if you get caught in the rain.

When you commute you will also discover different restrictions on things you can do during the day. Running errands may be a bit more of a challenge in part because of the time it takes to get moving and get unloaded for work and in part because of storage issues. If you're running out for lunch you'll need a place to stick the container where it won't leak all over your luggage and a drink container that has a top. Remember that when you run out at lunch or for an errand you will need to put on whatever gear you need to ride, perhaps unlock your bike, and possibly prepare your luggage to hold whatever you'll be acquiring. When you arrive at your destination you'll need to lock your bike, find something to do with your helmet and gear, then get whatever you've acquired into the luggage. When you return to the worksite you'll need to un-rump, lock up, and stow your gear. All this is a far cry from rushing to your car, throwing everything in the back, and rushing back to work. I'm not suggesting that all this makes riding to work a chore. Far from it, the ride to and from is often one of the highlights of my day. It is, important, however, to plan well. You probably won't want to ride your bike on the day you're scheduled to pick up your new lawn mower.

When you commute on your bike you will need waterproof storage for anything you want to transport back and forth. There are lots of options, but you want to be sure you use at least one of them. On a bike without luggage you may choose a waterproof backpack or a regular backpack with a rain cover. My backpack also has a built-in water reservoir and a drinking tube to make it easy to stay hydrated on long, hot rides. I actually have a couple of them, one for use under rugged conditions and one for easier rides. Both are brightly colored to make me more visible on the road. If you have luggage on the bike you may not need the backpack, but you will want to be sure that whatever you use is watertight. Some cases are either waterproof or water resistant in themselves. The Givi luggage on my KLR is a good example. Other luggage offers either an outer or inner bag. The outer goes around the entire piece of luggage and tightens down with some sort of drawstring or other device. Inner bags assume that at least some water is going to get through the luggage and provides a second line of protection. Either works well, but you should practice the installation a couple of times before you are forced to use it in a real life situation. Trying to fit a bag around important materials in a driving rain under an interstate overpass tries both ones patience and vocabulary. At least, that's what I am told. I, of course, am far too wise to have ever been caught unprepared like that!

When you choose your method of protecting materials for commuting it is important to understand just how protective they are. Some luggage is considered waterproof. You can take these cases and dunk them in a pool of water. Everything inside stays dry. Other materials are water resistant. They stop rain and splashes, but will not stop water from seeping in through cracks and crevices should the bag be submerged. Still others offer little resistance to water and require an external protector. If you already have a bag and aren't sure which it is, take it out in the back yard and turn the hose on it. Place it in a position that simulates water coming down, up, and from around it, because that's how it happens on the road. If you soak it good for 15 minutes or so and the interior is still dry you are probably in business.

We need to talk about leather a bit here. Leather must be waterproof, right? Otherwise cows would have soggy intestines after every rainstorm. Fact is, when leather is processed most of the good stuff that protects cow's innards is taken out. The result is a material that rain will penetrate, and will penetrate at a disturbing rate if the rain is hard and persistent. Many of the leather bags you buy for bikes are pretreated so that water will not seep through the material. If yours isn't pretreated you can buy products that will make it repel water. You should also be aware that water will seep through seams and will splash up under lids that don't seal. If you're using leather luggage that isn't guaranteed watertight an inner or outer protective bag is an excellent idea.

Remember our discussion way back a few paragraphs ago about how it takes more time to get ready to travel on a bike than in a cage? Consider that point in the light of what we just discussed about weather conditions. Now think about other variables you may need to consider. Now think about the things you haven't thought about. Riding to work is well worth the extra time an effort, but remember that the extra time and effort is required. Both you and the folks at your place of employment will be glad that you did. That's true unless you are the boss, of course. If you're in charge it may be that everyone would prefer that you took your sweet time.

Packing up for a day trip

I made two major discoveries when I packed for my first day trip. One was that I had less room to pack than I thought. The second was that I needed to pack less than I thought. The second discovery made the first much less important. I must confess that I went all Boy Scout when I planned: be prepared. I sat down and made a long list of everything I could possibly need, fetched everything into a pile on my bed, and started to (tried to) get it all in. It wasn't long before I realized that it wasn't going to work. I unpacked everything, went through the list and marked off things I thought I could do without, and tried again. Wash, rinse, and repeat. After the fourth cycle I finally got everything in. I went out, had a great ride, and used only the lunch I had packed and a couple of granola bars. For me, that was one big lesson on preparation.

Let's talk about the general types of things you might pack and the number of them that you are likely to need. Let's start with clothing. We're talking day trip here. The first question is, what are the temperatures likely to be? In the summer it's going to be hot. Depending on your adherence (or lack thereof) to the Motorcycle Safety Foundation's advice, you may either wear a light jacket or go without. If you're going to wear it all day you won't need any luggage space. If you're going to ride without it at some point you're going to make sure you have a place to put it. If you aren't going to use a jacket at all you don't need the space but you put yourself at greater risk for road rash and other nasties if you happen to go down.

Cold weather is also pretty easy to plan for. Just look at the coldest temperature you expect to encounter and the warmest temperature you expect to encounter (love my Weather Channel iPhone app) and take the amount of stuff you need for each. There are a couple of ways to save space when you do this. One is to wear electric clothing. Another is to wear a jacket and trousers that layer with liners. If it starts or turns a little cool, crank up the electricity or add a layer. As it warms up, take out a layer, turn up the juice, and unzip something that allows you to remain decent. Yes, you can do this with plain old layers of long underwear and sweatshirts, but they take up lots of space when you start peeling things off. Plan for the likely warmest and coolest temperatures, then figure out the way to manage them with the least possible gear.

Rain is, of course, also an issue. I recommend a good pair of waterproof boots that are tall enough to extend up under your rain pants, a compact rain suit like Frogg Toggs, and a whole-head helmet. Under most conditions those items will keep you snug and dry. If the rain lets up you can just take off the suit and crack the visor on your helmet to enjoy the bright sunshine.

What food you'll take on a day trip is also an important consideration. If you're traveling a route you know well that has shops and restaurants scattered along the way you may choose to take no food at all. Alternatively, if you will be riding an isolated area where meals and snacks will be scarce you may want to pack a lunch and some munchies.

I find that I like to stop for both breakfast and lunch. Eating on the road gives me a few minutes off the bike to stretch my legs, enjoy the scenery, and get to know a few of the locals. I typically pick a restaurant that is both appetizing and frugal or find some special local place that I've never tried before. I pack some fruit and granola bars in case it takes me longer to find a place to eat.

If you pack food you will need to think about how weather conditions, particularly temperatures, may affect what you pack. If it's hot and you're in a cage you can throw everything in a cooler. You can strap a small cooler on some bikes, or can throw in an ice pack in a plastic bag to lay against your sandwiches. If I choose to carry food with me I take things that won't be affected by the weather conditions. I stay away from mayo and other things that spoil quickly, avoid chocolate in hot weather, and avoid small containers of liquid when it's very cold. I also choose foods that are filling and won't take up too much luggage space.

If I'm going to be riding all day I make it a point to take some kind of drinkable liquid with me. It's important to stay hydrated. I usually just throw in a couple of PowerAids. I will sometimes take a hydration backpack. I know folks who take along a plastic bottle of water and several of those small packets of electrolyte powder to throw in. And yes, I'll admit it, I've been known to throw in a Diet Coke or two. They aren't the best choice for hydration, but they do hit the spot on a long, hot day.

When you pack for a day trip it's time to start thinking about things you might need to manage emergencies. Things I try to think about include first aid supplies, repair supplies, and medications I may need.

There are many different first aid kits of many different sizes. Most that you can fit on a bike without taking up way too much space will handle many small emergencies. Some of the larger ones offer things like pads to stop bleeding from substantial wounds and wraps for injured joints. Many include tape and popsicle sticks that can be fashioned into a splint. There are some pretty darn good kits out there that will handle many first aid situations. Most bikers I know don't carry a very large one if they carry one at all. I have two, one small and one large. I tend to carry the smaller one on smaller trips and the larger one on larger trips. I'm not sure how good my logic is for that, but so far it has covered any need I have had.

Repair supplies can also take up lots of space or only a little. For day trips I count on the little tool kit that came with my bike. I also pack a small tire repair kit. I'm sure almost everyone who has spent more than two hours on the road had a different opinion of which and how many tools you need. I tend to take minimal tools (with the exception of tire repair) and my AAA card. So far I haven't encountered much I can't handle with those things on board.

One of the things I find many bikers tend to leave behind is their meds. For many conditions this isn't much an issue for day trips. For others it is much more important. I take a blood pressure medication every morning. On the few occasions I forget I'm fine to catch up later in the day. If I'm on a day trip I can wait until I get home with few ill effects. Other folks need more medication more regularly and need to plan to take it with them. They also may need waterproof containers and some sort of refrigeration.

Day trips can involve easy navigation, or not. My favorites are usually the "nots". Because of my rural surroundings it's pretty easy to spend a day cruising along back country roads that run anywhere from straight and smooth to switchbacks and gravel. The Tail of the Dragon in East Tennessee has an awesome and well-deserved reputation for its twists and turns, but come to my place and I'll top it. You may, however, want to bring a dual sport, some of those one car ridge runners get a little rough.

For navigation I like to use a GPS. I have a Garmin Nuvi that serves me just fine It isn't made for motorcycles so it isn't waterproof, gasoline proof, shock-resistant, with built in satellite radio and prearranged guided tours. It also doesn't retail for almost $800 (the current price tag of Garmin's "made for bikers by bikers" model). Don't get me wrong, I'd love to have one, but I've already pretty much obliterated my five year budget on things i thought I needed more. I have strategies for handling the deficiencies of the Nuvi. I carry a watertight bag. I don't spill gasoline on it. I don't drop it. I listen to the sounds of the bike and wind, and I arrange my own spontaneous tours.

What are spontaneous tours? I'm glad you asked! I load up for a day trip, snap my Garmin in place, and head for a place known to me. When I get there I switch on my Garmin, set it for a place unknown, and head out. If there are no places unknown nearby I set it for a place I know and ask it to give me a route through unknown territory.

I love these kinds of day trips. I have two words of warning, however, OK, maybe three, OK, maybe four. First, make sure you take along some form of backup navigation. Yes, I know I said that I cover my Garmin in the rain, don't spill gas on it, don't drop it, etc. But what happens if one day, smack in the middle of nowhere I (gasp!) do? I could probably find my way home, but given some of the little country lanes and dirt roads I travel that could take much longer than I'd like. My backup navigation is really pretty simple. I take my iPhone along, complete with it's GPS app and backup car charger. If I didn't have that I'd take a map, but I've never (yet) been in a spot that my phone GPS didn't handle. I should probably add that, in the places I ride, phone and GPS service can get a little spotty, but it is never spotty for long. Ride a mile or two and the lovely computer-voiced lady is "recalculating", shortly picking up the route as though the signal had never missed a beat. If I lived in an area where service interruptions were a major issue I'd probably take along a map that had lots of detail of the local area.

Second word of warning, make sure you have your cell phone. Most of your trips will be pure fun and pleasure. Occasionally, however, you may encounter a situation that presents a challenge. If you ride a big bike, for example, and are riding alone in a remote location, what happens if you drop it? Can you pick it up by yourself? Is someone likely to pass or be nearby who can help you? Will the character of your helpers be something you want to deal with? (You done took a wrong turn, boy, this river don't go to Raintree!) If you're riding solo in remote areas be sure you have a means of communication along. If it's your cell phone be sure you have it in a secure place, bring a watertight bag, don't drop gasoline on it, don't drop it, etc.

Word of warning number three: if you're going to be in very remote areas make sure someone knows where you're going and about when you expect to get back. I don't see this as much of a problem where I live, but I can see it as a significant issue in the desert, mountains, and other sparsely populated areas. I don't mean that you should anticipate disaster on day trips (sorry about the "Raintree" reference) but some pretty simple things can go wrong that can make it a challenge to get help. The simplest and most frequent examples are running out of gasoline or having a mechanical issue with your bike. If either of these happen, you're alone, and no one is anywhere around it would be nice to be able to get help with a phone call.

My fourth word (and final word of warning is don't be shy about asking for directions and guidance. Yeah, I know the macho thing is to just keep going and figure it out for yourself, but asking a few simple questions about road conditions and routes can make your trip much easier. I've been in spots where a local could have told me which route to take and made my ride much easier. I'd rather suck up my male pride at a fork in the road and ask the guy at the gas station which way to go than suck it up when I'm stuck on a gravel trail full of potholes and call him to bring his truck to haul me out.

OK, enough words of warning, Let's talk for a minute about other systems of navigation. Maps work just fine and I do use them from time to time. There are a couple of issues, however, that make me prefer GPS. The first is, unless you have some means of holding your map in a convenient place for viewing, you'll need to stop, pull it out of a bag somewhere, consult it, fold it back up, and then move on. This can be solved with a tank back that has a clear, watertight top made to hold maps while making them visible. The second issue, however, is that it just isn't safe to spend much time trying to analyze a map while rumbling along at 45 miles per hour. If you use a map and a map holder, be aware that you're going to need to stop and look a lot. It works fine, and the stops may help to assure that you don't need to use that cell phone backup we talked about a couple of paragraphs ago.

Loading for the long haul

So what's a long haul? I guess I'm defining it as anything beyond an overnight trip. The very fact that you won't be home that night creates some extra needs. There are, after all, only so many hours that a single pair of skivvies is tolerable. You will also face greater potential for weather changes, breakdowns, thirst and hunger, and the need for something to occupy your mind. You will need these things, and will need to plan for them when you pack, but the chances are good that you will need fewer of them than you might think. The trick to packing with limited space is making sure you have just enough, without a whole lot more. At the same time it's nice to have enough, so careful planning for a long trip is a definite plus.

Yes, you will need clothing for your long trip. The highway patrol in every state frowns on nude motorcycling and bugs that smack you at 70 mph in certain unsheltered places really, really hurt (or so I am told). You need clothing, but you just won't have space to include lots of wardrobe options. When it comes to clothing I try to make it simple. A couple of pairs of jeans three pairs of underwear, three pairs of socks, and three shirts usually do it for me. If I'm going to be gone for more than three days I plan to stay in a place with a washer and dryer or stimulate the local economy by using a laundromat. Why two jeans and three of everything else? I like to have enough stuff to give me backup against the unexpected, but be conservative enough that I have room for other stuff. Does this always work? No, but it seems to handle most situations and give enough flexibility for improvisation when necessary. I also pack shorts and a tank top for hanging out in the hotel room if I'll be staying in one.

Toiletries are, of course, also a necessity. You won't need as many as you need at home. I usually pack a toothbrush and toothpaste, floss, and my allergy meds. I put my prescription meds in the same container, typically a high-tech water resistant device such as a freezer bag. I like to rely on the hotels I stay in for soap, shampoo, and conditioner. If I'm staying someplace where they are not offered I pack small containers of each. If I'm camping I take all the above plus at least one large roll of toilet paper. In hotels you won't need towels, washcloths, etc. If you'll be camping you may want to find a way to squeeze these in.

The National Weather Service does a pretty fair job of predicting a couple of days worth of weather. Beyond three days it gets a little more shaky. After about 6 days it seems to me that you might need to rely on the Farmer's Almanac or Aunt Bessie's bunions. Either seems likely to be a little more accurate. You need to pack for temperature extremes or rain, remember that the gear will consume a lot of space, but it's probably gear that you will want. There's some pretty compact stuff out there. We talked about some of it in an earlier chapter.

Some people ride without a thought for tools and tires. If they break down they call AAA. I tend to do that on short jaunts, but on longer trips where I don't know the area I prefer to be as equipped as I can. In addition to the onboard tool kit that came with my bikes, I also have a compact kit that I bought that includes a broader selection of tools for both the bike and the tires. It has most anything you might need to deal with just about any situation that can be fixed by the side of the road. With all the right tools in hand all I have to do is pray for someone to come along who knows how to use them. Seriously, my tool kit has paid off for me as well as for some other stranded travelers. I recommend carrying something similar. For tires I carry a patch kit and a can of Slime. The can of slime has an advantage even if you never use it on a tire. If the conversation lags with your biker buddies just pull it out. That can is sure to spark the 1 millionth rendition of the age-old "will Slime ruin your tire" debate. If you don't like Slime, there are also lots of small compressors out there. I recommend that you carry one or the other.

We've also talked about carrying hydration options

and food. Most of what we discussed earlier is true for long trips, except that it may be even more important. When you're traveling in unknown territory having ways to quench your thirst and raise your blood sugar on board is more important than it is a little closer to home. Yes, your GPS will help you find shops and sources, but GPS devices sometimes fail (gasp) and convenience stores in the middle of nowhere sometimes disappoint. It's better to have some of what you want and need along for those kinds of occasions.

When I'm gone for a few days I also like to make sure my hydration options are rich in electrolytes. If I'm using my hydration backpack there are several mixes available. You just pour in the mix and add water. Gatoraid and PowerAid also do very well. A couple of long, hot days on the bike often leave me with leg cramps in the night. A few pints of electrolyte replacement and I have cramps no more.

I also like to take things along to occupy my mind when I'm traveling. Many bikers like to get up early and park it in the late afternoon somewhere on the slow side of a city's rush hour traffic. If you choose to travel that way you may find yourself kicked back in a hotel room around 3:30 or 4:00 wondering just what in the heck you are going to do for the rest of the day. I like to take a pair of walking shoes so I can get in my daily exercise and some combination of iPad, Kindle, iPod, and iPhone to make sure I can write, read, watch movies, surf the net, and listen to music. If the (cheap) hotel I have selected has limited cable options I have lots of ways to entertain myself and (gasp!) even be productive if I so choose.

Looking back over my choices of entertainment, one might notice that all are electronic. This brings to mind that I want to be very aware of my charging options on long trips. I have three. The first is at least one cigarette lighter style power outlet on every bike. The second is one of those little portable units that you charge up later connect to your device to pass along the charge. The third is a little bag that includes both an Apple charger (with both AC and DC options) and a universal charger. As long as I remember that almost every time I hit a room it is time to plug something in the power supply and my rolling entertainment system works just fine.

If you plan to camp rather than stay in hotel rooms you'll need quite a bit more stuff. Tents, sleeping bags, air mattresses (or pads), cooking supplies, and other campsite necessities take up a good deal of space. Camping on a long bike trip is beyond the scope of this book, but let's touch on a couple of issues.

First, make a list of everything you need. Your requirements will depend to a large extent on what kind of camping you'll be doing and how eager you are to rough it. You may also want to consider your priorities in case lack of space influences your selections. My own priorities of being warm, dry, and well fed prompt me to pack my credit card on preparation for Microtel or Best Western. You may be happy with a pup tent and an MRE. You'll need to decide and pack accordingly. I would recommend the list, however. Once you set up camp for the night you may not want to load a bunch of things back on the bike to make a run to town for whatever you forgot.

Second, figure out how you're gonna pack. There's more space on and around a bike than you think. For example, you can strap on things like a tent and sleeping bags over the top of the rear wheel or on other luggage. When you strap, however, keep in mind things like the heat of the exhaust and the way in which your strapping may influence mounting and dismounting. The exhaust gets very hot and can melt plastics and actually catch some materials on fire. When you add things on be sure they don't wind up close to the exhaust. Also, what you use to strap is very important. Bungee cords were one of God's greatest creations. God did not, however, have motorcycles in mind when he made them. Bikes vibrate and sway. Bungie cords stretch. The combination makes loads shift and sometimes come apart. Bungie cords are a great, inexpensive alternative for many situations, not so much for packing a bike. If you're going to add stuff on, invest in a good set of straps. Your return on investment will be in the form of a secure load, without stops to tighten it or pick up your tent that is decorating the middle of the Interstate.

Third issue for strapping stuff on: decide how you're going to keep it dry and make sure you make a good decision. Have you ever slept in a wet sleeping bag? Trust me, I have and it isn't something I'd want to do again. Invest in good, watertight bags and make sure you secure them correctly.

Fourth, consider how you're going to manage your power issues. By this I mean the ways you'll choose to manage your electronic devices, including your cell phone. If you're camping you may or may not have an outlet to use for charging. If you have an outlet it may or may not be in a spot that is sheltered from the rain. You can certainly manage electronic devices while camping. It just takes some extra thinking and effort.

I'm all about checklists when preparing for long trips. I like to start the list a couple of weeks in advance to allow me to add things I may have forgotten. I keep the list on my cell phone so that I'll have it close at hand if I

194

think of something. I also have a template that I use that I have put together on previous trips. When I start to plan for a new trip I save it under a new name then modify it as necessary until it's time to pack.

You'll work your own preferences out over time, but lots of bikers I've talked to like to plan their trips around rush hours in major cities. They stop for the night just shy of a major community, get up early and ride through it before the traffic hits, stop for breakfast when they're in the clear, hit their planned stops along the way, and stop for the night just short of the next major AM and PM traffic crunch. The next day it's wash, rinse, and repeat. A few things to remember. One, unless you have a death wish you'll stop to eat your meals. Eating a burger and fries while trying to tend to the brake and clutch is really not a smart thing to do. Stopping for meals will also give your butt a little break and let you check out the community a little. I like to give my mid-day meal a little early or a little late so that I can spend more time exploring the area or heading toward my next stop than waiting to be served. I also like to plan my meals around things I'd like to see along the way. I like to eat in a local or famous or different kind of place, visit something I haven't seen before, then hit the road again.

When you're on trips, be sure to watch your gas gauge or attend to the setting and resetting of your odometer. When you're close to home you'll probably know where the gas stops are. When you're some distance away you may not have that luxury. The old man strongly advises against running til you hit the reserve tank, or even til you get close. My Can-Am has a gas gauge. I fill up when I get two notches from the bottom. My KLR and Virago are gas-gaugeless. When I fill up I reset the trip odometer to 0 and ride until about 175. I fill up, reset the odometer, and take off again. Yes,

I could probably get away with a few more miles, but running out of gas in an unknown spot is not my first choice of the way to spend my vacation. I recommend frequent, planned visits to gas stations.

One other observation about long trips. You'll probably find that you cover fewer miles in a day on two wheels than you would on four. You'll need to make more gas stops, probably more stretch-your-leg stops, and, if you're traveling for pleasure, more stops to look around than you would in a cage. It really isn't a big deal, and some people manage to travel just as far. My advice, however, is to plan for fewer miles a day. I think you will enjoy your trip more as a result.

Gaining confidence and control

In large part the process of moving from learner to rider is a process of gaining skill and confidence. Looking back, I can point to a few occasions on which my confidence grew. Without exception, it came at a point when I realized my skill had increased, or that I had gained greater knowledge and trust in what the bike could do. I think you'll find this to be true for you as well. Here are some examples of "aha" moments I experienced when I realized I had taken one more step form learner to rider.

I think I've mentioned that the Motorcycle Safety Class was one of the most difficult things I've ever done. It was miserably hot and my riding was miserably bad. I was embarrassed at how poorly I was doing, something the instructors didn't manage particularly well. It was a long, tough weekend. I did notice, however, that the next time I got on a bike my skills had improved significantly and my confidence was much higher. I'm convinced that all those hours in the saddle and the input of the instructors helped me gain a lot of knowledge and skill in

196

a very short period of time. You may or may not enjoy the course. I hated it. My son just got his certificate and enjoyed it thoroughly. If you're like I was you will wish a hundred times between the moment it starts and the moment it finishes that you were somewhere else. When you leave the range with your certificate in hand you may feel as though you haven't gotten much more than a piece of paper. If your experience is like mine, however, the next time you step onto your bike you will find that you have taken a major step from learner toward rider.

I've already told the fascinating story of my experiences at the ATV park with my son. That was a very difficult day, yet when it was over, a wrong turn put two noob riders half way down a mountain on a path that suited experienced ATV riders just fine, but left us noobs longing for the comforts of home. We had a very rough day. We did lots of power walking, had a lot of practice starting and stopping on hills, and rode through sand and gravel and water. We dodged 8 foot deep holes and edged our way along narrow ledges. We were in thoroughly and completely over our heads. It was a very rough day, but when we were done we were both much better riders.

What I learned that day was that my skills were better than I thought they were. Interestingly, it was limping my way along those hills and ridges without another rider in sight that gave me the confidence to move into high traffic situations. I think one of the keys to knowing your true skill level is making sure your rides include some challenges. Looking back, I constantly did things that pushed the envelope a little. Some of the pushed were accidental. Others were more than "a little". Overall, however, it was trying things I hadn't tried yet at a reasonable time in my progression that really helped me improve.

Another big learner-to-rider moment for me happened when I started riding to work. For some reason it was important to me that I was actually riding to a defined place with a defined purpose. The first night I parked the bike in the garage after a day at work something was different for me. I think it was the most defining moment for me. I think that day I thought, "I am now a rider".

Riding to work kind of automatically produced another step for me. I remember the first morning I got up to a light rain. I had rain gear. I had a watertight container for the things I wanted to transport. I had everything I needed, and I had doubt in my heart.

I'm sure all those people who warned me about how dangerous it is to ride on a wet road meant well. Technically, they were correct. You need to be a lot more careful about corners and stops and what other people are going to do than you need to be on a dry street. Still, the warnings get pretty extreme. As I looked out my window at the falling rain I had visions of Zombie tentacles (Do zombies even have tentacles?) stretching up from storm drains to drag me and my rain soaked bike off to a crash in zombie hell. Fact is, roads are slick when they get wet, particularly during the first several minutes of rain when the oil deposited on the road during drier times is rising to the surface. Fact also is, if you allow yourself a little extra time to stop, watch your driving distances, and be aware that other people may not be able to stop as well as they think, you will be just fine.

The first few trips in cooler weather were also an adventure. 55 degrees in a short-sleeved shirt is pretty comfortable for me. 55 degrees in a short-sleeved shirt at 55 miles per hour is a different matter entirely. The second 55 degree experience is just plain cold! It took me several rides with varying degrees of discomfort to figure out what I needed to wear, when. Lots of people told me I'd never enjoy riding in cold weather. Some said I should never get on a bike when the temperature dropped below 60. They were all wrong. It was a real eye-opener to me the day I pulled into a friend's driveway in my Under Armor and leathers and he, a long-time rider, said, "Wow, man, you are really a hard core rider." Nope, I just had enough semi-comfortable miles under my butt, errr, belt, to let me know what I needed to ride. Still when a guy who had been riding since he was a kid told me I was hard-core, it did something for me. I realized I had taken yet another step from learner to rider.

Yes, I understand that gravel isn't weather. I'm going to talk about it here, however, because well-intentioned people talk about it like they talk about rain. You need to listen to what they say, but if you listen too closely you will begin to believe that the zombie-tentacled rain monster has a fearful cousin, Frankenstone, who is waiting right in the middle of a small pile of rocks just waiting to clamp his irresistible grip on the tread of your back tire. Yes, gravel requires caution. Yes, it will make your rear wheel spin or slip to the side. It can enhance a good lean to the point of pellet production. It can make a stop last a lot longer than you had intended. Still, gravel is quite manageable when the proper management steps are taken. Slow down before you get to it, not on top of it. When you brake, do so gently and forget that God ever gave you a front brake. Accelerate more slowly when you depart from a pile of gravel. If your rear wheel slips a little from an unexpected encounter with Frankenstone, don't panic. It will probably correct itself. If not, just steer through it. A friend of mine warned my son, "Watch out for gravel. Just one little gravel (sic) out there on the road can put you in a ditch." This is possibly true, but highly unlikely. Exercise caution around gravel, just as you should on wet roads. If you do you will find the Frankenstone monster isn't nearly so fearsome as some may have warned you.

Another step for me on the trail from learner to rider was my first long ride. It wasn't really a day trip, but did last about 4 hours counting stops for food and gas. It was both a psychological and motorological step. It was psychological in that I felt like I had done what the big boys do. I had taken a long ride purely for pleasure and enjoyed (almost) every minute of it. It was motorological (having to do with the knowledge and skill base of motoring) because I made real-life use of the reserve tank, survived a school zone full of parents who were obviously in a hurry and must have been on crack, and successfully navigated a very windy country road that seemed to have developed new and better curves just to make me feel welcome. I strongly recommend these kinds of rides. I find that they are good for the soul, good for skill development, and good for your self-esteem as a biker.

Perhaps the second biggest event in my progression from learner to rider was my first Interstate trip. I mentioned it in an earlier chapter. My son and I took a ride through Nashville (complete with the mandatory stop at the Loveless Cafe), down the Natchez Trace to Natchez. We then cut across Louisiana and east Texas to visit my brother and his family in the College Station area, finally heading back home through Arkansas and west Tennessee. Counting side trips we rode a little less than 2500 miles. I really didn't see it as a big deal at the time. When we got back and I told some biker friends about it, it was clear that their level of regard for me as a rider had increased. As it turns out, several of them had made those kinds of trips. Even more, however, had not been outside the state lines on their bikes. I had taken another step not only in my mind, but in the minds of my comrades.

Let me make it perfectly clear that I am not claiming a high level of skill here. My neighbor demonstrates a high level of skill when he rides his motocross track in preparation for weekend races. MC clubs show a lot of skill when they ride in formation at 90 miles per hour at distances as little as 18 inches between them. They move almost as one, like a school of fish or a flock of geese. That's skill. I'm not a highly skilled rider. I am a capable rider who does some things pretty well and needs some work on others. I am, however, a rider. I have progressed through several experiences that have brought me to the point that I now am willing to say that I still learn, but I am now a rider. Put in enough saddle time and, if you have any doubt after day one, you will feel that way, too.

Kickstands down

In this chapter we've talked about progressing from learner to rider. The process is different for everyone, and the speed of the progression varies as well. Give yourself "seat time" in different settings and under different circumstances. Ride as much as you can and for whatever reasons you can. The way you feel about riding will change. Soon you'll swing your leg over your bike with every intention of riding while knowing that you may learn a few things along the way. You will look back on the days you mounted up to learn, hoping that one day you would be comfortable calling yourself a rider.

In the next chapter we'll talk about riding alone, behind, and with. Even if you like to ride alone it's sometimes good to have company. Chapter 8 will provide some insight on how to meet people to ride with and what to do with them when you travel.

Chapter 8

Riding Alone, Behind, and With: Companions for the Road

Somewhere along that path from learner to rider you may find yourself wishing that you had companionship, someone along to talk to about the things you see on the road or the things you think about while your mind is free associating to the mantra of the engine's roar. When this happens the question becomes "With whom will I ride?" This chapter will suggest some options for you.

Companions on your rides may join you in one of two ways. They can either sit on the rider seat behind you (We'll call this riding behind) or they can join you on a separate motorcycle (We'll refer to this as "riding with".) My most frequent "rider behind" is my son. As I am writing this he is 14 and just successfully completed the Motorcycle Safety Course. He'll turn 15 in March and will be on his own bike, so I guess I'll need to look for a "ride-behind" or just stick with the solo thing.

Riding alone

Actually, I like to ride alone. I don't mean that I mind company, and company can certainly be nice at the end of a day's ride, but there's just something about solitude on a bike, particularly in remote areas, that just plain soothes the soul. Mt penchant for solitary rides and lonesome country roads is one of the reasons I suffer from what my friends refer to as MBD (Multiple Bike Disorder). For that kind of riding I much prefer the Virago or the KLR. For long highway rides there's just nothing like the Can-Am.

Riding alone does have some inherent

disadvantages. If you break down, have a flat tire, drop your bike, or experience some other emergency you are on your own. Careful planning, however, can compensate for most of these. I make sure I have my cell phone, a tool kit, tire patch stuff, and a stash of food and drink. If I'm headed for sparsely populated places I also make sure someone knows where I'm going and when I'll be in touch.

Riding alone also has its advantages. When I'm riding alone I stop where I want, see what I want, eat what I want, get up when I want, and sleep when I want. There's something about solitary runs that is good for the psyche and the soul. Thinking back to the beginning chapter "Why We Ride", riding alone is by far the most therapeutic for me. There's a peace in the solitude and an assurance that my communion with the natural world and my Higher Power won't be interrupted by those whose minds are in other places.

I'm not going to say much more about riding alone because that is specifically what this chapter is not about.

Riding behind

Before you start to think I'm totally antisocial, let me clarify that I also like riding behind.
It also has its advantages and disadvantages and, if you're headed for a romantic weekend for two, you really need to have someone else on the bike with you. Otherwise, you are headed for a romantic weekend for one.

When I say riding behind I am referring to traveling with someone riding behind you in the passenger seat. Thus, it's the person back there, not you, who is riding behind.

Riding behind is really very comfortable. I've done a little of it and, though I prefer to be turning the throttle, the passenger seat is a great place to enjoy the fresh air and the freedom.

Riding in the passenger seat has an undeserved reputation. Some guys just won't do it. Old school bikers call it "riding bitch" because that's where a man would put his bitch when they rode. I'm not much of one to use the term. It is, of course, sexist and offensive to many women. It also is a pretty poor measure of a male's masculinity. While some old school bikers speak demeaningly of "riding bitch" others, equally old school, insist that men of sufficient endowment don't mind the passenger seat at all. I, of course, am comfortable in either seat.

Your early rides will probably be taken alone. You'll want to build up your skills before you take responsibility for someone else's well-being. Sooner or later, however, you may want company on some of your rides. You will then face a major decision. Who will be your first passenger? Despite the fact that this decision is absolutely none of my business, I think the OMSYOAR (Old Man's Save Your Own Ass Rule) is worth a mention. If you are married, have a significant other, or are even in the early stages of trying to muster the courage to ask someone out, you would do well to make that person your first invitation. If you are hell-bent on bringing emotional disaster to your relationship, or potential relationship, pick out a beautiful (or handsome) alternative and ask that person first. Otherwise, ask the love of your life first and do so in the most endearing manner possible. Something like, "There's no one else in the world I'd rather have be my first passenger than the love of my life.", is adequate, but way short of flowery.

The only possible exception to the OMSYOAR might be your children. Kids can usually safely trump a significant other. Still, for my money, I'd let the SO know first. "Honey, I can't think of anything I'd rather do than have you ride with me. The kids are so eager, though. Would you mind if I took them first?"

Of course, if you are married or with a significant other the first question may need to be, "With whom will I not ride." You'll enjoy your bike a lot more if it isn't a source of marital discord or an issue to be resolved in a property settlement. Pulling into your driveway with a beautiful (or handsome) face that your spouse or SO does not like is probably not the best way to gain support for your future riding endeavors.

By the way, you may think it odd that an old, single guy who has been single for the greater part of his life is offering advice on the management of your SO and your bike. You might even tend to question his judgment and right to comment on such issues. Feel free to ignore me if you wish, but I wash my hands of whatever happens next.

Whoever takes that first (or any) ride behind you, be sure that both you and your bike are ready. I would recommend that you be well along the path before you take a passenger. This isn't because having someone on board is difficult. In fact it's quite easy if nothing goes wrong. From the riding perspective all you need to do is to ask your rider to lean when you lean. If they do that there's no issue. If they don't you just lean a little harder. You also need to allow a little extra time for stopping and for reacting in certain situations, but if you're used to riding on wet streets you won't find that to be a problem.

The biggest safety issue when you are carrying a rider is what might happen in unexpected situations. If things go wrong a rider adds another variable to the experience. It's more than just extra weight. It's the fact that you don't know what that other person may do. I don't mean that a passenger is likely to cover your eyes or try to grab the handlebars, but any reaction to a crisis situation adds one more variable to an already challenging situation. When you're new there are plenty of variables to manage when time is short. Wait until some of those are second nature before you add more.

When riding behind you need to either have Bluetooth or some system of communication worked out. If you try to talk at 70 miles per hour the conversation will probably go something like this. Passenger, "Do you <unintelligible phrase> if <unintelligible phrase> maybe we <unintelligible phrase>." Rider, "HUNH?" Passenger, "<unintelligible phrase> I think <unintelligible phrase>. Rider, "HUNH?". The conversation will likely end with both parties thoroughly dissatisfied. The strange thing is that it will take about 10 to 12 minutes until the impossibility of communication has been forgotten. I have actually timed it. All too soon either passenger or rider will try again. The results will be no prettier than they were the first time.

If you want to talk while riding behind, spring for a couple of Bluetooth units. Otherwise, wait until a stop to talk about purple mountain's majesty. Work out ways for each to tell the other "I'd like to eat soon." or "My bladder has expanded to three times its normal size." Three pats on the shoulder works just fine to say, "I'd like to stop at the next exit, please."

Packing to ride behind presents another set of issues. This isn't, of course, a big deal for a day ride, but a single night on the road complicates things substantially. Make it a trip of several days and storage space can really get tight. Unless you're riding a big dresser and pulling a trailer there's only so much space available. On some bikes there's very little. Packing for one demands a fair amount of planning, packing for two even more. You'll need to figure out what things you can do without and share, as well as the best way to fit in what you are taking.

Also remember that some things can be lashed to racks or the outside of bags. If you're taking rain gear, for example, it can often be bagged and strapped to something outside your luggage. Small backpacks are also an option, as is adding tank bags or handlebar bags.

When you're riding behind, it will probably also help keep the peace if you plan together for some stops, places to stay, meals, and sightseeing. Think of conversations you have had during long distance travel with other people while in a cage. You may have experienced something like this. "So where do you want to go for lunch?" "I don't know, where do you want to go?" "I don't care, you pick." "It really doesn't matter to me. Why don't you choose?" "OK, let's go to Wendy's." "Naw, I'm not really in the mood for Wendy's today." Now imagine that conversation at 70 miles per hour with no Bluetooth. I think you see my point.

Information about places to eat, stay, and visit are readily available from several sources. MapQuest, Google, Earth, and your own GPS are excellent sources. Online biker forums are often great places to ask. I'm an AAA member and often use them as a source of recommendations for both routes and stops. Gather the information you need then sit down and put together a plan. You can always change the plan but having some agreement about where you are going next is likely to make your trip more pleasurable and conflict-free.

Riding with

I really like riding with. When I say riding with I mean riding with other people who are also riding on their own bikes. I like the freedom of being alone on the bike. That probably sounds a little strange, but having someone back there means that I have to be mindful of them, at least a little bit aware of what they're doing. On long rides I've had people fall asleep on the seat behind me or had them scare the pellets out of me because I had forgotten that they were there and they wanted me to know that nature was sounding an urgent call.

When you're riding with, you get all the benefits of solitary riding as well as all the benefits of having company. If you want to talk you can get Bluetooth. If you want silence you can turn off the sound. For breaks and when you stop for the night you have friends and companionship. If you break down, help is only two wheels away. To me, riding with is a great way to go.

If you're going to travel with another bike or two and don't have Bluetooth it's best to agree on some basic communication signals, or at least on scheduled stopping points. Bladders tend to operate on different schedules. Different bikes tend to use gasoline at different rates. Someone may notice a spot they want to stop to check out. Probably the most common means of non-verbal communication is for the front driver to simply pull off the road to the needed restroom, gas station, or vista. Riders to the rear can signal others by simply passing and leading the pack to the desired destination. This works better on straight roads and Interstates than it does on windy country highways. Some folks prefer a more elaborate set of signals, usually made by hand. Three waves with the extended left arm, for example, may mean "my bladder is screaming" or an arm extended above the head may mean "I need gas soon". A return signal is also needed, something to say, "I saw your signal and will stop ASAP."

You may also want to have a "where to meet if we get separated" plan in place. This is more important when there are several bikes traveling together than when there are only a couple. If you're going to be out overnight and are headed to a common destination you can simply meet up there if you get separated. If you want to stay together, however, it's good to have contingencies in place. An agreement like, "If we get separated meet at the McDonalds at exit 253." allows everyone a chance to catch up.

Traveling with also allows you to have a little more space in your baggage by spreading your emergency supplies around. Tools, first aid kits, and tire repair supplies can be distributed across bikes, allowing each rider a skosh more room. Of course, this system works best if you plan on staying close together. A first aid kit 60 miles further down to road really isn't very useful.

When traveling in a group a plan is even more important than when riding behind. A plan could be as simple as "Susan is in charge of planning." to a series of stops selected through discussion and vote. Some sort of organizing force is needed to be sure everyone is on the same page and no one gets left out.

If you do get separated or someone gets lost there is an easy solution. Cell phone check-ins will solve the problem. If you become separated from the crowd and have no idea how to find them just pull off the road in a safe place. Try to reach your friends by cell from there. If you can't reach them, you can always kill time by calling someone else and complaining about them.

Whether you ride alone, behind, or with you need to take things along to provide entertainment during any down time. We talked about this in another chapter, but I think it is important to provide a reminder that it's good to have both solitary and group recreational options. These options can be as simple as an eBook and a deck of cards.

Some people I know like to travel in packs. If you meet them on the road you meet a group of 5-6 bikes, each with one or two riders. They nearly always travel together and have a very organized approach to planning. One person or couple plans the route and the places to stay. Another plans meals. Yet another individual or couple selects recreational activities along the way. Someone else handles the games and portable recreation. There is, of course, some occasional good-natured grumbling about a poor meal choice or a recreational stop that sucks, but the system seems to work very well and, after years of traveling together, these folks seem to have no inclination to change.

Meeting people to ride with

So you want to travel with but you don't know any other people who ride? There are plenty of ways to meet travel companions. You can join clubs, go on benefit and special occasion rides, participate in sponsored rides by dealers, join online forums, and meet other folks on the road.

There are lots of clubs and motorcycle organizations out there that promote riding and allow opportunities to meet other riders. Some of those organizations are built around ownership of a particular brand of bike. Probably the best known examples is the Harley Owners Group (HOG). HOG has a very active national organization as well as numerous local chapters. The local chapters are built around dealerships. Most HOG members actually own Harleys. I don't currently own a Harley, but I am a member of national HOG because I enjoy the benefits it provides. I've been told I would be welcome in the local group, but just haven't felt comfortable representing myself as the owner of one brand of bike when I own three others. There are organizations for riders of other brands, but the ones I'm familiar with are not so closely linked with the manufacturers and tend not to be as stable. I, for example, have attempted to contact members of both a Can-Am riders group for Tennessee and the national organization for folks with Viragos. No one has responded to my call and emails. Ooops, here's an update, I just got an email back from the Virago folks. It's been months since I applied to join the site. Apparently I missed or never got the welcome email they sent. I have had great success with the KLR 650 folks through online communications. I'll say more about that in a couple of paragraphs.

There are lots of other types of clubs out there. My absolute favorite is the Patriot Guard Riders (PGR), a US organization. The PGR is a group of folks who ride escort and provide other supportive activities for fallen soldiers and former soldiers and their families. My schedule usually precludes my ability to join the rides but since i have been a member I have known the PGR to provide escorts for funeral processions for military funerals, serve as a human wall barring protesters who attempted to disrupt the funerals of fallen heroes, provide hospitality for family members of soldiers, and participate in national rallies to honor our troops. Joining and riding is a great way to honor those who have served on our behalf and also provides a way to meet other riders. Even if you can't ride often, your participation and financial support (even if it's only through the very moderate membership dues) are welcome. If you don't know how to find riders in your area, a Google search will quickly lead you to their website. Join the organization and you will quickly hear from them. They are great folks, and perform a wonderful service for passed veterans and their families.

Special occasion rides are offered by many organizations in many communities. These rides are typically built around holidays and occasions that warrant fund-raising.

Boswell's, our local Harley dealer, recently sponsored their second annual Toy Parade to raise money for Christmas gifts for disadvantaged children. The Baxter Medical Clinic, one of the few free rural medical clinics in the country, is currently planning a ride to support its activities. One of the local bars, Boondocks, frequently puts together events to raise money for community members who have extraordinary medical needs of families who lack the ability to pay funeral expenses. I usually find out about these rides by stopping at motorcycle dealers and sponsoring organizations and looking for flyers. I also try to get on email distribution lists (easier than I'd like it to be) where these kinds of events are advertised.

I've met some great folks at rallies. Rallies are massive get-togethers where bikers of all types and sizes plan to meet in a certain city or town and engage in a variety of planned and unplanned activities for anywhere between a day and a couple of weeks. Two of the more famous national rallies are the Sturgis Motorcycle Rally in Sturgis, South Dakota and Bike Week at Daytona Beach,

Florida. As I'm writing this, the Black Hills Motor Classic (Sturgis) is advertising its 72nd annual rally to be held in 2013. Daytona Bike Week is advertising its 75th. Both draw amazing numbers of riders from all over the world. Daytona, for example, hosts approximately 500,000 people during its 10 day event. Both have races, organized rides, concerts, parties, street festivals, and massive vendor displays. Famous bikers are on hand, as are the average riders of the world, perhaps folks like you and me.

There are several national and regional rallies each year. Most can be readily identified with a web search using some clever descriptor words like "motorcycle rally". I just did a Google search adding Tennessee to those descriptors and found 6 pages listing 22 rallies scheduled in the state of Tennessee between now and next August.

My first rally was the Tellico Biker Rally in Tellico Plains, TN. My son and I rode over for the weekend and got a room in a nearby community. Even though we didn't participate in any of the rally events (many are limited to folks over the age of 21) we had a great time riding the Tail of the Dragon, the Cherohala Skyway, and other Smokey Mountain roads. We met lots of nice folks, ate excellent local food, and stayed far enough from the actual rally camp site that we could sleep in comfortable beds without the sounds of the evening frivolities.

Meeting people at rallies is really easy. Want to strike up a conversation with a biker? Try a clever line like, "Nice bike!" or "So how long you been riding?" Most are eager to talk riding and will throw a few questions your way in return. I've also found that many are impressed by the fact that some of us later-life folks have decided to mount up. You can also ask about local rides, restaurants, and accommodations. Chats about biking lead pretty easily into conversations about jobs, families, and homes. I've found it pretty easy to make friends in the biker world.

I've also found it pretty easy to meet other riders on the road. Most riders are eager for a quick chat and may be willing to join you for a meal or an end-of the-day drink. I have been handed business cards while gassing up and asked to stay in touch by riders in several states. I've responded to many of these and have developed a network of friends with whom I occasionally correspond by email and with whom I may ride when I travel. Some of them have stopped off for meals or a local ride as they pass though my area. We also serve as sources of information for one another about good routes, places to stay, and places to eat in our own parts of the country. Yes, I know the dangers of strangers on the road, but so far I've swapped business cards only with very nice folks who have been completely non-invasive and have been content to chat a bit, share a drink or a meal, and stay in touch only under very appropriate circumstances.

I have found online forums to be an excellent way to meet other riders. I'm a member of forums for both the KLR and the Can-Am. In each someone posts regional information about rallies and rides. After a few posts you get to know others and develop some pretty good online friendships. I attended my first rally as a result of an invitation from a regular in the KLR forum. I've also found local bikers who are looking for riding companions. Again, I do recognize that meeting folks online is a bit of a risk, but it seems to be less so when you are meeting fellow-bikers in an environment where lots of folks know one another such as the online forums.

What if you meet people from an Outlaw Club?

"What do you do if you run into the Hell Angels or some other motorcycle gang?". I hear that question a lot. The answer is, I give them a biker salute if I'm riding, nod and say hey if I'm not. I am respectful of them and their rides. I don't go out of my way to have a deep heart-to-heart, but I don't avoid an interesting conversation if the opportunity arises.

Truth is, there are some fine people in MCs who want to be left alone to ride and live free. There are some MCs that engage in criminal activities and some that are composed of law enforcement personnel and law-abiding veterans. There are MCs for firefighters, first responders, and other groups.

MCs that engage in criminal activities range from smaller, local organizations to statewide and national groups. The larger, more famous clubs are sometimes called "outlaw" clubs or "one-percenters" because they welcome felons and people who an old American Motorcycle Association article allegedly identified as the "one-percent" of motorcyclists. You may recognize names like Hell's Angels, Mongols, Pagans, Outlaws, Sons of Silence, Warlocks, Highwaymen, Banditos, Free Souls, and Vagos. I rarely encounter these folks on the road. When I do, I act exactly as I said earlier. I greet them and move on. I don't go out of my way to strike up a conversation, but I don't snub them, either. I have yet to have a negative encounter with any of them. I'm sure none of them find an old guy on his Can-Am much of a threat.

How will you know when you meet a MC club or one of its members? Usually, they are pretty easy to recognize because of their "cuts". A cut is a vest or jacket, usually leather but sometimes denim, that contains the patches that identify the club, the local chapter to which the wearer belongs, and a large graphic patch that is the club's symbol. The patch containing the club name, usually curved, goes at the top of the back, approximately across the shoulder blades. The location patch goes near the bottom. The graphic patch goes in the center. The cut may also include other, smaller patches that indicate things like whether the wearer is an officer in the club, whether or not the wearer is an outlaw or a member of an outlaw club, or some other piece of information about the wearer. Nomads are members of a specific club that don't affiliate with a specific chapter. Their bottom rocker usually says "Nomad" rather than including the name of a chapter location.

There are non-outlaw clubs who wear cuts and colors. Groups like the Vietnam Veterans Motorcycle Club, the Blue Knights (police officers), the Expendables (first responders), and the Red Knights (firefighters) are among them. If you see a rider in colors it is probably best to assume that they are from an outlaw club until you know otherwise. One easy-to-recognize clue is an American Motorcycle Club patch worn on the front of the cut. Some riders use these patches as a way of communicating to outlaws that that they are not one-percenters and are, therefore, not a threat.

If I see a rider or group of riders wearing colors and don't know the name of the group, I usually give them lots of space until I find out for sure. I never ask one of the riders. That might be interpreted as disrespectful and could lead to a confrontation. My most frequent solution was to do an Internet search for the club name. Most clubs of any size, even local clubs, can be found in this way.

Some Never, Evers of Interacting with MC Clubs

Never, ever, touch a biker's cut or colors.

Never, ever, touch a biker's ride.

Never, ever, hit on a biker's old lady.

Never, ever, say anything demeaning or insulting.

Never, ever threaten or bluster.

Never, ever stick around for long if someone else does any of these things.

A Lone Wolf is someone who identifies with many aspects of the biker lifestyle, but does not affiliate with any club. For some folks it is a statement of their preference for solitude. The Lone Wolf patch isn't offensive to most MCs, but to include a lower rocker with a location name would be. The rocker would be like claiming that you, as a lone wolf, own and defend that territory.

MC Cut Terminology

Cut- The vest or jacket worn by a MC member that contains the patches identifying club and location.

Colors- The patches on the back of the cut, including the upper rocker, the lower rocker, and the large graphic club patch. The word is sometimes used to indicate the entire cut.

Upper rocker- The patch located at the top of the back of the cut and including the name of the biker's club.

Lower rocker- The patch located at the bottom of

the back of the cut and including the location of the biker's club or chapter.

Club patch- A larger, graphic symbol selected to represent the club.

Officer patch- Worn on the front of the cut and indicates the office (if any) held within the club.

One percent patch- A diamond-shaped patch including the 1% symbol. This indicates that the biker is an outlaw and one of the one-percent identified in an early American Motorcycle Association article.

There are lots of books by and about outlaw motorcycle clubs. I love them. Sonny Barger, president of the Hell's Angels, is one of my favorite authors. I like the books written by bikers and the ones written about bikers. I've included a partial list in the appendix of this book.

Kickstands down

In this chapter we've talked about finding other people with whom you can ride. We've talked about the advantages and disadvantages of riding alone, riding behind, and riding with. We've discussed several ways to meet travel companions, including joining clubs, participating in benefit and special occasion rides, going on sponsored rides, joining online forums, and meeting other folks on the road. If you're like most of us you'll mix it up, sometimes riding alone, sometimes riding behind, and sometimes riding with. If you are going to ride behind or with you may find some of the ways of meeting people we've discussed here helpful.

In the next chapter we'll talk about riding on dirt. Many of the things I've said about street riding also apply to dirt, but if you're going to learn to ride in off-road locations there are some other things you'll need to know. We'll discuss some of those things in chapter 9

Chapter 9

Riding on Dirt

As I was putting the finishing touches on the draft of chapter 3, which I wrote after chapters 4-8 (don't ask me why, I don't understand it myself) it occurred to me that my little masterpiece was one chapter short of perfection. I had recommended a dirt bike as a good option for learning to ride, but had said virtually nothing about riding on dirt. Consider this chapter the wrench and screwdriver of my manuscript repair kit. Here's what I know about riding on dirt.

How to prepare your bike for dirt

Dirt bikes come straight from the factory ready to ride on all kinds of surfaces other than asphalt. You can wheel it off the trailer (I'm assuming you aren't going to ride it home from the dealership.) and ride right off the driveway onto the grass, soil, or sand that is your back yard. Since many dealers aren't famous for overfilling gas tanks you may want check your fuel level, but they should have done the pre-ride check for you before they let it out the door. Just start it and go.

Unless you have a pretty big and very diverse back yard, however, you will soon want to go in search of distant vistas and unknown trails. When you do there are a few minor additions for your bike that you may want to consider. The availability of these items will vary according to your bike's year, make, and model. Your dealer may or may not know. If the salesman is an avid rider and has a bike like the one you've purchased she or he may be able to help. If not, try surfing online vendors and joining online forums.

Why would you want to make modifications to your

brand new bike? Fact is, although manufacturers do a pretty darn good job of getting them ready for most off-road conditions, the rougher or more varied the terrain the more likely you are to encounter something the designers hadn't planned for. There are also a few things that can happen even on easy rides. If you want to prepare for such events you might consider some of the following.

Grips may seem like a minor thing, but they are very important for two reasons. First, they help you hang onto the handlebars when the going gets rough. The last thing you need when your rear wheel slides is the handlebars slipping out of your hands. Grips made of the right material and with the right waffle pattern help you keep the hold you need. Comfort is another important factor. Riding produces a lot of vibration. Riding on irregular surfaces adds a lot of bouncing and jarring. It doesn't take much of that to cause your hands and arms to become fatigued. The padding in a good set of grips cuts down the fatigue surprisingly well.

Changing grips is easy if you know how, annoying and time consuming if you don't. Different people remove them in different ways, but I just whack the old ones off with a utility knife. When you get the old ones off you'll find that some spots of the adhesive that kept them in place remain on the handlebars. You can buy an adhesive remover to get it off. I've found that it usually peels off easily with a tool as common as my fingers. Clean the grips with alcohol (rubbing, save the bourbon for other purposes), slap on a new layer of grip glue, and work the new grips onto the handlebars. You don't want to over-apply the glue. A little goes a long way and a lot goes all over the front end of the bike.

Brush guards protect your hands from tree limbs, bushes, and flying objects. They also do a nice job of helping keep your hands warm on chilly days. We talked about brush guards in the chapter on accessories for your bike. I mention them here again because they are nice for the road, but even nicer for the trail. They are not cheap and can be a challenge to install, but the first knuckle whack they absorb from a passing limb makes them worth every penny.

Hand levers can usually be adjusted to fit your grip. You want them to be in a position close enough to the grip to let you reach them with a finger or two, yet far enough from the grips that you can brake or clutch without touching the back of your hand. There will be times when you need your first two fingers for braking or working the clutch and the rest of your hand for twisting the throttle or turning the handlebars.

Buy some extra hand levers the day you buy the bike. Sooner or later the handlebars are going to take some kind of hit and you'll break a lever. Brush guards will help but you'll still manage to break one off sooner or later. Levers are easily replaced and bikes are difficult to ride when they are missing. Take them with you every time you ride.

Foot levers (your gear shift lever and rear brake) should be adjusted to positions that work best for you. It's usually a matter of turning a screw or adjusting a nut. On some bikes you may want to consider replacing one foot lever or the other. If you have big feet or wear extra thick boots, for example, you may want to get an extended shift lever. I have one on my KLR and it works magic for slipping my 10 1/2 Thor off-road boots under the lever. If you can't seem to get the height of the brake lever right, consider either replacing it with an after-market or asking a welder to modify the one you have. A friend of mine has a locally-manufactured accessory for his brake lever.

It's a simple metal box with a hole in the bottom and teeth on the top. The distance from the bottom of the box to the top of the teeth is probably about 1 1/2 inches. It was attached to the stock lever by drilling a hole in the foot pad to match the one on the bottom of the box. A short bolt passed through both, and a lock washer on the bottom keep the modification in place. My friend now has no problem getting to the foot brake any time he needs it.

You may discover that the *foot pegs* on the bike you buy are not exactly what you'd hoped for. Good foot pegs are crucial to successful off-road riding. As time goes by you'll learn to shift in the seat, rise into a crouch, and stand upright to manage certain situations. You need a strong, stable grip for all these maneuvers. Metal grips with teeth on the tops are usually your best option. Many riders also prefer a broader surface than is typical of stock pegs. There are lots of options from several manufacturers depending on the bike you have. A quick Internet search will give you some idea of the options.

Crash bars are not the usual fare for dirt bikes. They're more common on dual sports and adventure bikes. If you do install crash guards they should be close to the body of the bike and as unobtrusive as possible. You want them to protect your engine but not snag on trees in narrow spots.

Brake protectors, sometimes called shark fins, protect brake rotors from rocks and flying debris. They probably aren't necessary for jaunts around the back yard and easy dirt roads, but as the terrain grows rougher they become more important. Rotors are costly to replace and if yours takes a serious hit your ride is probably over. I commend them to your attention.

Shark fins are accessories that protect the rear

disc on off-road and dual purpose bikes. Their name reflects their shape, and their shape reflects their function. They extend out from the axle far enough to shield the disc and are curved to follow it's contours. The result: a piece of aluminum that resembles the fin of a shark.

Chain guards, also called chain guides, protect the chain of a chain drive bike from both damage and derailing. Like shark fins, chain guards are not as important on easy terrain as they are in rougher spots. If you have any doubt at all about the safety of your chain, invest in a chain guard.

Skid plates protect your engine from flying rocks and ground strikes. Given that off-road bikes may have anywhere between 7 and 15 inches of ground clearance at their lowest point it probably seems unlikely that you'll bottom out and damage the engine. This would probably be the case if not for the 5-12 inches of suspension travel your bike will have. All that suspension travel makes for a more comfortable ride, but it also means that the engine of your bike may be as close to the ground as two inches at times. Skid guards protect your engine from things you might hit when your suspension is fully compressed.

Suspension travel refers to the degree to which your suspension will compress in response to the bounces and jolts you experience when you ride. Off-road bikes are built tall both to allow the bike to clear logs and rocks. They are built with a lot of suspension travel to keep your coccyx (base of your spine) from being relocated to your shoulder blades when you hit a big bump at high speeds. When you hit a bump the suspension compresses, preventing the lower portion of your anatomy from coming to a sudden, crashing stop.

There's actually a pretty good chance that your bike came equipped with a skid plate. There's an even better chance that the skid plate is made of plastic. It's probably a rigid, strong plastic, but it's nowhere near as protective as metal. Most serious riders I know install a metal plate before they ever ride their bikes. If you're only going to buy one piece of after-market protection to your bike this is the one I recommend.

Yes, your bike has an *exhaust system*. No you probably won't need to replace it. You do, however, need to be sure it's noise level and spark arrestor comply with any local standards that might exist in the places you plan to ride. State and National Parks, for example, often have very strict standards. If you're going to ride in them you need to be sure your exhaust system is in compliance.

This list of protective options for off-road and dual purpose bikes is nowhere near exhaustive. I listed and described the ones that I thought would be most important for most bikes. If you want to learn more I recommend that you do some reading and talk to some people who ride off-road. You probably don't need to worry about most of these devices when you're learning, but as your skills grow and you try more challenging rides you will need to begin to consider them.

How to ride on dirt

The basics of riding on dirt aren't much different from those of riding on the road. You steer, accelerate, decelerate, and shift gears in the same ways. The manner in which you do those things, however, varies considerably depending on your circumstances.

When you're off the pavement you need to be

even more aware of your *speed* than when you're on it. Response time is usually more limited. It will take you longer to slow and stop on most surfaces, and some will makes turns more difficult. You'll need to be aware of the composition of the trail, the potential for rocks and holes in the ground, and of any ruts or obstacles that may block your path. You'll need to be sure your speed is at a level that will allow you to control the bike if you encounter any of these conditions.

The nature of the surface and the changes that may occur in the surface on which you're riding are very important factors. Riding on packed dirt is very different from riding on sand. If you pass from dirt to sand while negotiating a turn at a high speed the probability of a fishtail is great. Gravel, water, and loose soil also make fishtails more likely.

Fishtail really isn't an exclusively motorcycle word, but it is an important concept to understand. You fishtail when the rear end of your bike (or car or truck) slips off to one side while the front continues to move in the original direction. Fishtails aren't usually difficult to control and are actually pretty common when riding off road. They are easier to manage at slower speeds, however, and when you are aware that surface conditions may cause them to happen.

The average fishtail isn't really a big deal. It's something that's going to happen sooner or later if you ride off-road. Truth be told, it's probably going to happen sooner. The main things to remember when your rear end (no, not your's, the bike's) slides are: 1) don't panic, 2) don't brake, and 3) keep your front wheel pointed in the direction you want to go. If you need to decelerate, roll off the throttle. You should be able to control the slide with minimal effort. Obviously, control is easier at moderate speeds.

Clearance is also an important consideration. If you have a dirt bike the center of the area between the two wheels is pretty high off the ground. Still, if you try to ride over a limb that is too thick or mount a ridge that is very tall and narrow, the bike could high-center. Be aware of holes, ridges, rocks, and limbs when you ride.

A vehicle is said to have high-centered when its center hits or comes to rest on an obstacle or piece of ground. High-centering can lead to loss of control of the bike.

You might encounter an *obstacle* most anywhere you ride. Obstacles include things like rocks, trees, limbs, and critters. When you encounter an obstacle you need to make a decision as to how you will manage it. One option, of course, would be to stop and check it out a little before proceeding. In unfamiliar territory this is often the best option for an inexperienced rider. If possible, you might also steer around it, jump it, or ride right over it. The important thing is to assure that your speed and skills are at levels that make the obstacle manageable.

Gravel roads and trails have a special place all their own in my heart and on my backside. Gravel can get you when you slow down, speed up, turn, or ride in a straight line. The issue is the relatively small contact point between your tires and the gravel. Gravel simply isn't very stable. It will always react to the contact point by moving. The only questions are which direction it will go and how much it will move. If enough gravel moves in some direction other than the intended path of the bike your wheels will go with it. When you brake the gravel moves, perhaps producing a skid or a slide. If you accelerate fast enough your rear wheel may throw a batch of it at whatever is behind you while you fishtail your way from your starting point. Gravel calls for more caution than does a packed or solid surface. It isn't hard to ride on, but it does require more caution, a greater stopping distance, and a higher tolerance for rabbit pellet moments.

The contact point is, very simply, the point at which your tires touch the ground. When you're on two wheels and the two wheels are comparatively small, as they are with motorcycle tires. Less contact point means less stability because when something goes wrong in that area, there isn't much other space to grip.

Sand is similar to gravel in some ways. A thin coating on a hard surface can be downright treacherous, flip-sliding like the tiny bits of gravel it actually is. Deep sand creates a different problem. Deeper sand shifts to make space for your wheel. As the tire sinks deeper it is more difficult to control your direction. The front wheel tends to wobble, sometimes to the extent that it will slip from your grip if you are not wary.

Mixed surfaces can really get your attention. You can sometimes find yourself moving from dirt or gravel to sand in quick succession. You need to be ready for the changes or run the risk of having your bike take a nap while you roll on the ground wandering how you got there.

Bike naps are one of the ways you hear off-road riders talk about their crashes. This is one of the interesting differences in road riders and dirt riders. Road riders do their best to never, ever go down. Although dirt riders try to always stay upright, they are also aware that given the challenges the terrain they face will bring, they will sooner or later lay it down. The emphasis then is in minimizing damage to self and ride when the bike takes a nap. Bike naps aren't nearly as frequent on easy trails composed of solid surfaces. If you're starting on dirt I commend them to your attention.

If your bike does go down there's no reason for panic. It happens to everyone off-road sooner or later. Just make sure you are OK then, as quickly as possible, get to your bike and stand it upright. If it wound up on its side it is likely to be slowly leaking gas, something you'd like it to stop. Once it is upright there won't be a leak. Then check the grips, levers, mirrors (if you have them) and anything else that might have gotten knocked askew. Most of the things that get knocked out of place can be put back with a screwdriver and a twist. If you break a lever, just replace it. See, I know you have one with you because you took the old man's advice to bring along some spares. You may also find that the bike is a little difficult to restart. This is normal and usually the result of flooding the engine. Just let it sit quietly on its kickstand for a couple of minutes and it should start just fine.

Going up and down hills is best done with a little movement in the seat. You want to keep as much weight as you can on the uphill side so going downhill you slide to the back. Going uphill you slide and lean to the front. On slopes it's good to be particularly aware of bumps, holes, and obstacles. Not only can they be harder to see, but hitting one at the wrong moment can do you in.

Crossing streams that are a few inches deep isn't very difficult. Just slow down so you don't get wet and head on through. Some folks lift their feet to keep them out of the water. You do need to be aware of things like underwater obstacles, hidden drop-offs, and rushing currents. Some stream bottoms are also very slick. If you're riding with someone who knows the stream it's probably safe to proceed. If the area is new to you, better to check it out before you hit a submerged rock or ride into an underwater hole.

I have given you only the most basic of information about off-road riding. Honestly, that's about all I know. I've ridden a few trails, dirt roads, and farmer's fields, but I am far from an expert. If you're going to use dirt for learning the basics of riding I've probably told you enough. If you want more I recommend Carl Adams' book *The Essential Guide to Dual Sport Motorcycling*. Although the title says dual sport, most of it is equally applicable to dirt and adventure bikes. There are also classes available at several private facilities around the county. You can find them through an Internet search or by asking around in an off-road forum.

Dressing for off-road riding

We covered the basics of dressing to ride in an earlier chapter. With such a vast storehouse of knowledge in your hands we need only say a little more about off-road gear.

You can ride off-road with the same *helmet* you use for asphalt. Some are, however, a little safer than others. The dirt bikers I know who use road helmets use either whole head or modular models so that their entire face and head is protected. Most seem to prefer a modular. The only downside to either helmet is that in cold or steamy weather the lenses tend to fog, or your glasses may fog inside the lenses. There are some very good anti-fog products available at bike stores and eyewear shops. Some are good for plastic, some for glass, and some for both. Be sure you buy what you need and are careful to use it only on the correct surface.

Body protection is also very important for off-road. You will see people zipping along trails at high speeds in shorts and t-shirts but the serious off-road riders I know would never do that. They might ride a relatively easy trail at moderate speeds in jeans and a t-shirt, but none of that breakneck, nearly naked stuff.

For jackets and slacks you want to be sure there is high-quality armor in the knees and elbows. Some also pad the shoulders and the base of the spine. If you might hit it, it's good to pad it. In my opinion the best material out there is textile of the Cortechish variety. It is waterproof, yet it breathes, and it is amazingly abrasion-resistant. Some people like separate knee and elbow armor. If you're riding hard these are probably a good idea.

If you want serious protection for serious riding there are additional pieces of body armor that protect the chest, back, spine, forearms, and shins. These may be more than you need for those beginning easy rides, but they are something you may want to consider as you amp up the difficulty of your rides.

Gloves may be leather, textile, or a combination. Lots of folks prefer gauntlets for improved wrist protection and padded knuckles. You also want to be sure that the gloves are flexible enough to be practical and small enough to allow you to operate the controls on the bike. I have a pair of winter-weather street gauntlets, for example, that I can use on the Can-Am because the switches for the turn signals, dimmer switch, and other essentials (like the radio volume control) are large and far enough apart that I can manage them. On the Virago, however, the control panels are more compact. Trying to wear those gauntlets on that bike makes me a danger to myself and others. You usually have fewer switches and buttons to worry about off-road, but the principle is the same. Optimize your protection, but don't sacrifice too much utility.

Gauntlets are gloves that extend beyond the wrist to some point on the forearm. You see them for wet and cold weather in street gear, but they are much more frequent in off-road gloves. They offer better protection for the wrists and forearms and help keep out water in the rain or when crossing streams.

A good pair of dirt *boots* is like a prop from a space movie. They are tall, heavy, think, and padded in all the right places. They offer extra protection for the toes, ankles, and shins. They typically snap or ratchet on rather than using laces. Dirt boots are very protective. As a result, they are also notoriously stiff and hard to break in. No joke, I have a friend who buys them, boils them, and beats them with a three-pound sledge before he wears them to ride. I wouldn't personally go that far, but many off-road boots need some serious break-in before serious riding.

Big, thick, heavy boots demand big, thick, heavy socks. In most cases you'll want them to stop just short of your knee when you pull them up. The thickness helps protect your feet and legs against abrasions from the tough boot surface. Don't skimp on the socks. You may spend several hundred dollars on top of the line off-road boots. Might as well invest $20 to $30 more in a great pair of socks.

Where to ride on dirt

Riding on dirt is great, but you may find that you need to give some thought to where you can do it. Sure, you can make your first few runs around your back yard, and a few trips up and down the driveway are certainly recommended. Soon, however, you'll hear the call of

233

broader vistas. In order to respond you'll probably need to do some research. Here are a few ideas.

You may know some people with parcels of land who would be willing to let you ride on them. If you don't know folks who are that generous, perhaps you can find someone who will let you ride for a fee. Whether it's for free or for pay there are some basic rules you'll want to follow. First, consider your safety. If you are going to ride on land you aren't familiar with and you aren't an experienced rider you may want to walk it first. Walk it with an eye to riding. Notice the hills and valleys, the nature of the soil, the frequency of rocks, and the nature of other obstructions you might encounter. Plan out a route and walk it a couple of times. You will probably notice things the second or third time around that you missed the first. When you do ride, ride slowly at first. Get used to moving around on your bike to adjust for hills. Notice how your wheels react to depressions in the ground, holes, and obstacles.

Safety is of primary importance, but you should also consider courtesy to the landowner. Riding the same path too often and too hard will leave a trail. Wet conditions make it happen even more quickly. Ride in mud and you will create ruts and gouges. If you ride on someone else's and you need to be sure both parties understand what the expectations are and you need to be considerate of the owner's preferences.

Some areas may have private areas where unlicensed riders can ride off-road bikes legally and safely. I mentioned one example a few chapters back when I talk about my brother's community. Before you ride on any private land, be sure it is private and be sure you have any needed permissions to ride.

234

Some parts of the country still have public dirt roads that you can ride after you have gotten your license. These may be a little hard to locate, but I have been able to find some in my own state through Internet searches, talking to people at the American Automobile Association, and checking the off-road Internet forums. There's actually a network of such roads in the central part of the state. An enterprising biker has developed a map of this network http://dualpurposetn.com/Trail_Details.html.

Dirt roads often mean easy rides, but this is not always the case. I've been on trails that started out wide and smooth, but soon narrowed to the unmaintained, deeply rutted remains of roads once cut by loggers. Dirt roads may include streams to be crossed and changes in the composition of the riding surface. Because they are public roads they may also include automobile or truck traffic. If you try out a dirt road, try to talk to locals about its condition and what you may expect along the way. Remember to take it easy the first time. Careful riding the first time through helps assure that you'll be able to return for additional rides in the future.

Some state and national parks have roads with motorized access. You can check availability in your area by checking the park's website. There are a couple of things to be aware of when riding in parks owned and operated by any level of government. First, you will need to be sure your exhaust system complies with statutory requirements. If it doesn't you'll either not be allowed to ride or you will be subject to a hefty fine. In some areas you may be required to furnish evidence that you have paid the appropriate amount of sales tax on your bike. If it's a dual sport licensed for the road the license will cover it. If not you may be required to display a sticker of compliance on the vehicle or carry paperwork providing evidence of the payment. Another thing to keep in mind is that many of these trails are shared with people on ATVs and sometimes hikers. A busy trail with speeding four-wheelers and clusters of strolling two-leggeds means that you need to be on your toes when navigating these roads.

There are also private parks where you can ride by paying a daily fee or purchasing a more extended membership. Licenses are not required at these facilities. They are, however, generally shared with other motorized vehicles, some as small as children on child-sized ATVs, others as large as big-wheeled pickups. This mixture of user types presents challenges similar to those in the government parks. It also means a range of trail varieties from relatively easy rides to paths with gullies and holes too deep for a bike to cross and too wide for even a skilled rider to jump. Be sure you know which routes match your skill level and be certain you have a means of communication in case the level of difficulty gets to a point that makes it dangerous for you to continue.

Kickstands down

Where can you ride off-road? Fact is, you can do it just about anywhere. Dirt is a great place to learn to ride, so long as you take your time and are properly prepared. If you're going to ride off-road, make sure you have the bike you need and that your bike is prepared in the ways it should be. Be sure it has the protectors, guards, and other equipment that will keep both it and you safe on the paths you choose to ride. Choose your gear carefully; thinking through your level of skill and the difficulty of the rides you'll be taking. Spend some time educating yourself about the places you can ride and how they fit into your overall plan for skill development. Dirt is a great place to learn. You'll enjoy it all the more if you are prepared for the challenges you'll face.

In Chapter 10 I'll report the results of interviews with folks who have started to ride at or after middle age, who love people who ride at or after middle age, and who sell motorcycles and gear to people at or after middle age. Doing the interviews was lots of fun and I learned a lot while doing them. I think you'll enjoy them as well. These are good examples of some of the great folks you'll meet as you learn to ride.

Chapter 10
Let's Ride! A Brief Visit with a Few Who Do

This will be a brief chapter, but it may be the most important chapter in the book. In this chapter we're going to visit with some people who are either at or beyond middle age or who care about others who are. I thought this chapter might provide you some insight about biking other than my own sparkling wisdom, and could give you an idea of hat those who love bikers think about it. I tried to get a collection of perspectives, from folks who sell motorcycles to those who love people who ride.

Cody Ellis- my son, first a rider behind, soon to be a rider both alone and with

Cody is 14 and will get his learner's permit in March when he turns 15. He took the Motorcycle Safety course a couple of months back. Let me begin by humiliating him in front of a national audience (OK, maybe both you guys who bought the book and made it to chapter 10). I am so blessed to have Cody as my son. He is a good kid. Smart, funny, hard-working (Umm, maybe often hard-working), kind, and considerate. He honestly is a lot like me, but I think he is way better than I was at his age. I think he has the potential to be way better than I have been after I am gone. I love that he rides. I love that we ride together, and I love that he started this whole thing by trying to scam me into buying him a ring. Thanks for being my kid, Cody.

I interviewed Cody while sitting at the kitchen table on New Year's Eve. Although he is typically effusive when discussing motorcycling, he turned out to be a tough interview. I'm no Oprah, but I think we did pretty well. Here's what he said.

The Old Man: "How did you feel about your dad

starting to ride?"

Cody: "I thought it was a good thing for him to do. I knew we'd have something to do together as I got older. We've always played games and watched movies. We don't do those things together as much. Now we ride."

"I wasn't worried when he first started talking about riding or when he took the class. I started to worry a little when he started talking about how big the Road King was and how difficult it was for him to manage. When we talked about my worry he told me that he'd rather live having ridden than die someday having not ridden. I got that."

The Old Man: "How did you feel when you started to ride?"

Cody: "I was happy because I was fulfilling a dream I had since I was a young kid. The first time that I can remember that I saw a motorcycle I wanted to ride one. I wasn't nervous at all. OK, maybe a little."

The Old Man: "How did you feel about taking the Motorcycle Safety Foundation Course?"

Cody: "I was excited to get it done so that I could hurry up and get my license and ride. I was happy to be able to take the course because it meant I didn't have to take the license exam. Some of the people I know flunked that thing 5 or 6 times."

The Old Man: (Shameless, inappropriate, paternal leading question) "Weren't you happy to learn about how to ride more safely?"
Cody: "Well duuuuh, of course. It was a safety course!"

239

The Old Man: "What was it like when you took the Motorcycle Safety Course?"

Cody- "It was a very slow-paced course for an experienced rider but a nice, easy pace for a new rider. The instruction was simple and clear. I was the only teenager in the class but I felt welcome and a part of things."

The Old Man: "How did your mother feel about it when you started to ride?"

Cody: "She was really worried about me. She said she wasn't worried about what I would do. She was worried about other people. You have to say this part: she said she was worried about people like her."

The Old Man: (shamelessly inappropriate for other reasons) "Oh, I can assure you we'll put that in. How about your friends? What did they say?"

Cody: "They were encouraging. They liked it. A lot of them ride or want to ride. A few were critical. They didn't like my bike because they said I'd outgrow it or it was too small."

The Old Man: "How did you handle that?"

Cody: "I told them to shut up and get over it. I'd get a bigger bike when I was ready for it."

The Old Man: "What do you like best about riding with your dad?"

Cody: "I like going to new places to see if they'll be good places to ride in the future. I really like the feeling of freedom I get when we ride."

The Old Man: "You and your dad took a trip last summer of about 2500 miles. It was a long, hot ride. What did you think about that?"

Cody: "I thought it was a good trip once you got past the 100+ degree weather and the slow pace of the ride on the Natchez Trace. On long days it sometimes felt like we would never get where we were going."

The Old Man: "What do you like least about riding with your dad?"

Cody: "Falling asleep behind him on those long hot rides. It scared me a little."

The Old Man: "How did you and your dad handle that?"

Cody: "He would yell back and ask me if I was OK. Sometimes he would reach back and tap me on the leg to be sure I was awake. We stopped a little more often. When I knew I needed to stop I would pat his left shoulder three times."

The Old Man: "What would you like to tell other people who are your dad's age and thinking about riding?"

Cody: "I'd tell them to pick their first bike carefully. They need to get a nice easy starter bike. (smart kid!) I'd tell them not to just think about it. Do it."

The Old Man: "What would you like to tell people your own age?"

Cody: "Don't listen to people who are critical.

Some people put down my bike and what I was doing. Do what you want to do and don't listen to people like that."

The Old Man: "Want to have some pizza?"

Cody: "Yeah."

Judy Rice Covington- my friend since second grade, she loves to ride behind

I walked into my second grade classroom all those years ago and was delighted to sit down by the sweetest, most beautiful girl in the room, Judy. There have been long gaps over the years in which we've lost touch, but the closeness I felt to her back then has never left. I don't think it ever will.

Judy is someone who loves to ride, and loves to ride behind. We'll talk about that more during the course of the interview. I talked with Judy by telephone on New Years Day. Here's what she had to say.

The Old Man: "How long have you been riding?"

Judy: "Oh gosh, let me see. I rode a little bit in my teens, then for a couple of years in my 20s. I started riding again about 5 years ago."

The Old Man: "Back when you first started to ride, what made you want to do it?"

Judy: "My husband had a bike that we rode some as teenagers. We got a different bike and rode for a couple of years in our twenties. We stopped because we almost had an accident and it scared me. We had a baby and I thought she needed her mom and dad so we quit.

242

The kids are all grown, so we decided to take it up again a few years ago."

The Old Man: "What do you like about riding?"

Judy: "When I ride I can almost feel Mother Nature hugging me. I feel the wind and the heat of the sun. I smell the smells of the world. When you're riding you're out there in nature. I have some health issues that limit my physical activities. Riding gets me in touch with nature like nothing else I can do."

"It's almost like a ritual to me. When I ride I stick my arms out to the side and feel the wind. Sometimes I have to do that, feel the wind. Like I said it's like Mother Nature hugging me. I'm absorbing nature, sun, smell, all of it."

The Old Man: "What do you dislike about riding?"

Judy: "Hmmm, well, I have short little legs. It's hard to get on and off, mount and dismount, sometimes. I also worry about the "other guy", the other drivers. Sometimes they don't even see you."

The Old Man: "Have you ever thought about riding alone rather than with?"

Judy: "I only ride behind. I've thought about trying it but I didn't think I was strong enough to hold the bike up. I've thought about a trike. I sat on one, rode on one, and I felt safe and secure. I still get a lot of pleasure from riding. It doesn't really matter to me that I am behind."

The Old Man: "Do you like riding with other couples."

Judy: "Yes, I do like it. There's a lot of camaraderie in the group. People are alike, have things in common. You ride, stop, have conversation. We usually had a destination like a festival or a place to eat. It's a lot more fun with other people."

The Old Man: "What advice would you give to women who want to start to ride?"

Judy: "Just do it. Get on, relax, trust the driver. Make sure you can trust the driver. I've ridden with one who scared me. I'm glad I won't have to do that again. Women who are older may get stiff and sore after a long ride. Just walk it off. Be sure to wear good boots. I wore flip flops when I started. My toes got really cold at night. They weren't much protection. Be sure you wear good gear and clothing."

The Old Man: "What advice would you give someone at or after middle age who want to learn to ride?"

Judy: "Start to ride in the evenings when there's less traffic. Work up to longer rides little by little. I have one female friend who will not ride behind. She will only ride alone or with someone else behind her. I'm very proud of her. She rides the way she wants to. That's what everyone should do." (Judy's friend Martha provided one of the other interviews in this chapter.)

A couple of days after the interview Judy sent me a text telling me that she hadn't said enough. She wanted to talk about Dan, her brother-in-law who died of cancer several years ago, and what riding had meant to him. I asked her to write it up and send it to me. Here is what she said.

"I witnessed firsthand the medicinal power of riding. My sister's husband was diagnosed with colon cancer and was given a timeline of 9 months. Riding his Yamaha Verago transformed him from a suffering, sick man to a man with a purpose—to ride until he could ride no more."

"My husband and I made the 1 hour trip at the drop of a hat when he felt the need—the need to ride. We traveled many back roads in Jefferson County, KY, without a care in the world focusing only on the ride. He was King of the Road and felt the power! His weak body was running out of power."

"It was a sad day when Dan could no longer have Sandy ride behind. It became a ride for men only. I am grateful for the bond we formed during our rides. We were there to witness Dan's last ride. He was so determined, but too weak to complete it. He went off the path and down an incline. He was unable to stop and went down."

"The doctors' prediction of his timeline was correct. I am convinced that riding was the perfect outlet for him to slip away and deal with his fate, his way; the way of a rider."

Brownie and Jane Grissom- A couple who ride together and who own a leather and motorcycle accessory store near Baxter, TN.

I've probably known Brownie for a couple of years now. I met Jane more recently. They are simply

245

delightful, both individually and as a couple. Brownie is 72, Jane is 59. They've been together for 32 years and show the amazing and elusive characteristics of a couple in love for that long: respect, shared humor, mutual interests, and an inextinguishable love of life and fun. Their communication skills as a couple are amazing. They listen to one another, respectfully respond to one another, laugh together, agree joyfully, and disagree gently when they don't see eye-to-eye. It made me want to go back for a whole bunch more interviews in the future.

You've already met Brownie a couple of chapters back. Remember the guy who can cut leather chaps like a champion and who makes fun of my size-selection from the Internet? That's the one.

I talked with Brownie and Jane in the second floor sitting room of their shop, Leather Worx, off the Highway 56 exit of I-40 near Baxter, TN. We chatted for an hour, sometimes sticking to the interview, but often wandering off into stories of bike trips past. Here's some of what we talked about.

The Old Man: "How long have you guys been together?"

Brownie: "32 years", turns to Jane with a smile. She nods and smiles back, "32 years. We dated for a couple of years, then got married."

The Old Man: "How long have you been riding together?"

Jane: "We started riding together in 2003. You got a Honda, right, Brownie?"

Brownie: "Yeah, it was a Honda."

The Old Man: "What was it like the first time you rode together?"

Jane: "The first ride was a little anxious. He was worried about me. I think he was afraid he'd scare me off from riding."

Brownie: "Yeah, I was afraid I'd do something stupid and she wouldn't want to ride again. It went well, though." (Jane nodded.) She is a great rider. Not everyone is. She's a natural. Leans at the right times and in the right places, doesn't do anything to throw you off. Not everyone can do that, you know."

The Old Man: "What are some of the places you've been?"

(Brownie and Jane had a brief discussion about whether they would talk about long or short trips first. They decided on short trips first.)

Brownie: "Our short trips have been to places like Helen, GA and the Tennessee State Parks. We have a beautiful park system here. We love to ride to them, then ride around inside."

Jane: "Our long trips would be things like the Natchez Trace and the Blue Ridge Parkway. Brownie loves to ride. He will just go on and on and on."

The Old Man: "Tell me about the Natchez Trace trip."

(At this point a couple of customer entered the store. We had already agreed that Brownie would get up and attend to customers if any came in during the interview. Jane and I continued.)

Jane: "It was a great trip, but a learning experience. It was 38 degrees in Nashville, 98 in Natchez. I packed heavy clothing, long sleeves, everything we needed for 6 days of cold weather. We nearly burned up."

"We left on a Sunday morning, got back on Wednesday or Thursday. There are lots of interesting places of interest along the Trace. We stopped all the time. It's an interesting place to ride for many reasons. No advertising is allowed, no billboards, I mean. That's great because of the view. It makes it a little difficult to find good places to stay, though. You just have to get off on a exit and search. Sometimes it's a long way to a restaurant or hotel, and you never know what you're going to get. I remember one place where I told Brownie, 'You can use the bathroom, but you aren't going to shower in that place. You can shower tomorrow night.'"

The Old Man: "When my son and I rode the Trace we scheduled stops at Bed and Breakfasts along the way. There's a guy who does scheduling with all of them. We stayed at one in Huston, MS and another in Natchez. They both were great"

Jane: "I'd probably have to convince Brownie to do something like that. He likes to just ride and ride 'til we're ready to quit. Back when we had a travel trailer and went to Alaska I'd ask him, 'Where we gonna be tonight?' He'd just laugh quietly and say, 'Honey, I don't know where we're gonna be tonight."

The Old Man: "So he's a true free spirit on the road."

Jane: "Oh yeah, a true free spirit. (Brownie rejoined us at about this point.) We've also learned to pick a bike up together. Everybody drops a bike once in a while. We've learned to put our backs against it and push."

The Old Man: "Yeah, you guys have a heavy bike. Mine are light, except the Can-Am, of course, but you can't drop it. The KLR and the Virago are easy, just grab the handlebars and stand them up."

Jane: "Brownie, remember when I used to ask you where we were gonna be that night and you'd just laugh and tell me, Honey I don't know where we'll be tonight."

Brownie: (Laughing what I'm sure was that same soft laugh.) "Yeah, I remember."

The Old Man: "What was the Blue Ridge ride like?"

Jane: "Fun, foggy, damp. Foggy and damp even though it was in the summer. That is such an beautiful place. we loved it. We like to explore the unexplored. "

Brownie: " That's one of the great things about riding. When you go there on a bike it's like the first time there. You can smell the air, feel the openness. It's like riding a horse, freedom.

The Old Man: "What do you like most about riding?"

Jane: "It's different. It's freedom. The only thing I don't like is rain. We did the Tail of the Dragon in the rain. Water was streaming down my helmet and visor and I told Brownie I wanted it to be over. He just laughed and said, "We're not far from home."

Brownie: (Laughing) "Yeah, I said that. We were close. It's definitely the freedom. Again, it's like when you go there, you're going for the very first time."

The Old Man: "What percentage of your customers are age 40 or over?

Brownie: "I'd say probably 50-60%. It's a lot."

Jane: "The guys he rides with are all over 70."

Brownie: "One guy is about 80. He rides a Can-Am. They are amazing machines."

The Old Man: "I love mine. They can certainly extend your riding life."

Brownie: "Yes, they can!"

The Old Man: "What challenges does riding beyond middle age bring?"

Brownie: "I actually think there are fewer challenges. I'm more comfortable now."

Jane: (laughing) "Well, maybe getting your leg over the bike. He has to get on first, then I put my foot on the peg and step over. I have to kind of grab my pants leg and help lift my leg over."

Brownie: "Age isn't a handicap, or even a challenge. I think at that point you appreciate the pretty country and the freedom more. Health issues can create challenges, but otherwise I can't think of any."

Jane: "Maybe getting over-tired."

Brownie: "You have to know your limitations. I have pushed myself beyond the point of over-tiredness. that's when I tend to make mistakes.'

Jane: "Pretty much the only time he makes mistakes on a bike."

The Old Man: "What advice do you have for people who want to begin to ride at or beyond middle age?

Jane: "Take the (Motorcycle Foundation Safety) course. Be sure you get the right equipment, DOT helmets, jackets, and so on."

Brownie: "Get a bike that's comfortable for you. One that fits you. Know your limitations and stay within them."

I ended some of my interviews by asking people to tell me a story. I didn't have to ask Brownie and Jane. We'd already swapped several. Here is my favorite. I'm telling it in narrative form. They told it together, laughing the entire time.

"I was on Mount Mitchell, the highest point in the US east of the Mississippi. I rode to the top, then stopped to look around. I enjoyed the beauty, then got on my bike. 'Click, click, click. Click, click, click. It wouldn't start. I was trying to decide what to do when a local guy suggested that I try coasting. He said I could make it to Waynesville, that there was only one spot where there was a hill. He told me, as you get to the exit do not slow down, even if you think you're going a little too fast. Just keep up your speed and you'll make it through the hill. I tried it and he was right. Coasted 8 miles and got it fixed."

Brad Nelson- General Manager of Boswell's Harley, Cookeville, TN

Boswell's Harley Davidson is a dealership in Middle Tennessee with locations in Nashville, Madison, and Cookeville. I have dealt with them since day 1 of my (second) riding career. I have to say that every interaction I have had with them has been very positive. Don't get me wrong, they like to sell you stuff, and are not shy about trying. They are, however, honest, fair, and helpful. I like to go in there and harass them even when I'm not going to buy anything. Brad also flips a great burger at their outdoor events. He swears he's going to put me on a Heritage Softail one of these days. We'll see, Brad. Maybe if the price is right.

I wanted to talk with Brad because as someone who both manages a dealership and sells motorcycles there he has the opportunity to talk to people of all ages who ride or who want to ride. He can offer a perspective on this whole getting older and riding thing that most of us cannot. I met with him in his office at the Boswell's Harley Davidson on Interstate Drive in Cookeville, TN.

The Old Man: "How often would you say you sell a motorcycle to a new or relatively inexperienced rider of age 40 or more?"

Brad: "I'd say maybe 10% of my customers fall into that category. That's quite a few people over time."

"I've been around motorcycles for years. I've been a machinist and a mechanic. Motorcycling is a great release for us. No matter how you feel when you get on your Harley everything just melts away."

The Old Man: "What reasons to people like that give for wanting to start riding at this point in their lives?"

Brad: "For a lot of folks it's like a bucket list. People get to 60 and say, "I may have only 10-12 good years left. There's gonna be things we wish we had done. I remember an old Harley commercial with a grandfather telling his grandson. The guy said, "Instead of doing that (other things) I spent my money on a Harley."

"Some people start to ride because they've experienced a tragedy and want to start doing things differently. I tell them, starting to ride will change your life. I hope it will be good. I can't promise it won't be bad. But I can tell you it will change your life."

The Old Man: "What are older riders looking for in a bike?"

Brad: "I'd say it varies. The most important thing is to get a bike that fits. It can be a little intimidating to walk into a Harley store. We want people to sit on bikes, get the feel of them. You need to feel comfortable on your bike."

The Old Man: "What advice do you give new riders?"

Brad: "Several things. I need to know a little bit about their pocketbook to help them find something in the right price range. I want them to sit on the bikes and find what feels comfortable. We can custom fit most anything by changing out shocks or seats or handlebars. I tell people they need to find their comfort zone. I you don't feel comfortable on your bike you aren't going to be safe on it."

"I've had people tell my customers, "Don't start with a Harley, it's too big and powerful. I tell them that it's about comfort. Buy the bike you are comfortable with and the one you want to ride."

"I also tell them to take the (Motorcycle Safety Foundation) course. No matter how old you are, no matter whether you're new, you need to take the course. Take both the beginner and the advanced. You just don't learn some things until you take the course, things like braking and weight transfer."

"Taking the course needs to be a good experience for you. At Harley we offer the Rider's Edge. The dealers hand pick the instructors, people they know and who have been through the courses themselves. I tell people to take the course. It will make them better and safer riders."

The Old Man: "What do older riders say to you about the bikes they buy and their riding experiences?"

Brad: "I ask them, 'Has it changed your life?' They say, 'It has.' I don't know of anyone that has told me it has been a negative experience."

"I tell them to join the Harley Owners Group (HOG). That gives them people to ride with and to talk to about riding. They may feel a little disoriented at their first meeting but they soon find themselves surrounded by a whole group of new friends."

"Our Upper Cumberland Chapter of HOG is great. We are very supportive of the town and the community, We do benefit rides like the annual toy ride and the one to support people who have Alzheimer's Disease."

"I tell them to plan great rides. They can ride with HOG or use the Ride Planner on the Harley Website. We're very lucky here in the Upper Cumberland. People spend lots of time and money to ride in places like the ones we ride through everyday. Every state park here is a great ride."

(Our conversation wondered off into side topics from time to time. During one of those verbal side trips I commented about a friend of mine who is sometimes very nasty about the fact that I don't currently own a Harley. Brad shook his head.)

Brad: "We all share the same sun and wind. I love Harley, but we can all ride together. I know this, when you get on that bike you feel like you're 10 feet tall."

Martha Wells- a woman who rides alone or with, but never behind.

Schedule conflicts prevented a face-to-face meeting with Martha, so she completed the questions on her own and returned her answers to me via email. Here's what she said:

The Old Man: "How long have you been riding?"

Martha: "I started riding in April of 2010."

The Old Man: "At what age did you begin to ride?"

Martha: "I started riding at age 46."

The Old Man: "What provoked your interest about

learning to ride?"

Martha: "I have several friends that ride and one of those friends was going to trade his bike for bigger bike and offered his small bike to me to purchase. I had never had the thought of riding before this offer."

The Old Man: "What was the most difficult thing about learning to ride for you?"

Martha: "Having to ask for help from others and advice from licensed riders. I usually don't like to ask for help for anything....."

The Old Man: "What were some other things that you found challenging about learning to ride?"

Martha: "I had to come to terms that I had no protection from other vehicles while on the rode on a bike."

The Old Man: "What were some things you enjoyed about learning to ride?"

Martha: "I LOVED the process of learning to ride. I could do something that others had only dreamed of doing....Some people put limits on themselves and I never put limits on myself or my son....I am a single parent and I found the thought of "NO LIMITS" very important!!"

The Old Man: "How often do you ride now?"

Martha: "In the spring and summer and fall I usually ride 3-4 times per week.....always on the weekend...."

The Old Man: "In what ways do you think riding as a woman is different from riding as a man?"

Martha: "Our physical strength is one thing that we have to keep in our mind constantly....I don't ride if I have a serious issue on my mind....I devote my full attention to my safe riding....I have often heard men say they need to take a ride and think something over but I never ride if i need to "think something over"

The Old Man: "Do you ride alone or with others?"

Martha: "Both, but I won't take the time to call lots of others to set up a ride....takes to long....if others call and are leaving now for a ride I will go....but I won't stand around and wait on a group!!!!"

The Old Man: "Do you belong to any motorcycle clubs or organizations?"

Martha: "No!!!!"

The Old Man: "What advice would you give someone at middle-age or later who wants to learn to ride?"

Martha: "DO IT..........what are you waiting on???"

The Old Man: "What advice would you give to women who want to learn to ride?"

Martha: "Do it....take the safety class offered in your city and go for it........advice to all riders....RESPECT the bike and the danger that can happen if you don't watch for other riders and VEHICLE traffic.........most people don't give any respect to motorcycle riders."

The Old Man: "Please tell us a story about an experience you have had as a rider."

<u>Martha</u>: "Bad experience.....hadn't learned to "lean" into curves yet and nearly was hit by a truck.....pay attention while riding and listen to all advice given to you by other experienced riders!!!!! My good experience is all the fun of each and every ride.....if you make it back home IT was a GOOD ride!!!!!!"

"Thanks for taking the time to send me the questions.....i sooo enjoy riding my bike and encourage EVERYONE that would like to learn to hop on and get moving......"

Eric Deebanks- Friend and salesperson extraordinaire at Midstate Motorsports in Cookeville, TN

Eric has sold me a couple of dirt bikes and nearly sold me a dual purpose and a couple of street bikes. In that process he has become a friend. I trust Eric, respect his judgment, and know I can always count on him for good advice, whether it means he will gain or lose a sale. I recently traded my Can-Am for a Victory at anotherdealer. I know Eric would have loved to sell me a bike, but I had fallen in love with this Victory and his shop didn't carry that line. When I told Eric he was eager to see it, looked at it admiringly, and wished me the best on my new ride. He's a good man and a good friend. Eric's interview brings dirt and dual purpose bike expertise to the chapter. Thanks, Eric, for your contribution.

The Old Man: Tell me a little bit about your work at Midstate Motorsports.

<u>Eric:</u> I have worked for Midstate for a little over 6 years. I started in the service department as a service writer. When a customer needed service on their bike or ATV I set up the appointment and took them in. I did that

258

for about a year and a half. I've been in sales ever since. Our days here can be anywhere from very busy to very slow. It mainly depends on the weather. We sell Yamaha ATVs and motorcycles, Kawasaki ATVs, motorcycles, and jet skis, and Kymco products. Mostly I enjoy working around these products that I absolutely love.

I enjoy the variety of people I meet and I think I get more excited when someone we sell. As far as percentage of sales goes, I would have to say that sales of dual purpose bikes has really taken off over the last three years, but dirt bikes have slowed down.

The Old Man: How long have you been riding? How often do you get to ride now?

Eric: I started riding ATVs and dirt bikes when I was about six or seven. I started riding on the street when I was about 13-14, nothing major because I wasn't legal yet. I don't get to ride as much now as I used to because I sold my street bike. I do have access to a few, though!

The Old Man: What kinds of things do you think a new rider should know and do?
What things are particularly important for older riders?

Eric: First, stay out of busy and congested areas. Definitely take the Motorcycle Safety Course and get plenty of saddle time before doubling (riding with a second rider behind you). Always be defensive as a rider. Stay out of very large groups and never let your ego determine how you ride. As far as older riders go, always keep learning. I always tell people that 75% of your stopping power is in your front brake.

The Old Man: What are some of the things you

can do to help?

Eric: The most important thing is choosing according to your riding experience, then what the customer is planning on using it for. If someone comes in wanting a sport bike I never suggest a 1000 or 600 unless they have plenty of riding experience. I suggest starting on either a dual purpose bike or if they want sport, a Ninja 250 or 300. For older riders it's definitely important to consider the bike weight and seat height.

The Old Man: What do older riders say to you about riding after they have learned?

Eric: They tell me that, if they had known how fun this would be, they would have done it 20 years ago. I hear that a lot. That's funny because when I say it to people they think I am just being a salesperson.

The Old Man: How is riding on dirt different from riding on the road? Are there any special concerns for older riders?

Eric: Riding on dirt is very different. You learn that when your rear wheel is loose (slips a little) it isn't that big of a deal. The basic concept is the same. I think everyone should learn on dirt, if possible. It's a whole lot more forgiving than concrete. When you get a street bike and you have a dirt background you don't freak out when you see a little bit of gravel. In the woods you learn to constantly scan ahead of you. Older riders who start on dirt should buy all the safety equipment they would but for street. If you ride on dirt you are probably going to hit the ground from time to time, but you are also going to develop the skills you need for the street.

The Old Man: How is a dirt bike different from a dual purpose bike? How is an adventure bike different from either of those?

Eric: A dirt bike is titled for off road use only. The tires and the suspension are different. There are no turn signals. A dual purpose is tuned a little more for the road. It also has blinkers, speedometer, headlight, tail lights, and brake lights. An adventure bike is usually quite a bit bigger and is a lot more road oriented. It has more comforts like ABS, heated grips, and sometimes traction control.

The Old Man: What advice would you give someone at middle age or later who
wants to learn to ride?

Eric: Take the Motorcycle Foundation Safety Course and see if you enjoy it. Then get a bike that fits you. Don't let friends try to persuade you how to ride or what bike you need.

The Old Man: What else do people at or after middle age who are going to learn to ride need to think about in order to get started?

Eric: Take your time and keep everything in perspective. Take time with your gear selection, insurance, and preparation. Be sure to plan for a lot of time off worbecause once you start that is all you will want to do! Enjoy yourself. It will take you back to when you were in your 20s.

Kickstands down

In this chapter we've talked to some folks I know about riding. I've tried to include a good mix of young and older, male and female, rider and non-rider. I can't tell you how much I enjoyed my time with these folks. I'm sure you've enjoyed them as well.

So what now? Why, write the publisher, demand a second book, demand book signings and television appearances and coast-to-coast publicity rides. Naw, just kidding. Now go ride and, if I am ever so fortunate that our paths may cross, please say hey. Let's have a cup of coffee or a bite to eat and talk about riding. See you on the road

Chapter 11

Biking and Spirituality: Seven Devotional Thoughts

Where is God? Certainly, different people would answer that in different ways. My answer is that He is always here right beside me. I am simply more aware of His presence at some times than at others. There are times when I am particularly aware; such as sitting in my office struggling to understand the hurt that has damaged a client, such as walking quietly in an isolated wooded place, such as puffing my pipe and watching the sun rise, and such as riding my bike down a lonesome but lovely stretch of highway. For the Old Man, biking is a spiritual experience, one that cannot replace prayer and meditation and ritual, yet one that is no less powerful in making me aware that He is with me every moment.

Yep, I know some of you guys aren't going to like what I say here. You may not like that when I use the word God I'm leaving it to you to decide Who I'm talking about. You may not like that I call God "He". In fact, you may not like the fact that I talk about God at all. Let me say a few words about this before I get into the whole spirituality thing. First, if the whole notion of God makes you want to do a face-plant at 75 mph, just forget that I brought it up. This is the last chapter of the book and is easily skipped. I'm not writing to convince you of anything, just to talk about my own experiences with God and what I've learned about Him while biking. If He doesn't show up when you mount up, feel free to skip straight to the appendices.

Now for the whole "tell you who God is" thing. That really isn't my job here. I know who I think God is, although I must admit that my understanding of Him has changed as I have changed over the years. I'd like to invite you to read with your God in mind, not mine. Even if you don't like mine I think you'll find that many of the experiences He and I have shared are very much like your own.

Now for a word about the "He, She, It" thing. Yes, it is more than a tad sexist that I'm calling God "He". Trouble is, I'm writing in the English language and have only those three options, He, She, and It. There just isn't a single, short word for saying "The One Who is neither Male nor Female, yet is Both Male and Female". Therefore, with apologies to those who see God as androgynous or as female, please hang in there with me. I welcome you to substitute any pronoun you choose throughout the chapter. Betcha you still find that much of what I experience is what you experience.

So let's talk spirituality and bikes. Much to your relief, I'm sure, I've given some thought to how to approach this topic. Almost everyone I know who rides has described some sort of experience that I would call spiritual. If you listen closely to what they say you find many of the themes of the faiths of the world imbedded in what they describe. Here are the themes we'll discuss: darkness and light, love and grace, woundedness and healing, sin and redemption, solitude and community, independence and interdependence.

Darkness and Light

The sun is setting as you ride. Dusk enfolds you like the goodnight hug of a doting momma. You are suspended in that duality that is neither light nor dark. The peace of God's world, sometimes inevitable, often fleeting, descends.

Truth be told, this is peace on peace. The wind and the sun and the life around you have already muted

264

the voices of cares and sorrows. God has whispered in your ear as the miles have passed, and you have heard His voice.

The world is both dark and light, a place of struggle, a place of evil, a place of pain. Yet it is God's world: a place of peace, a place of love, a place of incredible joy, and in the descending darkness you see both. Inevitably, you also see the hand of God there to lead you through it.

We, too, are both dark and light… creatures of the earth, yet children of God. The dusk reminds us that we must have the courage to face both. It also reminds us that God is there to help us with both. We are spirits of love and goodness and light, placed here to shine God's love into the darkness. We are also masses of anger and selfishness and pride. When we are able to see both, and to live in the grace of God, we can both shine and be healed. To deny either is not to choose darkness, but it is to know less of his peace and to share less of his presence than we might.

Ride, and Know that I am God

I rode with God tonight,
Found Him rushing there beside me
On his carriage of spirit-metal, both simple and shining, both awful and wonderful.

As we rode, God showed me love and hate, sorrow and gladness, peace and chaos.
He reminded me that I am not simply to see them or bear them.
He told me that I am to thrive in them, and accept the touch of his hand wherever I walk, and whatever I see about myself and the world.

265

He reminded me that He is always there.

God rides with us, every moment of every day.
In the darkness of our ride we cannot know what
lies beyond our lights.
Demons of madness lurk, hoping to crush our
hearts and souls.
Angels attend, ready to bring us hope and help.

Yea though I ride through the valley of the shadow
of death
    I will fear no evil
    I will revel in His love.
    For every day I ride with God.

Freedom and Bondage

As we've seen throughout this book, bikers often describe joy in the freedom they experience while riding. It really is a glorious feeling, out there in the wind feeling the sun and enjoying nature as you speed through it. Automobiles are, after all, known as cages. Sure, their walls and wheels offer protection against all kinds of threats. They are also one more way of cutting us off from the world. Folks riding in cages often cannot fathom this. Folks on a bike cannot deny it. We live behind the walls of our homes, work behind the walls of our places of employment, and visit in the homes of our friends. We also build walls in our hearts to protect tender spots against the harm the world or even we ourselves might inflict. For a time those walls are like a fortress, shielding against the onslaught of our emotional enemies. Often, however, the walls outlast the onslaught. Our enemies retreat and the walls, once our saviors, are reborn as prisons. We cowered behind them safe, yet in rage and fear when our enemies came. Yet when our enemies departed the walls remained. Our faith in them and in the power of our enemies kept us behind them and kept them in place. Years after we may yet peek from behind those walls, scanning the horizon for an imaginary enemy who came, but will never come again. Often we long ago gained the strength to make the walls obsolete, yet the walls remain because we believe we need them.

Our fortresses once kept our enemies at bay, but our prisons become training grounds for jailors within. These jailors are our thoughts and beliefs about the world. "Look," one whispers at the sight of a very good person, "That one will steal away your heart and leave you emotionally destitute, get away!" "Watch out," cries another, the world is a fearful place from which you must hide yourself." "You might as well give up hope," adds another. "It isn't ever going to get any better than this." Because we believe the walls we also believe the voices, and sink toward an isolated, immobilized despair. We may or may not ever reach that awful bottom, but so long as the walls remain we will never approach the top, either.

It was our faith that raised these walls. It is also our faith that can remove them: faith in God, faith in ourselves, faith in the inherent goodness of some of the world and some of the people in it. Faith imprisoned us. Faith can set us free.

The wind in my face is a Word from God, telling me that I can be free. The walls need not stand. The prison can go. God will stand with me. The lessons I've learned from the past can help guide me. My friends will stand with me. I can be free.

Freedom Ride

Wind on my face, a rough caress.

Turns my jaw scarlet,
My hair a blowing mane.
Yet kindly whispers in my ear,
"You are free. Be free."

At sea, the wrath of Poseidon.
In grasses, King of the Fae.
At Pentecost came wind with flame,
Tongues to tell of freedom unearned.
Today in wind it comes again:
Echoes of temple fires unleashed .

Unfettered, I race into the wind,
Mindful of the One who meets me there.
Come, oh come Emmanuel
Your gusts take my sorrow, my fears, and my
wounds.
Meet me in the wind.
Set me free.

Love and Grace

I understand and accept but a pittance of the love and grace God offers me. Yesterday I knew Him less. Tomorrow I hope to know Him more. But for today, just for today, I accept what I can and be who I am. That, I am sure is enough for me, and know is enough for Him.

Why do I speak with such confidence about my relationship with God? Let me assure you that it is not about me. It is about Him. I am no spiritual giant. I have known soaring moments of spiritual connection and delved deep into the pits of depravity. I have known angels and demons. At times I have probably resembled both.

But it isn't about me. That's the good news. God

doesn't base His love on my fickle nature. He bases it on his immutable, totally consistent nature, and the ferocious, unfailing love with which He pursues me. It is that same love with which He pursues every one of us.

In many ways coming to know the love of God is like learning to ride. When we start, we may do well, or we may do pretty awful. A lot of how we do depends on what we bring to the experience. New bikers who start young before they have developed fears and bad habits learn fast. So do older folks who have done things with transferrable skills, like riding ATVs with standard transmissions. Even after you learn to ride well, however, there are opportunities for developing skill and becoming more comfortable. I find that I learn something, or push my comfort zone just a little, almost every time I ride.

Some people seem to find it easier to understand and accept the love of God than do others. Many of us learn about God from what we see in our parents. If our parents are loving and supportive and forgiving, we tend to first see God in that light. If they are rigid and unforgiving we often assume that God is like that. If we are children removed from our homes and bounced from place to place without solid and stable parental figures in our lives we may begin with the belief that God is capricious and unstable and impossibly distant. As we go through life our experiences with authority figures and other people of faith reinforce or refute what we believe. The result is an imperfect faith, full of fear and doubt and misconception.

The good news is that whatever our experiences have predisposed us to believe about God and his love, God wants us to know the truth. The truth is that His love exceeds our every doubt, our every fear, our every sin. He loves us when we trust him. He loves us when we rage against Him. He loves us when we turn to him with open and hungry hearts. He loves us when we turn away from Him. Wherever we turn whatever we do, God is there.

I was a particularly bad rider when I sat on my bike at the age of 56. I was not afraid. I was terrified. I couldn't go through the motions of even starting the bike without stopping and thinking, doing and redoing. When I rode I made mistakes, serious mistakes, often born of my fear and my inability to trust what the bike would do. As I rode more I learned to trust. I came to understand the bike. My fears melted and my mistakes lessened until I reached the point that I now ride with confidence… most of the time.

I've made lots of mistakes when it comes to understanding the love of God. My rides with Him have been bumpy and frightening with lots of setbacks and a few times when I just got off His bike, pretty sure it wasn't the ride for me. Every time I got off and went to bed pissed I got up the next day or a few days later or a few years later and found Him standing right there beside me, holding that spiritual bike and saying, "Ready to try it again?" Eventually, I have always answered with a "yes", however reluctant or enthusiastic. I was ready to give up over and over again. God never gave up on me. He never, ever will.

One of the most difficult parts of accepting the love of God for me has been honesty. Like many folks, I'd like to pretend that God doesn't know what I'm like. Fact is, He knows me even better than I do. The things I hide from myself, even try to hide from others, God already knows. He does not love me because of who I am. He loves me because of who He is. Knowing that requires a lot of trust, overcoming a lot of fear, and ignoring the influences of people past and present who try so desperately to tell me who He is and what He is like. I really don't need their opinions. He has already told me. He loves me.

Ride Like a Child

Sunburned child, immersed in glee...
Mounts pintsized bike, imagination set free.
Parents close to help and to hold...
A new journey begins, a new life to unfold.

God help us to mount and to ride like he...
The bike with which you bring eternity.
Help us to know the love that You are...
And that though we dismount we cannot go far.

For You are there.

Woundedness and healing

Every one of us is wounded. Some wounds are greater than others. Some seem to have a greater effect even though their appearance is small. Some of us carry our wounds pretty well, looking bold and confident and strong. But for all of us the wounds are there. Some are very deep, and most interfere in some ways with our ability to love and laugh with people and with God.

The wounds we experience come most readily at the hands of those we love and trust. A parent may deny our infant selves the constancy and comfort we so desperately crave. Over time we learn that we are not worthy of comfort, and come to doubt our capacity to love or be loved. The childhood dreams of a tender spouse and a picket fence may be crushed by a mountain of alcoholism and violence and debt. We may survive a storm only to find that it stalks us in our dreams, stealing away the peace and rest our bodies crave. We may be called to war, returning broken and hopeless and haunted by the demons and ghosts of the atrocities we lived. Each cut goes deeper. Each drains away the person we were and might have been.

Often our wounds are concealed or fortified by guilt and shame. We cannot be healed because we believe in the awfulness of what we have done or the fearfulness of being so vulnerable. It may be that we fear appearing weak in the eyes of others.

Some of us are oblivious to our wounds, believing the hurt to be normal and inevitable. In fact, we often protect them, forestalling healing through our belief that we need those wounds to protect or drive us. Shamed by our wounds, trusting in their elusive benefits, we live with doubts and fears and guilts that do not belong to us. Long ago we might have healed, if only we had known how. Fact is, God knows how. He is able to heal.

Emotional wounds affect us in several ways. Of course, the obvious way is what they do to our emotions and behavior. People respond with deep depression, severe anxiety, sleeplessness, symptoms of physical illness, and hypervigilance. Relationships are destroyed. The capacity to love is hampered. Sexual desire may vanish. Even the capacity to seek and know God may be diminished or completely sublimated. In the mind the wounds appear in two ways. They affect the things we think, but they actually affect the functioning of the brain as well.

Our wounds affect the way we think by causing us to see ourselves, our worlds, and our futures in ways that we have not seen them before. We come to perceive ourselves as less than we are, the world as worse than it is, and the future as more threatening than it is. Think about my experiences in learning to ride. A few weeks and a few terrified rides into the process I realized that my fears were due to a roll-over truck accident I had experienced on black ice several years earlier. I had escaped with virtually no physical consequences. My mind had been harmed, however. Perhaps I suspected it when I drove past the spot in subsequent months. The touch of nausea and faint sound of crunching metal should have been a warning to a seasoned therapist. I didn't really get it, however, until I sat in the seat of that big Road King. "You can't handle this," something inside me screamed. "You're too old. The bike is too heavy." Another voice warned, "There are other drivers out there, and gravel just waiting for a chance to knock you down." "You are gonna wreck for sure!" another chimed in. It's just a matter of time until you go down and go down hard." I wasn't fully aware of these thoughts at the time. In retrospect I can see them clearly... false ideas about myself, my world, and my future. The ideas raced through my mind, creating fear and affecting my motor skills. My wounds had remade my world.

We also know that when we experience unresolved trauma there is a physical impact on our brains. The neural networks in our brains stop functioning the way they are supposed to function. As a result we are unable to access the range of responses we should have to threatening situations. The part of the brain that tells us we must fight, flee, or freeze dominates. Alternative, more functional responses come to us very slowly or not at all. In the case of my riding experience I got stuck in freeze, and my tendency to freeze made riding a bike a dangerous thing for me. The neurons in my brain were no longer firing correctly. My brain had actually experienced a small amount of physical damage. This damage affected my thoughts, my emotions, and even my ability to react physically.

As with my biking experience, our wounds keep us from experiencing the freedom, joy, and peace we might otherwise know in our lives. They can even inhibit our ability to relate to God. He made our brains in such a way that we are able to love and trust Him, as well as accept His love and trust. When they are damaged we simply cannot experience those things to the fullest. It isn't that God ever goes away or isn't there to be experienced. He never moves. It is that our ability to recognize and accept His presence is impaired.

The good news is that our brains can be made well. Our walks with God can be enhanced. Our wounds can be made whole. This is promised in every faith I've ever studied. Here's one of the things Christianity (and Judaism) have to say about it.

"Surely he hath borne our grief's, and carried our sorrows: yet we did esteem him stricken, smitten of God, and afflicted.

But he was wounded for our transgressions; he was bruised for our iniquities: the chastisement of our peace was upon him; and with his stripes we are healed." (Isaiah 53:4-5).

Some interpret this as meaning that we are cleansed of our sins. I agree with this interpretation, but I also think it is far too limiting. I think it means that God has both the power and desire to heal the wounds to our hearts and minds that hurt and trauma and betrayal have produced. I really don't mean to oversimplify. I don't mean that every wound we experience will miraculously vanish. I do mean that, in his nearly inescapable love and mercy, God can make us better, and perhaps someday make us whole.

So how do we access the healing power of God? The first step is simple, yet incredibly difficult. We have to recognize and acknowledge our wounds, our own brokenness. We have to admit that there is something wrong with us. We have to be willing to accept the fact that we are emotionally weak and vulnerable, and that although we may carry it off well, we are walking today bleeding from the wounds of the past.

The second step is in asking God's help for healing. You will need his guidance and support, and will need him to help you find ways to live without the wounds. Strange as it may sound, being wounded feels "right" to most of us. After all, the wounds have been a part of us for a very long time. Some even prop us up when we need support or help us to avoid dangers that confront us. An example would be someone who uses anger to keep others at a distance so that he will not be hurt as he has in the past. You will need to both heal of your wounds and things to help you live well in the world when the wounds are healed.

The third step is the nuts and bolts. If you were working on your bike steps one and two would be like diagnosing the problem and consulting the owner's manual to make sure you know what to do. In step 3 you pull out the wrenches and go to work.

There are lots of ways to turn the wrenches in emotional healing. Meditation, particularly a system called Mindfulness can be remarkably helpful. Remember the ideas about self, the world, and the future we discussed earlier? It can be very helpful to identify and write down the thoughts that were created by and sustain your wounds. If you'd like examples, take a look back at the ones I mentioned that pertained to my accident. You may also want to seek out the assistance of a spiritual leader or therapist. Most importantly, you will want to seek God's help and support along the way. Remember that you are changing not just the way you act and feel, but also the way you think and the biological functioning of your brain. It's a big job, but the help you need is yours. Remember, "by His stripes we are healed".

The Healing Hand, The Healing Road

Ride with me and we will find
A way for You to touch my mind,
A way to see the depths of pain
Upon my hand my heart 's blood stain.
From whence I sought to staunch the flow
From what I abhor but can't let go,
The wounds that scar my soul and mind
The ravages hurt has left behind.

And when I see, help me to know
That what I need You will bestow.
If courage lacks You will attend
Where wisdom fails You will extend
The truth You held ere time was made
The Might by which was Darkness staid.
When I behold the hurt I bear
Bring those to light my path through care.

The tools you place within my hand
And in my world by your command
Gird my heart and clear my mind
As hand in hand my wounds we bind
Help me to see and learn to wield
The grace by which my stripes are healed.
The hurts I knew all left behind.

Whole in thought and whole in mind.

<u>Sin and Redemption</u>

The thought that God sees our sins could be very frightening. So many people have been so ready to remind us that God is there and He is pissed and we'd better watch our steps or we're gonna get fried. Authority figures model that characteristic for many of us, and we wind up with a sadly perverted view of God as some cosmic bad guy who delights more in punishment than He does in grace. Fact is, exactly the opposite is true. God wants more than anything else in (or out) of the world to be in love with us.

Some folks were probably uncomfortable, if not downright put off, by my selection of words in the last paragraph. I see it going through a few minds: "God gets "pissed off"? Oh, He doesn't get pissed. He gets full of wrath and glory." "Wait! How can you say a "perverted" view of God? I just say what the preacher says and He says it's from the Word of God. You've got a lot of nerve calling that perverted."

Fact is, there are at least as many opinions about what God is like as there are churches. Probably more. You can just pick one and go with it if you want. I think God is probably just fine with that. Each of those churches develops a package of ideas about what God is like and an associated package about what is good or not good for us to do. Some of those ideas are correct and some are not. Each church will assure you that its ideas are the correct ones. Each will say that it's what the Bible says. Funny thing is, they can't all be right.

I've been talking about Christianity here. Obviously, it gets even more complicated when you add in the other faiths. Most of them have some sort of concept of sin. Many seem to think their own thoughts about sin and God are correct and that the rest of us poor bastards are just gonna get fried. Again, everyone can't be right.

Religious groups create a culture, a system of beliefs that include a group of social rewards and sanctions. Once you hook up with them you have to either live in a manner that is consistent with their belief system, conceal the fact that you do not, or experience the consequences that group chooses to impose. All that has very little to do with God and lots to do with being human. There are many benefits to being a part of one of those systems. Obviously, there are also serious downsides. You can live your life within a system if you so choose, or you can choose not to. Some of what I'm going to say about sin, however, will probably go against some of what they say. You get to decide what you think about what I say as well.

I do believe in sin. I think it distances us from God. I think it's best if we don't do it. I also think the way sin is treated in many religious groups is more about social control than it is about loving God.

In my own little system of beliefs I find comfort in the fact that God knows the sins of my past and of my future. People may worry about trying to control my decisions through guilt and shame. God never does. He has forgiven me. In His eyes I am not guilty, not shameful. I'm just one of his kids that He loves.

When I think about God and my walk with Him I think about teaching my kid to ride a bike. I was still wet behind my moto-ears when I started teaching him. I had the safety course fresh in mind, my experiences close at hand, and knew a LOT about how not to treat him from the way I had been treated. I think I also learned a lot about the way God treats us.

My kid actually got me into riding. I would never have thought about getting back on a bike after all those years. He was dying to learn so I was dying to help him. Bought him a little Yamaha 125 dirt bike. Sold it after he outgrew it. I've wished a thousand times I hadn't. That little bike would haul my oversized backside up and down mountains at breakneck speeds… OK, so maybe breakneck was only on the way down. Anyway, we started him in the driveway. Worked with him on startup for a couple of days, then went to power walking. We wore the driveway out, first with me walking beside him, then with me watching. One day he wanted to try the grass. I sucked it up and said "OK", like I really had a choice. He did great! Soon he was flying around the yard (about 2 acres, great place to start) and I was out whacking bushes to make him a trail. When he'd struggle with something we'd talk about how to fix it. He rode and rode, and got better and better.

Eventually we swapped the 125 in on a 250 dual purpose. He was a little insecure at first, but I watched and gave him tips and started to ride with him. After he got his permit I rode along behind and watched his technique. We'd stop at local restaurants and discuss his progress. He made some mistakes, but did lots of things very, very well. A couple of days ago we rode to one of our favorite little country restaurants, the Rose Garden. We ate fried food and chatted. After a while I noticed that I had no suggestions to make. He had made a perfect ride, or at least as close as you can get to perfect.

I think that's the way God is, even about our sins. I don't mean to suggest that I'm very God-like, or that He couldn't have done a better job with the ride training, but I think God is more eager to help us through our walks in life (or rides) like a loving daddy than an evil ogre. He loves us, coaches us, teaches us, dines with us, and forgives us when we don't measure up. That's how I think God treats our sins.

Let's go back to religious groups for a minute. One of the things I think is a serious problem for many is the way they pick out "pet sins". You can be one of them so long as you don't engage in certain sins. If you chose those you are sanctioned and relegated to some kind of "lesser" status. You may even get kicked out. I don't think God is like that. I don't think He has pet sins, and I don't think He ever stops loving us.

Probably even more insidious than group pet sins is our tendency to have personal pet sins. Many of us have sins that we believe are worse than others. We want not to do them, we try not to do them, yet we find that we return to them against our want and will. Afterward we are mired in guilt and shame, God is right there beside us, hugging us, holding us up. Sadly, we cannot feel His presence. We are too wrapped up in feeling our shame and guilt.

God has no pet sins. He forgives all. Sin is a powerful force. Yet it pales and flees before the light of God's love. His redemption is not so small, his grace is not so weak. We are forgiven. We are redeemed.

Willing Heart

Willing heart, eager to ride, eager to know the God it seeks.
God is there with hugs and heart and immeasurable love.

We ride a while basking in his grace,
And then we fall.
With broken heart, by our pain more than by our
sin
God strokes our hair and takes our hand and
helps us right our lives.

Come, He says, let's ride again.
And so we mount and twist the throttle,
Knowing God but not knowing He is there,
Ignoring His whispers and comforting touch
Because we think He cannot forgive us
When in fact He cannot help Himself.

God help us know your love,
Never failing, never waning.
Grace without measure.
Redemption above all that we can do or be.
Scarlet sins washed white as mountain snow.
Forgiven… ever and always hopelessly in love
with You.

Solitude and Community

Jesus surrounded himself with people. His disciples followed him, he ate meals with all kinds of folks, He spoke to the masses. We know that people followed Him everywhere. Community, the company of others, was definitely a part of his life.

Yet Jesus also sought solitude. I'm sure we don't know of every example, yet the Gospel writers speak of a few, perhaps most notably his time in the desert and his private time of prayer in the Garden of Gethsemane. Clearly He knew something we often lack. (Among many things, of course!) He knew how and when to seek both solitude and community.

This way of seeking both solitude and community can also be seen in the lives of many of the great leaders of other faiths. There's a balance in there to be had: the support of a group of people we love and trust and enough love and trust of ourselves to be able to spend time alone. For many of us, it's not that we don't know that we need both, it's that we don't know how to find either, or what to do with them once we've found them. There's another issue, too: one about God. We have to love and trust Him enough to deal with being alone or being with others. Those are the three critical elements: being with self, being with others, and being with God.

Think of all this as it relates to riding. Again, there are three perspectives. The three are riding alone, riding with others, and riding with God. To live and ride in a balanced manner, we need to be comfortable with all three.

In one of the earlier chapters we talked about riding alone. Many things about it are freeing, exhilarating, and set the mind in just the right state for contemplation. Yes, you do have to pay attention to what you're doing and what's happening around you, but something in the back of your mind just kind of settles down. The voices that constantly vie for attention in other times and places gradually become quiet. In the stillness that results you find peace, rest, and a remarkable openness to the still, small voice of God. You have moved beyond loneliness the place where aloneness was intended to take us. You have found solitude.

Fortunately for non-bikers, solitude can be found many other places. It may await you in the shelter of the woods, in the peace of a sunset, or in the comfort of your favorite chair. When you ride, the bike does some of the work for you. Stillness grows with every passing mile. Yet that same stillness can be found away from the bustle of the highway. Fact is, it doesn't exist on the bike or in the woods or on your favorite chair at all. It exists within your mind. The key to experiencing and enjoying solitude is finding that place within your mind.

There's also something very special and spiritual about riding with others. Your friends are there, people you care about and who care about you. You watch out for one another as you ride. You chat and walk together on breaks. You have meals together, enjoy the sun together, prepare for the rain together, and on longer trips, you begin and end the days together. Riding in a group brings feelings of closeness to others, camaraderie, and comfort. Yes, you can also find it other places than with other bikers. Some folks find it in family, some with close-knit groups of friends, some in churches or other spiritual groups.

There are times to be alone and times to be together. Some of us, however, find it difficult to do one or both. Some of the reasons for this discomfort are rooted in mental illness and may require the help of a professional (a form of community) to overcome. For most folks, however, it's quite possible to find ways to enjoy both solitude and community. Those who find it challenging will benefit from the following four processes: 1) learning to still the mind, 2) learning to be comfortable with self, 3) learning to be comfortable with other people, and 4) learning to be comfortable with God.

Learning to still the mind

Learning to still the mind is easier than many of us think it is. Yes, there are lots of things to interfere. Most of them have to do with things that have happened in the past, or things we anticipate may happen in the future. Mental stillness is best achieved by finding ways to think about those things as little as possible. In order to find quiet in our minds three things are necessary, a focus on something in the present, persistence in focusing on that something, and the ability to accept some irregularity in the results.

Fact of the matter is, no matter how difficult you may think it is to still the mind, most of us already do it from time to time. Have you ever caught yourself staring out the window thinking of nothing at all? Have you ever gone fishing and discovered yourself staring at the waves and water with nothing on your mind except that moment? Have you ever been busy with a repetitious task and found that you were thinking of nothing else other than the movement of your fingers? If you've done any of these things you've stilled your mind. Now all you have to learn is how to do it on purpose.

To intentionally still your mind you need to sit quietly and comfortably and focus your mind on one single thing. Some people focus their minds on following the sensations of their breath. Others may choose to listen to the sounds around them. Others may focus on a brief favorite scripture or on some aspect of the nature of God. You sit quietly, focus on your chosen process or object, and breathe normally. After a time you will notice that your mind becomes more still. As it does, you find greater levels of peace. I said earlier that quieting your mind requires persistence because it does. Your mind is probably accustomed to running off to something that happened yesterday or something that could happen tomorrow. You may find that as you focus you need to gently return your thoughts to your chosen object again and again, but persistence will prevail. Ultimately, your mind will become more still.

I also mentioned that you have to allow yourself to be comfortable with irregular results. You may, for example, try to still your mind one day and notice it quieting right away. On other days you may find it a daunting task. What matters is that you are persistent, and that you take what seem to be the "good" days and the "bad" days as they come. The "bad" days may be much better than you think.

Learning to be comfortable with self

Stilling the mind is an important step toward learning to be comfortable with yourself. Much of our discomfort with ourselves is born of things we feel badly about from our past and things we are afraid we will not be adequate to face in our future. As our minds still and focus on the present we become more open to understand the healing power of God for the things we've done, and the power of God to help us deal with things we will face in the future.

We've already talked about our need to accept and trust the love and grace of God earlier in the chapter. Fact is, most of us find that process to be like peeling layers off an onion. We reach one level of healing from our guilt and shame, then discover other layers beneath. Each layer brings us closer to recognizing the constant and persistent presence of God. Each allows us to be more comfortable with ourselves.

It is also trust in the love and grace of God that allows us to overcome our feelings of inadequacy about the future. God doesn't promise us that we will not face challenges and hardships. He does promise that He will be with us through every one that we do face. He is adequate to face the things the future may bring. When

285

we ride with Him we are made adequate.

"Be still and know that I am God." Be still, and He will find ways to help you be more comfortable with yourself.

Learning to be comfortable with others

You can be very comfortable within a community. You can also be very uncomfortable. A lot of how you feel depends on what you think of the community and what you think the community thinks of you.

A couple of nights ago I was invited to a local bike rally to meet folks and to let them know about an upcoming ride to benefit a local charity. I thought I was going to be asked to speak to the group so I decided to dress in more conventional street clothing than in the leather and dew rags I knew would be prevalent. I met the other two guys who were supposed to join me to pass out brochures, only to discover that we were the only folks not wearing leather within a radius of several hundred yards. I also discovered that we were to speak to the same group, but on another night somewhere in the future.

I was surprised to find myself very uncomfortable. Understand, these were not outlaw MC folks. They were local business people and retirees. I even knew a few of them from outside the group. Nothing they did was making me uncomfortable. I managed to do it all on my own, somewhere in my mind. I quickly convinced myself that I didn't fit in, that they all thought I didn't belong there,   and that they would all prefer to see me get on my bike and roar off into the sunset. Turns out I learned that nothing could have been further from the truth.

I was uncomfortable. The bikers were standing around in groups chatting, chowing down on burgers and hot dogs, and listening to a very good local band playing live under a big tent. I decided to suck it up and distribute flyers. I started with the tables. While the bikers munched I greeted and chatted and distributed. The longer I kept at it the better I felt. It took about 10 minutes, but after a while I stopped feeling out of place and started feeling right at home. By the time I had passed out the flyers I felt like one of them. Funny thing is, I had been one of them all along. I just hadn't felt that way.

Being comfortable in a group, a community, requires getting your mind in the right place. Mine hadn't been at all. I was very concerned with what others were thinking. I was engaging in two mental activities that any biking therapist worth his gremlin bell would tell everyone else not to do. I was "mind reading", that is, deciding what other people thought without any information to work with whatsoever. I was also fortune telling. I was predicting how they would react, again, with no information whatsoever. Both are activities outside the present moment. They're about the future. As I chatted and interacted with people I came more and more into the present moment. I remembered who I was and why I was there and that God was standing right there beside me.

Feeling comfortable in community is often a lot about what is going on in our own heads. Next time you're in a group where you feel that you don't belong, check to see whether you are mind reading or fortune telling. My money says you are. Do something mind-stilling. Breathe and concentrate. Focus on something in the present moment. And take a moment to remember that God is there. I think you'll quickly find yourself comfortable in your community.

The folks you ride with are a community. You care about one another, support one another, laugh with one another, and when no one is looking, may cry with one another. The brotherhood of bikers is well known. If there's trouble on the road one of your brothers will be there.

I think it's also important to have a core group of people who are like family to you. Jesus had this kind of relationship with His disciples. Obviously, He didn't need their advice, but I think He valued their companionship and love. He trusted them with the personal knowledge of his life and many of His plans. Following his example, I have been blessed to fond a core group of people who surround me. I've known some of these folks all my life. Others I've known since childhood, still others I've met much more recently. Regardless of when I met them, they are family to me in every way that matters. Perhaps most importantly I find that, in moments when I cannot perceive the presence of God beside me, it is these folks who remind me. It usually isn't in what they say. It usually is in who they are, and the binds of love and forgiveness and hope and grace that hold us together. When I forget about God's love, it is their presence that never fails to remind me.

Learning to be comfortable with God

So we are back to this. Somewhere at the core of nearly everything about living is learning to be comfortable with God. It's about making God a part of our community. The closest people around us, the ones we trust and go to in times of need… we need to find a way to allow God to be one of them. In fact, we need to find a way to allow God to be even closer. Fact of the matter is, He already is even closer, closer than we will ever manage to be to another person. In seeking the quiet, in learning to be comfortable with ourselves, in learning to be comfortable in community, in all these things we learn to be closer to God. He is our core. He is our community. He is in the solitude and in the midst of community. Look beside you while you sit or walk or ride. God is there.

Solitude, Community, and the Great Rider

Alone at dawn, you ride.
Mists swirl in their futile rush away from the warming sun.
There is strength in the solitude, power in your moment alone.
The roads are bare, the houses dark, silent birds await the signal of light.
You ride… alone… content… at peace.

Other riders come,
Joining you from other ways and paths, falling into silent formation.
The strength of one becomes the might of many;
Friends to share the road and stand with you through tears and laughter.
You ride… in community… content… in peace.

The Great Rider joins.
In truth, He rode before you rose, it was Him you joined on the path.
His strength made loneliness into solitude, chaos into community.
In you, He rides through birth and death, through pain and joy.
You ride… in Him… content… in peace.

Interdependence and Independence

Bikers are, for the most part, very independent sorts. Some wear leather, some textile. Some ride a Harley, some a Victory, some a Yamaha. Some like two wheels, some three. They know what they like and they know why they like it, and they damn well insist on their right to like it. There are a few "conformity Nazis" out there who insist that what they like and buy and do is best, but the rants they sometimes muster are largely ignored by the rest of us.

For all their independence, bikers are also very interdependent. Their social activities usually include or even focus around other people who ride. They help one another and stand up for one another. A broken down biker by the side of the road is a brother or sister in need of a hand. A broken-hearted biker at the edge of the crowd is a brother or sister in need of a listening ear or a friendly hug. Love, respect, and brotherhood are common themes among most groups of bikers.

In many ways relationships among bikers mirror relationships among people of faith. We are independent of one another. We live separate lives, go to separate homes, are part of separate families, have separate jobs. Yet we are also interdependent. We come together to worship. We come together to pray. We come together to rejoice. We come together to weep. We are independent and individual, yet we depend on one another in many, many ways.

These relationships also mirror what our relationships can be with God. In many churches there's a cookie cutter somewhere between the profession of faith and the communion table with which we are all to roll out the spiritual dough and carve out our own copy of someone else's relationship with God. That's the relationship we're supposed to live with. Independence is sacrificed on the alter of interdependence. Despite the fact that everyone of us is different, despite the fact that God is so vast that no two of us could possibly relate to Him in exactly the same way. We mold our relationship with God into a shape that may or may not fit others well. As a result, we know Him less than we otherwise could. Christianity is not alone in this expectation; it is a common theme in many faiths.

The God who is beyond knowing cannot be reduced to a cookie cutter. The individuality He has crafted in each of us can be denied only at the cost of our mental health, creativity, and spiritual walk. We need the interdependence and guidance that Holy Books and pious counsel provide, yet we can sacrifice our own individuality only at the cost of our own spiritual paths.

We are taught to worship in the manner taught by tradition, often at the expense of the worship God lays on our hearts. We may offer the Lord's Prayer as a model in structure and content, yet forget that it was given more as a model of heart and spirit. Ritual and tradition have their place in a spiritual walk, yet they were intended to be signposts and supports to our paths, not the shackles by which we are dragged and driven.

I, of course, am no one to tell anyone whether their walk with God is all it could be. Mine certainly is not. Yet I am convinced our spiritual paths can be enhanced by both honoring revealed truth and by making our paths our own. God offers four beacons to light the path of independence in our relationship with Him: faith, wisdom, courage, and trust.

Faith, is, of course, the foundation of any walk with God. It is faith in God that leads us to a path. It is faith that sustains us. It also is faith that allows us to express individuality and independence in our walk with Him.

The writer of Hebrews told us, "Now faith is the substance of things hoped for, the evidence of things not seen." Today's path is something we cannot see. We don't know what will happen as we sleep, when we rise, or when we walk out the door. We also cannot know exactly what will happen when we set out to know God in a more personal way. Some things we can be sure of. We will make some good decisions. We will make some bad decisions. We will make some decisions that do not matter at all. Yet it is faith that allows us to take those steps, and it is faith in the love and grace and power of God that will lead us on our paths and sustain us as we walk.

Wisdom is also a key. Although we may lack it as we begin our walk, we gain it as we go along. There is also wisdom in the Scripture, wisdom in the counsel of spiritual leaders, and wisdom in the advice of our friends. I also think God's wisdom is available to us more directly than we think. He gives it when we take the time to ask, and when we are willing to listen.

Forging independence in our walk with God also requires courage. Facing the unknown can be a frightening thing. Change can be intimidating. Others may criticize our path, believing that abandonment of the cookie cutter constitutes abandonment of our faith. Steps toward a personal faith and walk need not come in leaps. God is pleased by our tottering baby steps. Where we lack courage to go, He is willing to lead. As we take small steps, our courage grows, our wisdom grows, and our faith grows. Our path becomes more clear, and our confidence to walk it grows stronger.

To know God we must learn to trust in God. We

trust that He will guide our steps. We must also trust that he will help us up when we stumble, and light the way back when we miss a turn. Forging your own relationship with God requires trust in his love and grace and constant presence, a trust that He is there even when we don't see him. He will forgive our failures, correct our misunderstandings, and sooth our broken spirits. God loves us fiercely, without limit or apology. In His love He wants us to know Him as best we can. It is in the boundless love and burning desire of God that we are able to place our trust.

Prayer for the Crossroads

In the hands of a loving God, I approach a crossroad,
A lonely choice if I ride with a borrowed God.
Which way will I turn?
Where will it lead?
What if my choice is wrong?
The arms of a loaner Lord are less shelter than I need.

The choice grows nearer,
The crossroad a way of opportunity.
I can turn and go back the way I have come.
I can take the road to a place I have been before.
I can ride where others want me to go.
I can take a turn to places I have never been,

God, help me choose a path that takes me closer to You.
A road beyond the cookie cutter,
To places where I walk with You more deeply and freely and faithfully than ever before.
Where I lack faith, help me to find it.
Where I need wisdom, lead me to it.

Where I lack courage, bolster my spirit.
Where I lack trust take me in Your arms and help
me know Your love.

I would not know You less than I might.
I would know You as best I can.

Kickstands Down

The end of the chapter. The end of the book. I hope you have found these thoughts on biking and spirituality helpful and enjoyable. I look forward to meeting you on the road, and on the path.

Blessings.

Appendix I
Books and Sites about Biking

This is a very partial list. There are lots of good books and site out there about riding. The ones I've included here will make a nice start. Please take a look at my suggestions, but also Google and search places like amazon.com and barnesandnoble.com for titles. If you want to get them from a great gear shop, my friends at whitehorsegear.com have a nice selection.

Again, there are lots of books and sites out there. I've included a few of the ones that I've read or visited and have benefited from.

Books

The Complete Idiot's Guide to Motorcycles, 5th Edition. The Editors of Motorcyclist Magazine and John L. Stein. Alpha.

The Motorcycle Safety Foundation's Guide to Motorcycling Excellence: Skills, Knowledge, and Strategies for Riding Right (2nd Edition), Motorcycle Safety Foundation. Whitehorse Press.

The Essential Guide to Motorcycle Maintenance: Tips & Techniques to Keep Your Motorcycle in Top Condition. Mark Zimmerman. Whitehorse Press.

Proficient Motorcycling: The Ultimate Guide to Riding Well, David L. Hough. Bowtie Press.

Street Strategies: A Survival Guide for Motorcyclists, David L. Hough. Bowtie Press.

Bathroom Book of Motorcycle Trivia: 360 days-worth of $#!+ you don't need to know, four days-worth of stuff that is somewhat useful to know, and one entry that's absolutely essential, Mark Gardiner, Bikewriter.com.

Coming and Going on Bikes: Essaying the Motorcycle. Jack Lewis. Litsam, Inc.

The Essential Guide to Motorcycle Travel: Tips, Technology, Advanced Techniques. Dale Coyner. Whitehorse Press.

Motorcycle Touring in the Southwest: The Region's Best Rides, Christie Karras, Stephen Zusy. GPP Travel.

Motorcycle Journeys Through North America, Dale Coyner. Whitehorse Press.

Motorcycle Journeys Through the Appalachians, Dale Coyner. Whitehorse Press.

Motorcycle Adventures in the Southern Appalachians: North Georgia, Western North Carolina, East Tennessee Book 1, Hawk Hagebak. Milestone Press.

Motorcycle Journeys Through New England: You Don't Have to Get Lost to Find the Good Roads, Martin C. Berke. Whitehorse Press.

Motorcycle Touring in the Pacific Northwest: The Region's Best Rides, Chrisite Karras, Stepehn Zusy. GPP Travel.

Hell's Angel: The Life and Times of Sonny Barger

and the Hell's Angels Motorcycle Club, Sonny Barger, Mark Zimmerman.

Let's Ride: Sonny Barger's Guide to Motorcycling, Sonny Barger, Darwin Holmstron. William Morrow Paperbacks.

No Angel: My Harrowing Undercover Journey to the Inner Circle of the Hells Angels, Jay Dobyns. Broadway Books.

Under and Alone: The True Story of the Undercover Agent Who Infiltrated America's Most Violent Outlaw Motorcycle Gang, William Queen. Ballantine Books.

Websites

All the manufacturers have websites. Rather than listing them all, the old man is jus gonna recommend that you do an Internet search by manufacturer name.

News and Reviews

http://msf-USA.org/
http://www.motorcycle.com
http://www.motorcycle-usa.com
http://www.nadaguides.com/Motorcycles

Gear

http://www.motorcycle-superstore.com
http://www.cyclegear.com
http://www.jafrum.com/Motorcycle-Gear
http://www.rockymountainatvmc.com/cl/45/Riding-Gear
http://www.aerostich.com

http://www.happy-trail.com
http://www,whitehorsegear.com

Forums

http://www.motorcycleforums.net
http://www.yamahamotorcycleforum.com/foru
m
http://www.motorcyclenews.com/MCN/commu
nity/Forums
http://www.mctourer.com
http://www.victoryforums.com
http://www.kawasakimotorcycle.org/forum
http://www.v-twinforum.com
http://www.motorcycleforum.com

ABOUT THE AUTHOR

Rodney A. Ellis, PhD, LCSW, CMAT, CSAT (known to almost everyone who speaks of him without expletives as Rod) is an associate professor of social work at the University of Tennessee and has a mental health practice working with folks who have PTSD and addictions in the Cookeville, TN area. He's the father of the greatest teenage son in the world and an avid rider of motorcycles. He likes to walk in the woods, smoke pipes, play MMORPs and hang out with his friends. He considers himself fortunate to be surrounded by an amazing group of talented and incredibly supportive friends, who help him in his endeavors, encourage him toward his goals, and provide a listening ear whenever it is needed. He has, indeed, been blessed.

11704658R00171

Printed in Great Britain
by Amazon.co.uk, Ltd.,
Marston Gate.